P9-CTP-070

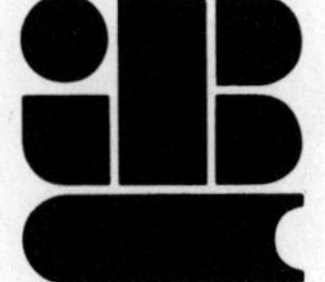

New Futures for Student Affairs

Margaret J. Barr,
M. Lee Upcraft,
and Associates

NEW FUTURES FOR STUDENT AFFAIRS

Building a Vision for Professional Leadership and Practice

Jossey-Bass Publishers
San Francisco • Oxford • 1990

NEW FUTURES FOR STUDENT AFFAIRS
Building a Vision for Professional Leadership and Practice
by Margaret J. Barr, M. Lee Upcraft, and Associates

Library of Congress Cataloging-in-Publication Data

New futures for student affairs : building a vision for professional leadership and practice / Margaret J. Barr, M. Lee Upcraft, and associates.—1st ed.
p. cm.—(The Jossey-Bass higher education series)
Includes bibliographical references and index.
ISBN 1-55542-298-5 (alk. paper)
1. Personnel service in higher education—United States—Administration. 2. College student development programs—United States—Planning. 3. College student personnel administrators—United States. I. Barr, Margaret J. II. Upcraft, M. Lee. III. Series.
LB2343.N394 1990
378.1′94′0973—dc20 90-41464
CIP

Manufactured in the United States of America

The paper in this book meets the guidelines for permanence and durability of the Committee on Production Guidelines for Book Longevity of the Council on Library Resources.

JACKET DESIGN BY WILLI BAUM

FIRST EDITION

Code 90102

The Jossey-Bass
Higher Education Series

Consulting Editor
Student Services

Ursula Delworth
University of Iowa

Contents

Preface

The rapid pace of change in society and in higher education demands thoughtful reflection about and careful planning for the future on the part of student affairs professionals. *New Futures for Student Affairs* is designed to assist professionals with this planning process. The book presents the ideas of a number of respected professionals regarding the future of our profession. It is our hope that these ideas will aid the reader in thinking about and planning for the future. Our task as professionals is to shape our response to the future in ways that will ensure positive outcomes for students, staff, and our institutions.

Both of the principal authors have a long-time interest in the future of the profession, and this interest has been stimulated by professional colleagues, new and provocative books, and the change we have experienced in our own professional lives. The work of Robert D. Brown has been particularly helpful as we consider the possibilities that lie ahead. Theodore Miller and Judith Prince in their 1976 book *The Future of Student Affairs* made an enormous contribution to the field and stimulated our thinking. These early works provided a stimulus to all of us in the profession and helped shape our ideas.

Much of our impetus for writing this book came from the publication in 1987 of *A Perspective on Student Affairs* by the National Association of Student Personnel Administrators (NASPA). We have included the original authors of that publication in our group of authors, believing that each had much more to share than could be included in the NASPA document—and we were correct!

Readers should find the contents of this volume stimulating and provocative. Not everyone will agree with us about the issues and forces that will influence the future, and that is as it should be, since no one can accurately predict the future. We can, however, carefully examine available data, observe trends, and make some fairly accurate predictions regarding the changes we will face. This book can aid in this endeavor.

Audience

We believe that this book will be useful to three groups. First are those professionals who serve as chief officers or middle managers in student affairs organizations. The issues and strategies presented in this volume will directly influence the professional practice of these individuals in the years ahead. Study of the issues that will influence our future can aid in thoughtful planning that will enable staff members to meet the inevitable challenges we will face.

Second, the book will serve as a textbook for graduate professional preparation programs in student affairs. The book can help individuals engaged in graduate study and graduate preparation faculty determine what the emphasis should be in graduate study and the issues that must be explored. We hope this volume will stimulate both students and faculty to address the complex issues that will face the profession in the future.

Finally, the book is intended for persons involved in higher education, both within and outside of student affairs, who are concerned about the challenges the future will bring. Change is an inevitable part of the agenda for higher education, and examination of the issues and alternative solutions to confront problems should be helpful for presidents, other institutional officers, and concerned faculty.

Overview of the Contents

This volume is organized into three parts. Part One assesses the foundation of our profession as we prepare for future change. In Chapter One, Upcraft and Barr identify the challenges for the future that are present in our current practice and review the ethical principles that undergird our work. In Chapter Two, Lyons examines in detail the assumptions and beliefs that guide student affairs. Upcraft and Moore in Chapter Three highlight student development theory and emerging theoretical perspectives that will be useful in dealing with future challenges.

Part Two identifies the major forces for change and the implications these have for student affairs. In Chapter Four, Kuh presents a careful analysis of the demographic trends that will influence higher education. Sandeen and Rhatigan in Chapter Five explore some major social issues and discuss the effects of these issues on student affairs. In Chapter Six, Fenske and Johnson examine the changing nature of the legal and regulatory environment of higher education and consider the implications for those we serve and how we serve them. Mills in Chapter Seven assesses the impact of the technological revolution on student affairs professionals and the students they serve. In Chapter Eight, Barr identifies new and developing career paths for student affairs professionals along with strategies for dealing with the changes.

Part Three outlines an agenda for action as we plan for the future. Barr and Albright discuss new organizational roles and approaches for student affairs in Chapter Nine. Chapter Ten delineates the paradoxical issues that will face the profession. Barr and Golseth suggest ways to improve our skills in managing change. In Chapter Eleven, Woodard and Komives provide an agenda for staff development, professional preparation, and working conditions that must be met if our staff is to be equipped to face future challenges. Brown discusses the importance of strengthening ties and developing collaborative efforts with academic affairs in Chapter Twelve. In Chapter Thirteen, Hanson considers ways student affairs professionals can improve their ability to meet future challenges through research, evaluation, and outcomes assessment. Finally, in Chapter Fourteen, the principal authors summarize an agenda for action in student affairs that will effectively serve our students and our institutions.

Acknowledgments

Preparing a volume such as this is not possible without the collaboration and dedication of many individuals. We particularly want to thank the chapter authors for the careful, stimulating, and insightful perspectives they have shared. Each of them has made an enormous contribution, and we are grateful.

Gale Erlandson of Jossey-Bass, who encouraged us in our quest, and Ursula Delworth, who helped us refine our thinking, both deserve praise and thanks. They aided us in producing a much better body of work. Sheryl Sclater, Carolyn Shapard, and Dianna Smith from Texas Christian University all spent untold hours putting this volume into its final form, and we are grateful for their help.

Lee Upcraft would like to acknowledge the constant and helpful support of his wife, Lillian, and his parents, Milton and Mabel Upcraft. In addition, he wishes to acknowledge the continuing support of William W. Asbury, vice-president for student services at the Pennsylvania State University.

Margaret Barr wishes to thank her colleagues at Texas Christian University for their understanding and support as work on this volume progressed, and she wishes also to acknowledge her family, especially her parents, who always encouraged her to attempt to be all she could.

September 1990

Margaret J. Barr
Fort Worth, Texas

M. Lee Upcraft
University Park, Pennsylvania

The Authors

Margaret J. Barr is vice-chancellor for student affairs at Texas Christian University in Fort Worth, Texas. She previously served as vice-president and assistant vice-president for student affairs at Northern Illinois University and as associate and assistant dean of students at the University of Texas, Austin. She received her B.S. degree (1961) in elementary education from the State University College at Buffalo, her M.S. degree (1964) in college student personnel from Southern Illinois University, and her Ph.D. degree (1980) in higher education administration from the University of Texas, Austin.

She is the author of over twenty-five articles, monographs, and chapters about student affairs and is currently editor-in-chief of the Jossey-Bass New Directions for Student Services monograph series. She is also the editor of *Effective Student Services: A Guide for Practitioners* (1985, with L. A. Keating) and *Student Services and the Law* (1988). Barr received the 1986 Professional Service Award from the American College Personnel Association (ACPA) and the 1986 Award for Outstanding Contribution to Literature and Research from the National Association of Student Personnel Administrators (NASPA). She is a former president of ACPA and currently serves as a senior scholar for that association. She was a member of the committee that authored "A Perspective on Student Affairs" (NASPA, 1987).

M. Lee Upcraft is assistant vice-president for counseling services and program assessment, a senior member of the graduate faculty, an affiliate associate professor of education, and an associate in the Center for the Study of Higher Education at the Pennsylvania State University. He obtained his B.A. (1960) in social studies and his M.A. (1961) in guidance and counseling from the State University of New York, Albany. He also received his Ph.D. (1967) in student personnel administration from Michigan State University.

M. Lee Upcraft has authored and edited *The Freshman Year Experience* (1989, with J. N. Gardner), *Orienting Students to College* (1984), *Managing Student Affairs Effectively* (1988, with M. Barr), and two quarterly sourcebooks in the Jossey-Bass New Directions for Student Services series. He is the principal author of two books, *Residence Hall Assistants in College: A Guide to Selection, Training, and Supervision* (1982, in collaboration with G. T. Pilato) and *Learning to Be a Resident Assistant: A Manual for Effective Participation in the Training Program* (1982, in collaboration with G. T. Pilato and D. J. Peterman). He has also written journal articles, research monographs, and book chapters and is currently the associate editor of the Jossey-Bass New Directions for Student Services monograph series.

Robert L. Albright has served as president of Johnson C. Smith University in Charlotte, North Carolina, since 1983. He received his A.B. degree (1966) from Lincoln University, his M.A. degree (1972) from Tufts, and his Ph.D. degree (1978) from Kent State University. He is the author of several publications on admissions and financial aid and was a member of the committee that wrote "A Perspective on Student Affairs."

Suzanne S. Brown serves as associate vice-chancellor for academic and student affairs for the Pennsylvania State System of Higher Education. She received her B.S. (1959) from Northwestern University, her M.A. degree (1963) from the University of Arizona, and her Ph.D. degree (1984) from the University of Nebraska. She is the author of several book chapters and has refereed journal articles on academic and student affairs relations and student affairs professional staff development.

Robert H. Fenske is professor of higher education at Arizona State University. He received his B.S. (1958), M.S. (1961), and Ph.D. (1965) degrees from the University of Wisconsin. He is the author of several book chapters, monographs, and articles in refereed journals on topics such as student financial aid, legal issues in student affairs, historical foundations of student affairs, and cultural diversity.

Anne E. Golseth is vice-president for student services at Ohlone college in Fremont, California. She received her B.A. degree (1959) from the University of Colorado, her M.A. degree (1962) from Cornell University, and her Ph.D. degree (1974) from Michigan State University. She served as a member of the committee that wrote "A Perspective on Student Affairs."

Gary R. Hanson serves as coordinator of research at the University of Texas at Austin. He received his B.A. (1965), M.A. (1968), and Ph.D. (1970) degrees from the University of Minnesota. He has published many monographs, book chapters, and articles in refereed journals on program development, student development measurement, value added assessment, and outcomes assessment. He is coeditor, with Ursula Delworth, of both editions of *Student Services: A Handbook for the Profession* (1980).

Edward A. Johnson is associate general counsel for the Arizona Board of Regents. He received his B.S. degree (1973) from Morningside College, his J.D. degree (1976) from Creighton University School of Law, and his Ph.D. degree (1984) from Arizona State University. He has published several book chapters, monographs, and refereed journal articles on fund raising, independent colleges, college trusteeship, financial management, and higher education administration.

Susan R. Komives serves as assistant professor of counseling and personnel services and faculty associate for the division of student affairs at the University of Maryland-College Park. She received her B.S. (1968) and M.S. (1969) degrees from Florida State University, and her Ed.D. (1973) degree from the University of Tennessee-Knoxville. She is a former ACPA president and has published monographs, book chapters, and refereed journal articles on professional staff development, graduate education, residence halls, development of women, and administration.

George D. Kuh is professor of higher education in the Department of Education Leadership and Policy Studies at Indiana University-Bloomington. He is currently directing the Colleges Experiences Study. He received his B.A. degree (1968) from Luther College, his M.S. degree (1971) from Saint Cloud State University, and his Ph.D. degree (1975) from the University of Iowa. He is the author or coauthor of more than one hundred publications, including *The Invisible Tapestry: Culture in American Colleges and Universities* (1988) and has also edited four books. He served on the committee that wrote "A Perspective on Student Affairs."

James W. Lyons was dean of students at Stanford University from 1972 to 1990. He received his B.A. degree (1954) from Allegheny College; his M.S. (1956) and Ed.D. (1963) degrees are from Indiana University-Bloomington. He received the Scott Goodnight Award from NASPA and is a member of the research team that conducted the Colleges Experiences Study. He served on the committee that wrote "A Perspective on Student Affairs."

Donald B. Mills is associate vice-chancellor for student affairs at Texas Christian University. He received his B.A. degree (1968) from Harvard University, his M.Div. degree (1972) from Texas Christian University, and his Ed.D. degree (1985) from the University of North Texas. He is the author of several monograph chapters on financial management in student affairs, residence halls, and leadership development.

Leila V. Moore is assistant director for the Center of Student Development and Leadership at the Pennsylvania State University. She received her B.A. degree (1961) from Carnegie Institute of Technology, her M.A. degree (1963) from Syracuse University, and her Ph.D. degree (1975) from the State University of New York at Albany. She is editor-in-chief of the Jossey-Bass New Directions for

Student Services sourcebook on student development theory and coeditor of a sourcebook on professional development in this series. She has published several book chapters and articles in refereed journals on cultural diversity, returning adult students, and professional education. She is the current president-elect of ACPA.

James J. Rhatigan is vice-president for student affairs and dean of students at Wichita State University. He is a former NASPA president and received the Scott Goodnight Award from that association. He received his B.A. degree (1957) from Coe College, his M.A. degree (1959) from Syracuse University, and his Ph.D. degree (1965) from the University of Iowa. He served on the committee that wrote "A Perspective on Student Affairs."

Arthur Sandeen has served as vice-president for student affairs and professor of educational psychology at the University of Florida since 1973. He received his B.A. degree (1960) from Miami University, Ohio; his M.A. (1962) and Ph.D. (1965) degrees are from Michigan State University. He is a former NASPA president and received the NASPA Fred Turner and Scott Goodnight awards. He is the author of *Undergraduate Education: Conflict and Change* (1976), is widely published in refereed journals, and is the author of several book and monograph chapters. He was the chair of the committee that wrote "A Perspective on Student Affairs."

Dudley B. Woodard, Jr., is the vice-president for student affairs at the University of Arizona. He received his B.A. degree (1962) from MacMurray College; his M.A. (1965) and Ph.D. (1969) degrees are from Ohio University. He is a former NASPA president and has published several monographs and articles in refereed journals on faculty advising, student outcomes assessment, precollege perceptions of freshmen, careers in student affairs, and student affairs cost studies.

New Futures for Student Affairs

PART ONE

Assessing the Professional Foundations for Growth and Change

The one certain element of the future is change. Our life and work in higher education and student affairs of the future will be markedly different than it is today. The causes of these differences will be many and are related to events, trends, people, and problems. And our effectiveness as student affairs professionals in dealing with the differences will rest in large measure on what we believe and know as well as on our ability to translate these beliefs and knowledge into practice.

In Part One, we are focusing on our current state of affairs as a profession. In Chapter One, we present an overview of the broad issues that will influence our professional practice, a brief history of student affairs, and the ethical foundations of our work; and we assess the current state of the profession and provide a framework for the rest of the volume.

The assumptions and beliefs underlying our work are identified by James Lyons in Chapter Two. This chapter expands on the work in "A Perspective on Student Affairs, 1987" (National Association of Student Personnel Administrators, [1987] 1989) and focuses our thinking on the beliefs that provide the foundation for our work. Often we do not carefully examine why we do what we do, and we assume that all student affairs professionals share the same belief system. Chapter Two provides an opportunity for practitioners to reflect on those concepts providing the foundation of our professional responsibilities.

Theory is a useful and essential tool for practitioners, and Chapter Three provides a broad overview of the theoretical perspectives that undergird our work. Lee Upcraft and Leila Moore provide an overview of the theoretical models that have helped us understand our students in the past. In addition, they provide information about the insights regarding evolving theoretical perspectives that will guide our practice in the future as new and different students come to our institutions.

Part One is designed to provide a shared basis of understanding among student affairs professionals regarding who we are, what we believe, and what we know about students and their development. This foundation and shared understanding is essential as we face the future. Forces of change will continue to influence higher education in the future, and our challenge as a profession is to build on our present as a foundation for this future filled with change.

Reference

National Association of Student Personnel Administrators. "A Perspective on Student Affairs, 1987." In *Points of View*. Washington, D.C.: National Association of Student Personnel Administrators, 1989. (Originally published 1987.)

Chapter 1

Identifying Challenges for the Future in Current Practice

M. Lee Upcraft
Margaret J. Barr

Identifying the issues facing the student affairs profession is at once easy and difficult. It is easy because those of us facing the day-to-day demands of our profession, whether as administrators, student development educators, or faculty, can readily identify many of the issues we face. On the other hand, it is difficult because our profession is very much influenced by institutional and societal issues that we may not fully understand and over which we may have little control.

Careful consideration of the future is essential for student affairs professionals. First, an analysis of potential issues and problems can assist in identifying both problems and opportunities that will be a part of our professional future. Second, study of the future can enable us to plan more effectively so we can respond to issues. Third, contemplation of future issues can assist the profession in developing strategies to prepare both new and continuing professionals to meet changing conditions. Finally, as professionals, we can determine our own needs and skill deficits as we contemplate a future with ambiguity and change.

This chapter provides an overview of the broad issues that will influence our professional practice as society and higher education respond to changing conditions. As we proceed, we will make references to other chapters in this volume where these issues are explored in greater depth. Second, we will trace briefly the student affairs profession's history as a foundation for our discussion of the future. Third, we will explore the fundamental assumption of ethical approaches to our professional lives. And finally, we will assess the current status of the profession as a stepping stone to the process of examining the future.

Predicting the future is an educated guess, at best. We hope, however, that we will challenge and stimulate the thinking of the profession as we prepare for the decades ahead.

Societal Context and Trends

One basis for understanding the future is to examine the societal trends that we predict will influence higher education and the student affairs profession in the years ahead.

Demographic Trends. Our country is on the verge of dramatic changes in its racial, ethnic, age, and cultural mix. For example, whites are declining as a percentage of our total population; and by the year 2000, the United States will be a nation in which one of every three of us will be nonwhite. In fact, several states such as California, Florida, and Texas will have nonwhite majorities by the early 1990s.

Most present minorities will increase in numbers and as percentages of our total population. Through a combination of larger birth rates and immigration, Asian Americans, American Indians, African Americans, Mexican Americans, and Puerto Ricans will all increase their percentages. Only Cuban Americans will have birth and immigration rates comparable to whites (Hodgkinson, 1985).

Second, the U.S. population will continue to grow older. Our declining birth rate, along with increased life expectancy, will gray our population. Today 29 percent of the population is over sixty-five, and that percentage is expected to continue to grow. As retirees continue to constitute a greater percentage of our population, the health, social, economic, legal, and political issues our country faces will change drastically.

Third, while women will continue to constitute about the same percentage in our population, their roles will continue to change. More women will be in the work force, demanding increased representation in middle and upper management positions and better fringe benefits such as child care, parental leave, and expanded health care, and they will insist on closing the pay gap between men and women. More women will also be in dual-career situations, some out of economic necessity, and some out of choice. Many will defer child bearing until their thirties, preferring to launch careers before families.

Fourth, the geographic distribution of our population will continue to shift away from the Northeast and toward the South and West. This shift will create geographic areas where economic and political influence will decline, thereby creating greater economic hardships for citizens in those areas. On the other hand, geographic areas with expanding populations, while accruing many economic and social benefits, will also have to deal with the problems that accompany overpopulated areas. Chapter Four in this volume provides a full discussion of these issues and the influence they will have on higher education.

Economic Trends. It is clear that we are moving toward a global economy. Multinational corporations are expanding, making economic boundaries based on geographic boundaries less important. The world stock exchanges are interconnected as never before, and regional economic communities are being created. In the United States, the increasing balance-of-trade deficit, coupled with increased foreign ownership of national assets, makes our economy more globally connected.

Second, our economy is changing from a production emphasis to a service emphasis. Even today, 75 percent of our labor force is employed in service industries, and by the year 2000, the figure will be 88 percent. About 50 percent of the service industry is dominated by informational industries such as high-tech computer businesses (Coates, 1986).

Third, our economy will be increasingly dominated by computers and information systems. By the year 2000, 90 percent of American homes will have computers, and we will use them for tasks such as mailing, shopping, and banking. Businesses also will become increasingly dependent on computers. Basic and applied research will be assisted by computers that can think as well as process. In addition, computers will create international communications capabilities (Coates, 1986).

Fourth, our work force will change drastically in response to changing needs. Jobs will become obsolete more rapidly, and knowledge needed to retain jobs will increase. Today, the half-life of an engineer is five years; that is, one-half of what a graduating engineer is taught in college will be obsolete within five years. Workers will need to retrain frequently, and second and third careers will become commonplace. In fact, people will change careers on the average of every ten years. In addition, more women and minorities will enter the work force (Coates, 1986)—a change that will have profound implications for higher education.

Fifth, our economy will be increasingly dominated by scientific and technological advances, some of which have been identified above. But there are other examples. These advances will be essential for dealing with our national and global environmental problems including the diminishing ozone layer, acid rain, and preservation of our natural resources including clean air and water.

This set of issues will create problems, paradoxes, and opportunities for higher education and student affairs (see Chapters Six, Seven, and Ten).

Social Trends. In our opinion, the social trend having the most impact in the near and distant future will be the changing family dynamics of our country. Divorce rates continue to rise, thereby creating single-family households and blended families. *USA Today* (1989, p. 1) reported recently that the percentage of children under eighteen living with one parent rose from 20 percent in 1980 to 24 percent in 1988. According to Hodgkinson (1985), of those children born in 1985, 40 percent will be born to parents who will divorce before the children are eighteen. There will be more single heads of households, particularly among minorities. And for those families with two heads of household, both will have to work to maintain economic stability. These dual-career couples will have special needs such as child care.

Second, health issues and health advances will also have a great influence on society and higher education. The health-related problems of our society today, including alcohol and other drug abuse, AIDS, nutritional disorders, and sexually transmitted diseases, are well documented (see Chapter Five). Advances in health care and technology will also have an impact. By the year 2000, we may have artificial blood, genetic engineering, brain cell transplants, bionic limbs, fetal viability outside the womb from the moment of conception, and other medical advances that will challenge our ethics way beyond their present capability to provide guidance (Coates, 1986).

Third, our society will become increasingly heterogeneous and diverse in its values. For example, the increased religious fundamentalism on the one hand and the decline of traditional religious values on the other hand will create stress among our people—as evidenced by the intensity and acrimony of the debate about legalized abortion. We may be entering a period in which our differences become more important than our commonalities. The increase in the nonwhite population of our country will amplify cultural, racial, and ethnic differences. Diversity rather than assimilation will be the predominant value; we will be creating salad bowls rather than melting pots. (See Chapter Five.)

Fourth, our society will have more time for activity unrelated to work. As workweeks shorten and the middle and upper classes have more disposable income, the leisure industry will grow. We will be able to engage in more leisure activities such as sports, aerobics, hobbies, and travel.

Political and Legal Trends. As we face the last decade of this century, we are in the midst of a conservative political climate. Conservatives have captured the last three presidential elections, and there is a tendency to rely less on the federal government to deal with our societal problems and issues. State governments and the private sector are being called upon more and more to deal with these issues.

Second, in the legal realm, our judicial system is much less inclined to exert its influence on social issues, so that task is left to our legislative branches. The collective rights of our society and the general welfare of our citizens are in ascendency over individual rights. We now worry as much about the victims of crime as we do about the so-called alleged perpetrators. As a society, we seem to be backing off civil rights issues, including affirmative action. (See Chapter Six.)

Third, world political events will continue to have an influence on our society, particularly as the global economy becomes more influential. Events in South Africa, international drug trafficking, the Middle East situation, the emergence of the Third World, and the more recent drastic changes in the Communist countries of Eastern Europe, the Soviet Union, and China will affect us in ways that will influence our political processes.

These societal trends, along with others not mentioned, will frame our society in the next decade and beyond. Their impact on higher education will be enormous.

Trends in Higher Education

In general, trends in higher education closely parallel trends in our society. Trends in higher education, of course, have even a more direct influence on the student affairs profession than do societal trends. Four of these trends, in particular, will have a real and direct effect on student affairs in the future.

Demographic Trends. Our students will be older, and more will be engaged in part-time learning. In Chapter Four, Kuh provides the background information on the graying of the American campus and on the growth in our populations of women, ethnic minorities, and part-time learners. These trend lines will have enormous implications for higher education and thus for student affairs. The changing characteristics of our students will influence whom we serve and how we serve them.

Further, the changes in demographic characteristics of students will profoundly influence who will be the future staff members in student affairs. Enormous challenges will face the profession as we seek to attract and retain qualified staff to work with our current and future students and institutions. (See Chapters Eight and Eleven.)

Enrollment Trends. Although enrollment trends are clearly related to the demographic trends described above, they have very specific ramifications and dimensions for all of higher education and student affairs. We must reexamine services, practices, and policies as our nation's colleges and universities cope with an increase in the number of part-time students and older students and with a reduction in the pool of traditionally college-age students. As that examination takes place, specific attention must be paid to the policies, practices, and programs that assist new students of whatever category in their transitions to our institutions. A growing body of evidence suggests that resources must be diverted to focus on the critical transition to the collegiate environment (Upcraft, Gardner, and Associates, 1989).

The process of recruitment is becoming so competitive that failure to aid students in that successful transition will result in untold costs to both institutions and students. And the problem of making that successful transition is not just an issue for the entering freshman of traditional age. Transfer students clearly have some of the same issues, but institutions, although dependent on transfer students, still have not effectively accommodated them. Some evidence indicates that transfer students have a lower retention rate than do native students, that they receive less financial support, and that they experience incongruity between their expectations and the reality of the new environment when they transfer (Harrison and Varcoe, 1984). Orientation programs clearly must be strengthened for both freshman and transfer students, but merely dealing with orientation will not be enough.

Finally, according to Schlossberg, Lynch, and Chickering (1989, p. 8), "The educational bureaucracy originally served only young adults who were in apprentice like roles dealing with dependency issues. Older adults who begin school or return to school are usually colleagues, mentors or sponsors in their families, jobs and communities. Suddenly these adults are Bill, Joe and Anna, and those in charge, sometimes younger and with less experience are 'Professor' or 'Doctor'. . . . The needs of adults and the character of colleges diverge: Adults want to feel central, not marginal; competent, not childish; independent, not dependent; colleges and universities rely on rigid rules, regulations and policies. As a consequence, adults and educational institutions are out of sync."

For all of these new populations, something must change. Higher education must accommodate these new learners of whatever age, category, ethnicity, or race and must be intentional about those efforts by front-loading resources to assist them with the transition; otherwise, we will face even greater problems with retention of students than is currently the case.

Retention and reduction of attrition has become a national priority for higher education. Colleges and universities simply must do a better job of retaining students if they are to succeed in the decades ahead. The issue of retention is varied and complex and has been discussed at national conferences, symposia, and workshops. Current policies and practices must be modified if institutions are to retain students of all the categories they admit. Clearly, failure to grasp the consequences of high attrition rates would be a fatal mistake for colleges and universities.

Support of and confidence in higher education will inevitably decline unless the need to change enrollment patterns by reducing attrition is not met head on. Two resources in the literature are particularly helpful to institutions and practitioners struggling to reduce attrition—*Increasing Student Retention* (Noel, Levitz, Saluri, and Associates, 1985) and *Recruitment and Retention in Higher Education* (1988). The former provides an excellent discussion of the issues and provides suggestions for changes in practice. The latter, a monthly newsletter, shows the current state of the art in practice. Both are highly recommended as resources to assist in tackling the retention issue.

Economic Trends. First, it appears that institutions of higher education will have less support from governmental sources at the federal and state levels. Financing of higher education in both the public and private sectors will rely increasingly on private support or will involve increased costs borne directly by students and their families (see Chapter Six). The shift in the economy from the production of goods to the production of services will also influence higher education. There will be demands for changes in curriculum, and technology will assume an even greater role in how students learn and how we accomplish our own work. (See Chapter Seven.) Institutions will need to prepare to assist workers in retraining programs, and continuing educational programs servicing business and industry will grow in importance.

Finally, the global economy and interconnected business and governmental economic efforts will place new demands on higher education. More international students will attend our institutions, increased numbers of American students will study abroad, and more cooperative ventures will be established between institutions of higher education and foreign governments and between businesses and universities.

Social Trends. Many of the social trends that will influence higher education are connected to the changing demographic characteristics of our students, as described previously. Other social trends will affect higher education as well. Increased demands for student health care and research to solve health problems of society will influence the curriculum. The trend toward cultural and religious diversity and heterogeneity will also affect higher education, and we may be faced with greater conflict based on ethnic, cultural, and religious differences (see Chapters Two and Ten).

Our new students, as do our current students, will come to us bringing more complex problems and pathologies—students with problems including substance abuse, eating disorders, chronic depression, and suicidal tendencies and students who are victims of parental, sexual, physical, and psychological abuse. These kinds of health and sexual issues will continue to be an active agenda among our students (see Chapter Five).

Finally, the trend to increased leisure pursuits will mean that more students will want to receive academic preparation in these fields. Moreover, students will enter higher education with heightened expectations regarding the availability of leisure and recreational activities.

Political and Legal Trends. Political and legal trends will most certainly have an impact on higher education. The conservative trend of the last decade already has influenced higher education in many ways. Our students and faculty are less socially active—with some exceptions in areas such as the divestment issue and racial tensions. Students now come to college expecting to be a part of the great American economic machine. They do not come as agents of social change (Cooperative Institutional Research Program, 1988).

Second, state-supported institutions will be more accountable to their state and local governments. Support for public higher education is no longer automatic, and many legislatures and governors are demanding more evidence of the results of higher education in the form of state-mandated assessment programs. The public will continue to demand greater accountability, and the assessment movement in higher education will grow in importance. In the case of private institutions, they will be faced with balancing rising costs and reasonable tuition rates, and the search for private support will intensify.

At the same time, we can expect less judicial support for the rights of individuals and for programs that prevent discrimination and promote affirmative action. As a result, institutions of higher education will pursue such goals as a matter of choice rather than legal or legislative mandate. The courts, however, have taken a keener interest in recent years in such issues as alcohol host liability, high-risk student activities, and campus safety and security.

The trends in society and in higher education will provide enormous challenges for student affairs. We outline these challenges in later chapters. Our history as a profession, however, provides a foundation for us to encounter and productively confront the enormous changes we must face.

History of the Student Affairs Profession

From the very beginnings of higher education in the United States, colleges sought to develop the total person, not merely the mind. Godbold (1944) reported that colonial colleges were founded to provide a supply of clergymen and to assure "that youth . . . [were] piously educated in good letters and manners" (p. 5). Morison (1935) reported that Henry Dunster, the first president of Harvard, charged new fellows to the board of overseers by stating, "You shall take care to advance in all learning, divine, and humane, each and every student who is or will be entrusted to your tutelage, according to their several abilities; and especially to take care that their conduct and manners be honorable and without blame" (p. 19).

In fact, some historians argue that the development of the student character was substantially more important to colonial educators than the development of the intellect. For example, Rudolph (1962) reported there was a great concern in the 1760s that Harvard was "developing a dangerous liberality of spirit, which might be useful in the sharpening of the intellect, but which was unquestionably damaging to true and holy character" (p. 65).

Early American colleges attempted to develop character primarily through the concept of in loco parentis, whereby colleges acted on behalf of parents for the good of the students. The curriculum stressed traditional religious values that reinforced a Christian concept of good moral character. Outside the classroom, strict rules and regulations were enforced by rigid discipline (Rudolph, 1962).

Functions that might be regarded as the forerunners of student services were the responsibility of the president, the faculty, tutors, the priest-seminarians, or other so-called persons of the faith (Knock, 1985). Sometimes presidents insisted on living with their families in suites within dormitories—all the better to scrutinize the behavior of students (Upcraft, 1982). According to Knock (1985), "Student services were inseparable from the academic program and were performed by all who were viewed as capable of molding young men into Christian gentlemen" (p. 18).

Although the nature of higher education changed with the establishment of public colleges and universities in the early part of the nineteenth century, the relationship between students and their colleges remained dominated by in loco parentis. The advent of coeducation in the mid-nineteenth century presented the rule makers and enforcers with some new challenges. Women had to have special rules designed to develop them into young ladies; and, of course, men and women had to be kept from all but formal, chaperoned interactions. By the end of the nineteenth century, some presidents delegated the responsibility for supervising students and handling student problems to deans of men and deans of women. Their functions were to control and limit the behavior of students, which was perfectly consistent with the concept of in loco parentis. In fact, these roles and titles survived until the 1960s, when changes in the legal definitions of adulthood and the demise of in loco parentis in our courts resulted in the redefinition of these roles.

In the early part of the twentieth century, the application of the emerging disciplines of psychology and sociology to the collegiate setting resulted in the appointment of human development specialists, or *student personnel workers,* whose responsibilities focused initially on vocational guidance, and later on the more generalized needs and interests of students. So the student affairs profession was built upon two historical roots: the deans of men and women, who were concerned about general student welfare and the maintenance of campus order and morality, and student personnel workers, who were concerned with students' human development (Knock, 1985).

The Student Personnel Point of View (American Council on Education, 1937) defined the essential nature of the student personnel profession. This statement, and the 1949 revision (American Council on Education, 1949), imposed on colleges and universities an obligation to consider each student as a whole person and to conceive of education as including attention to the physical, social, emotional, and spiritual development as well as intellectual development (Knock, 1985).

From 1950 to the mid 1970s, the student affairs profession changed dramatically. Deans of men and deans of women gave way to deans of students. Vocational counselors were gradually replaced by counseling and clinical psychologists. Student development educators emerged to work in residence halls, to student activities, and in other student services, and student development theories and concepts were introduced in the sixties and seventies by such scholars as Erik Erickson (1968), Nevitt Sanford (1962), Arthur Chickering (1969), William Perry (1970), Lawrence Kohlberg (1971), and others. (See Chapter Three.)

The decade of the seventies, however, brought significant changes to the student affairs profession. First, in loco parentis, as the legal basis for our relationships with students, fell before the onslaught of students demanding that their constitutional rights not be left at the campus doorstep; and a series of successful legal challenges followed. Second, the age of majority was lowered to eighteen, making full adult citizens out of people who once were children in the eyes of the law. Third, the Family Educational Rights and Privacy Act (1974) strengthened the privacy rights of students and restricted many administrative practices.

By the end of the seventies, we had very little legal rationale for our profession. In public institutions, we could no longer intrude in students' lives on behalf of their parents, particularly if that intrusion violated students' constitutional rights. Fortunately for our profession, and for our students, the decades of the seventies and eighties brought an abundance of retention and developmental research, which showed a relationship between student participation in student services and programs and students' academic and personal development. The presumed benefits of our work with students were no longer acts of faith; they were clearly demonstrated outcomes of retention and developmental research.

In 1987, the National Association of Student Personnel Administrators issued *A Perspective on Student Affairs.* This statement articulated the assumptions and beliefs on which our profession is based (see Chapter Two) and defined the responsibility of student affairs professionals to serve both students and our institutions.

Additionally, throughout the decades of the fifties, sixties, seventies, and eighties, our professional associations have helped us confront our ethical responsibilities to students and to our institutions. As we face the future, it is imperative that we embrace the highest ethical standards in our practice. Failure to do so will hamper our ability to respond effectively to the forces of change.

The Issue of Ethics

Ethics is not an abstract concept for student affairs professionals. Our ethical stance shapes our relationships with students, colleagues, staff, faculty, students' family members, our many publics, and our governing boards. Ethical beliefs provide form and shape for policies, practices, and procedures, and they influence every aspect of our professional practice.

The future of student affairs will be filled with challenges and choices. Our primary task is to be sure that we confront each and every issue from an ethical point of view and that we exhibit ethical behavior in our practice. Fargo (1981) argues that the ability of an administrator to balance the rights of all concerned is the greatest skill and can be the most effective contribution we make.

Being ethical is much more than adhering to the law. Canon (1989) reminds us that "an informed professional cannot afford to be ignorant of the legal constraints on his or her practice or a professional decision. Happily, most of what is ethical is also legal, and a good portion of all that is legal probably conforms to minimal ethical standards" (pp. 75–76). Ethical behavior defines the manner in which we do our business, confront problems, and resolve issues. To meet legal standards is not enough. As Albright and Barr indicate later in Chapter Nine, one of the major roles of student affairs is to serve as the institutional conscience. Student affairs professionals carry a historical mandate to address "matters of individual dignity and worth, of fairness and of equity" (Canon, 1989, p. 58).

Kitchener (1985) has posed five ethical principles to guide our professional practice: respecting autonomy, doing no harm, benefiting others, being just, and being faithful. Often these ethical principles are in conflict, and we must try to balance competing principles against each other. For example, recent events involving the development of racial harassment policies at institutions often place student affairs professionals in the position of balancing institutional concerns and individual student rights. All five principles of respecting autonomy (of students), doing no harm (to members of the community), benefiting others (in creating a climate free of harassment), being just (treating all parties in a fair manner), and being faithful (to institutional and personal positions and values) come into play. The achievement of balance among competing principles is not easy. However, as we look to the future, the concerns that we must resolve will require that we achieve that balance; we teach ethical behavior, not only through our words, but through our actions. Upcraft, Gardner, and Associates (1988) reinforces the importance and the dilemma of acting when he indicates that one of the foundations of student affairs is managing in the best interests of everyone.

Ethical standards statements by professional associations such as the American College Personnel Association (ACPA) and the National Association of Student Personnel Administrators (NASPA) provide guidance as we try to respond in an ethical manner. But these standards also have limitations. "While formal ethical standards are important and helpful, they generally are useful only when the problem has a superior or clearly right solution; ethical standards can help give professionals backbone. In institutions where all the alternatives seem to be equally good or bad or where the ethical principles within a statement conflict, ethical standards have limited value. Ultimately, ethical professional behavior rests on the personal integrity of individual student affairs professionals and on their commitment to the values and ideals of the profession" (Winston and Dagley, 1985, pp. 63-64).

As we face the future, it will be even more important that the student affairs profession respond ethically and work actively to deal with ethical concerns beyond the boundaries of our individual campuses. Our future agenda as a profession and as part of higher education will mandate that we expand our concepts of ethical behavior and that we actively work to create communities within our institutions that support and foster ethical practice (Brown, 1985). Each issue examined in this volume will have ethical implications—issues including changing staff, new students, legal and regulatory environments, technology, research, organizational behavior, our relationship with academic affairs, and managing change. Each professional must examine his or her own approach to ethics and translate it into practice if we are to be successful in the future.

We cannot afford to let ethical statements and ethical practice remain abstract concepts. A commitment to ethical and responsible behavior provides the essential framework to guide our behavior in the future and aids us in approaching that future with optimism.

Current Status of Student Affairs

We are optimistic about the state of the student affairs profession at the end of the eighties, and we believe the prognosis is excellent as we enter the nineties and face the twenty-first century. That is not to say that our profession does not have its problems, or that we will not have to work hard to meet the challenges outlined in this book. But we are optimistic for several reasons.

First, we have survived the demise of in loco parentis, and we have established a developmental rationale for our existence. Our student development theories are expanding to include the diversity of students we face today and will continue to face in the future (see Chapter Three). The evidence of our effectiveness, as shown by retention and developmental research, confirms our importance to the educational process.

Second, in response to the changing student and institutional needs, our profession has become more specialized and now draws from the fields of psychology, sociology, anthropology, human development, business administration, medicine, nursing, computer science, management information systems, and many others. We will need to embrace these professionals as part of the student affairs organizations. (See Chapter Eight.) Further, our profession has expanded to be more inclusive of women, ethnic minorities, and racial minorities. And finally, we are actively examining methods to help our staffs better prepare to meet new challenges. (See Chapter Eleven.)

Third, we are connected with the academic side of higher education in improved and enhanced ways. More and more, we are seen as partners in the educational process, particularly as institutions admit more high-risk students. It is clear that the out-of-classroom environment, which is basically our domain, is critical to the academic and personal success of students. It is also clear that student affairs professionals can and do use the classroom as another way of affecting students' development. (See Chapter Twelve.)

Fourth, we are getting better at managing our enterprises. We have become more cost-effective and efficient managers, better able to defend ourselves in eras of stable or declining resources. We have become more skilled strategic planners, budget managers, human resource managers, consultants, and program assessors. (See Chapter Nine.)

Fifth, we have successfully responded to the outside forces

that have influenced and that will continue to influence higher education and our profession in the future.

We have been responsive to judicial precedents, civil rights legislation, student financial aid regulations, affirmative action, changing economic conditions, and other externally directed forces, and yet we have been able to continue to serve our students. (See Chapter Six.) There are probably many other reasons for our optimism; but in short, we enter the decade of the nineties in a position of strength. We will retain and expand that strength only if we acknowledge our past, are aware of our present, and are able to forecast our future, based on our best prognosis of societal and educational trends. The rest of this volume will explore the many agendas that will be part of our future as a profession. We hope the following chapters will provide food for thought as our readers view their own futures and those of their institutions.

References

American Council on Education. *The Student Personnel Point of View.* ACE Studies Series 4, vol. 1, no. 3. Washington, D.C.: American Council on Education, 1937.

American Council on Education. *The Student Personnel Point of View.* ACE Studies Series 4, vol. 13, no. 13. Washington, D.C.: American Council on Education, 1949.

Brown, R. D. "Creating an Ethical Community." In H. J. Canon and R. D. Brown (eds.), *Applied Ethics in Student Services.* New Directions for Student Services, no. 30. San Francisco: Jossey-Bass, 1985.

Canon, H. J. "Guiding Standards and Principles." In U. Delworth, G. Hanson, and Associates, *Student Services: A Handbook for the Profession.* (2nd ed.) San Francisco: Jossey-Bass, 1989.

Chickering, A. W. *Education and Identity.* San Francisco: Jossey-Bass, 1969.

Coates, J. F. *Issues Management: How You Can Plan, Organize, and Manage for the Future.* Mt. Airy, Md.: Lomond, 1986.

Cooperative Institutional Research Program. *The American Freshman: National Norms for Fall, 1988.* Los Angeles: American

Council on Education and the Higher Education Research Institute, University of California, 1988.

Erikson, E. H. *Identity: Youth and Crisis.* New York: Norton, 1968.

Family Educational Rights and Privacy Act of 1974, 20 U.S.C., sec. 1232q.

Fargo, J. M. "Academic Chivalry and Professional Responsibility." In R. H. Stein and M. C. Baca (eds.), *Professional Ethics in University Administration.* New Directions for Higher Education, no. 33. San Francisco: Jossey-Bass, 1981.

Godbold, A. *The Church College of the Old South.* Durham, N.C.: Duke University Press, 1944.

Harrison, C. H., and Varcoe, K. "Orienting Transfer Students." In M. L. Upcraft (ed.), *Orienting Students to College.* New Directions for Student Services, no. 25. San Francisco: Jossey-Bass, 1984.

Hodgkinson, H. L. *All One System.* Washington D.C.: Exxon Education Foundation, 1985.

Kitchener, K. S. "Ethical Principles and Ethical Decisions in Student Affairs." In H. J. Canon and R. D. Brown (eds.), *Applied Ethics in Student Services.* New Directions for Student Services, no. 30. San Francisco: Jossey-Bass, 1985.

Knock, G. H. "Development of Student Services in Higher Education." In M. J. Barr, L. A. Keating, and Associates, *Developing Effective Student Services Programs.* San Francisco: Jossey-Bass, 1985.

Kohlberg. L. "Stages of Moral Development." In C. M. Beck, B. S. Crittenden, and E. V. Sullivan (eds.), *Moral Education.* Toronto: University of Toronto Press, 1971.

Morison, S. E. *The Founding of Harvard College.* Cambridge, Mass.: Harvard University Press, 1935.

National Association of Student Personnel Administrators. *A Perspective on Student Affairs.* Washington, D.C.: National Association of Student Personnel Administrators, 1987.

Noel, L., Levitz, R., Saluri, D., and Associates. *Increasing Student Retention: Effective Programs and Practices for Reducing the Dropout Rate.* San Francisco: Jossey-Bass, 1985.

Perry, W. G., Jr. *Forms of Intellectual and Ethical Development in College.* New York: Holt, Rinehart & Winston, 1970.

Recruitment and Retention in Higher Education. (monthly newsletter) Madison, Wis.: Magna Publications, 1988.

Rudolph, F. *The American College and University.* New York: Vintage, 1962.

Sanford, N. (ed.). *The American College.* New York: Wiley, 1962.

Schlossberg, N., Lynch, A., and Chickering, A. *Improving Higher Education Environments for Adults.* San Francisco: Jossey-Bass, 1989.

"USA Snapshots." *USA Today,* Jan. 28, 1989, p. 1.

Upcraft, M. L. *Residence Hall Assistants in College.* San Francisco: Jossey-Bass, 1982.

Upcraft, M. L. "Managing Right." In M. L. Upcraft and M. J. Barr, *Managing Student Affairs Effectively.* New Directions for Student Services, no. 41. San Francisco: Jossey-Bass, 1988.

Upcraft, M. L., Gardner, J., and Associates. *The Freshman Year Experience: Helping Students Survive and Succeed in College.* San Francisco: Jossey-Bass, 1989.

Winston, R. D., and Dagley, J. C. "Ethical Standard Statements: Uses and Limitations." In H. J. Canon and R. D. Brown (eds.), *Applied Ethics in Student Services.* New Directions For Student Services, no. 30. San Francisco: Jossey-Bass, 1985.

Chapter 2

Examining the Validity of Basic Assumptions and Beliefs

James W. Lyons

Student affairs has a distinctive role in higher education. Those who work in it are teachers, yet they are ordinarily not regular members of teaching and research faculties. They administer complex organizations with numerous facilities and services, yet they are not usually regarded as administrators.

Certainly the administrative portfolio of student affairs is distinctive and includes programs and services such as orientation, residential life, judicial affairs, counseling and advising, emergency services, college unions, health services, and student resource centers. But others can, and sometimes do, run these things. Hence, it is not just the educational and administrative domains of student affairs that define its unique role.

In this chapter, I assert that a special set of assumptions and beliefs that student affairs professionals bring to their responsibilities makes the difference. These assumptions and beliefs explain why student affairs professionals do the things they do—their methods and approaches. No one of these assumptions and beliefs is unique to student affairs. Indeed, they are held by many others in higher education. But the combination of these assumptions and beliefs in our field is distinctive. Together they give special meaning to the role and work of student affairs.

Imagine a group of faculty and staff meeting to decide how to allocate student housing spaces when the demand outstrips the supply. What suggestions are likely to be advanced? The academic dean might suggest that students with high grades be given priority because this approach would encourage and reward good scholarship. The admissions dean would ask that new students be given priority as a way to help them adjust to college. A hardened science professor, a social Darwinist by nature, might urge that rooms be assigned on a first-come-first-served basis to reward the go-getters and those who pay attention to announcements. The foreign student, the disabled student, and the minority affairs adviser might team up to suggest that their respective constituents be given priority—both to help with their students' special needs for adjustment and access and to enrich the diversity of life in the residences. The business manager, ever mindful of her budget-balancing duties, might suggest auctioning off some of the spaces to the highest bidders. And someone else will invariably suggest a lottery in the interest of fairness. In this example, the participants, all educators, shared the need to decide how to allocate spaces in student residences. Yet many different solutions were suggested. That happened because each person in this meeting brought a distinct set of values to the task.

The assumptions and beliefs outlined in this chapter also provide a distinct set of values that shape our perspective as professionals and, hence, our work. They guide choices and priorities, and they influence our responses to new issues, changing times, different circumstances, and recurring events. Our assumptions and beliefs as professionals will influence powerfully how we respond to the changing agenda in our future.

In this chapter, I will discuss some assumptions and beliefs about the role of student affairs in an institution, about the nature of students, and about the collegiate environment's influence on learning. The chapter presents a version of the assumptions and beliefs that appeared in *A Perspective on Student Affairs, 1987* (National Association of Student Personnel Administrators, [1987] 1989). The list is not exhaustive, nor will all student affairs people agree that each point guides their work to the same degree; the higher education community is too diverse for that to be true. Yet these ideas have remained important and remarkably unchanged over time, and in a variety of collegiate settings. Many can be traced back to the keystone documents: *The Student Personnel Point of View* statements of 1937 and 1949 (American Council on Education, [1937] 1989a, [1949] 1989b).

Let us begin by discussing a fundamental assumption about the role of student affairs in an institution.

The Academic Mission of the Institution Is Preeminent. Colleges and universities organize their primary activities around the academic experience: the curriculum, the library, the classroom, and the laboratory. That academic mission is the fundamental reason for the existence of the enterprise. All other activities exist to support, promote, and enable the core business of the institution.

Academic missions differ from one college or university to another. The mission of a community college might be to provide, among other things, technical skills needed in the community it serves: computer technicians, auto mechanics, or dental assistants, for example. A liberal arts college, on the other hand, is likely to have a different and more general mission. And large universities may have multiple missions. In each instance, however, academic programs are organized to achieve the school's mission. Those programs become the preeminent activities of the school. When one hears the phrase "First things first!" in a college or university, it is usually the academic mission that comes before intercollegiate sports, club activities, and housing programs.

It would be a mistake, however, to conclude that other institutional activities are not important or even essential. Just as it takes many people in addition to a surgeon to make an operating room function, so too does it take many functions and roles to achieve the academic mission of an institution. Student affairs is one of those important functions; as a partner in the educational enterprise, it enhances and supports the academic mission. In fact, the primary test of the efficacy of student affairs is the extent to which it enables the achievement of academic goals.

This belief in the importance of student affairs is a formidable building block of many policies and practices in student life. It explains the requirement that a person be a student in order to have access to student resources or benefits. It is why intercollegiate athletes, organization officers, and on-campus residents must be students. It is why students who fail courses repeatedly are not allowed to stay. It is why many student services, psychological, medical, and recreational, are limited to students who are registered. It is why one test of whether a psychologically disturbed student may remain on campus is whether the student can do his or her academic work while being treated. Another test, incidentally, may be the extent to which limited resources, in this case the time and energies of a counselor, student friends, and others, are available to support the student without seriously depriving others.

Students affairs, then, is primarily instrumental; it succeeds when it supports and enhances the academic mission of the school. At its best, it also provides some intrinsically good secondary benefits to students in the areas of social, personal, and ethical development.

Let us turn next to some key beliefs about human nature and students in the collegiate setting. Student affairs professionals place special import on the uniqueness of the individual, on the relationships between thinking and feeling, on asserting the worth and dignity of all people, and on the power of personal involvement in educational experiences.

Each Student Is Unique. Of all the precepts of student affairs, the uniqueness of each student may be the one most widely embraced, simplest to explain, and yet the most difficult to translate into policy and practice. It leads the practitioner directly into one of the most vexing of institutional work zones: ministering to the needs and interests of the individual in the face of often conflicting norms and expectations of the collegiate community (see Chapter Ten).

Students are individuals. No two are alike. Each brings a unique history of personal circumstances. Some are from large families, some from small. Some grew up in cities, some in rural areas, and some in both. Some are the first in the family to attend college; others have long legacies of college attendance. Some are religious, some not, and rarely do those who are religious practice their faith in similar ways. All have an ethnic history, but the nature and power of their ethnic traditions and heritage differ, often significantly. Some have never known hardships; others have never known otherwise. They all look different from one another. Tastes in music, sports, and leisure-time activities are never quite the same for any two students. Each has a distinct personality. Some are men and some are women; some tall, some not; some physically able and some less so; some traditionally aged and some older. No two have the same ethical foundations and may not always agree on what is right and what is wrong. Some are socially mature; some are not; and some are in-between. And not all have benefited from good schools and scholastic encouragment and support from home and family. In sum, each brings a different history of successes and failures, strengths and weaknesses.

Given all of these differences, it is not surprising that each student's approach to college is distinct. Interests will differ, as will abilities to engage in the social and intellectual life of the campus; not all are equally ready. Students will not make the same choices, nor equally good ones. Some will need lots of help and encouragement; others will not, or at least not to the same extent. But in all cases, an institution's successes in teaching, advising, and promoting social and intellectual growth are strongly related to its ability to recognize and respond to the unique and special traits of the individual student.

Yet how blind institutions can be to these differences! They impose common standards of success or failure that ignore the reality that students start and progress differently. Students too frequently find themselves in large classes where anonymity prevails. Rarely do teachers, deans, and advisers set stages where students' names are learned, remembered, and used. How often we fail to recognize and acknowledge the importance of a student's race, gender, or ethnic background. The more common situation is one that discourages teachers and advisers from knowing the unique qualities of the student and from intellectually engaging the student on a deliberately groomed turf of common love and interest.

It is high on the agenda of student affairs to counter the impersonalization of the collegiate experience; to respond to the individual, yet avoid the cult of individualism; and to create social, physical, and organizational environments that allow the individual to show through and shine. Organizing and doing things on a human scale will, more often than not, nurture the very best social and intellectual development of students.

This belief in and appreciation of the uniqueness of each student accounts for many of the whys of student affairs. It is why there is a tendency to suspend judgment in individual situations and why we take time to learn more about the individuals involved. It is why residential communities are especially valued as a means to recognize, care about, and support the individual. It is why pluralism is held to be more natural and important than an imposed so-called mainstream model of student life. This belief is why those who work in student affairs must be very skilled at recognizing and mediating the intersections between the standards and interests of the community and the values and goals of the individual student.

Feelings Affect Thinking and Learning. Although students are in college to acquire knowledge through the use of their intellect, they feel as well as think. Students are whole persons, and how they feel affects how well they think. This is as true for nontraditional as for traditional-age students. While students are maturing intellectually, they are also developing physically, psychologically, socially, esthetically, ethically, sexually, and spiritually. Helping students understand and attend to these aspects of their lives can enhance their academic experiences.

This belief that students are whole persons and must be recognized and treated as such was one of the first to be articulated in the field of student affairs. The authors of "The Student Personnel Point of View, 1937" (American Council on Education, [1937] 1989) asserted that belief in words that are as fresh today as they were more than fifty years ago (allowing for the change in pronouns): "This philosophy imposes upon educational institutions the obligation to consider the student as a whole—his intellectual capacity and achievement, his emotional make up, his physical condition, his social relationships, his vocational aptitudes and skills, his moral and religious values, his economic resources, and his aesthetic appreciations. It puts emphasis, in brief, upon the development of the student as a person rather than upon his intellectual training alone" (p. 49).

When implemented, this belief is a powerful tonic for the academic mission of an institution. It is why no institution would organize the collegiate experience so that only the cognitive development of students received attention. Just as it is important for there to be activities that develop the intellect, so too must there be activities that help students mature in other areas of their lives as means to promote intellectual development.

Because how students feel cannot be separated from how they think, those in student affairs are charged to organize the physical, social, and ethical aspects of the student's collegiate experience with the same deliberate care used to design the academic curriculum. We know, of course, that student life can be organized in ways that promote social, physical, ethical, and other forms of development. We do this with the sure knowledge that such development can enrich a student's engagement with academics. Equally well known, but too often forgotten, is the fact that arrested social or psychological development can effectively eliminate the motivation and ability to perform academically.

How this organization is manifested in higher education is well known. Good institutions encourage students to live balanced lives by providing opportunities and encouragement for physical activity, for participation in organizations or groups, for having fun, for esthetic and ethical engagement, and for learning how to make and keep friends. Good institutions also provide an array of helping services that include orientation programs, financial aid, counseling and advising, and the teaching of learning skills. Good institutions make sure that people offer help when it is needed.

This concern for the personal development of students also accounts for policies and programs that prevent or reduce activities that can impede positive growth. Hence, there are programs that address drug and alcohol abuse, personal harassment, and threats to a student's personal safety.

Each Person Has Worth and Dignity. One of the most ennobling adventures that students face is learning to recognize, understand, and celebrate human differences. Colleges and universities can, and indeed must, help their students become open to the differences that surround them: race, religion, age, gender, culture, physical ability, language, nationality, sexual orientation, and lifestyle. These matters are learned best in settings that are rich with diversity, and they must be learned if the ideals of human worth and dignity are to be advanced.

Few nations are as diverse as the United States, and few are as unmarked by a continuing history of violent religious, ethnic, and racial strife. Indeed, there are divisions and tensions, but they pale when compared with South Africa's apartheid or the bloodshed in Lebanon, Ireland, or Afghanistan. Why is it that the American society can remain so relatively free of repressive laws and outright violence, even as it becomes more diverse? Perhaps it is because the United States is primarily a country of immigrants with a strong commitment to human rights. Despite our history of differences, tensions have not robbed us of the unifying belief that all among us have worth and dignity.

As the United States nears the fulfillment of another uniquely American dream, universal access to higher education, it follows that campuses are marked by increasing pluralism. Higher education has become host to the challenge and the hope to make pluralism work not only in the collegiate community but also in the larger society.

For a growing number of schools, the awesome task of diversifying the student population is nearing an end. Diversifying faculties, however, remains an elusive goal. Recent Supreme Court decisions indicate that the era of affirmative action is being pushed aside. We are faced with the challenge of creating collegiate communities that are pluralistic yet interactive, where differences are acknowledged and valued, and where all individuals share a sense of personal and collective worth.

Donald Kennedy (1989), Stanford University's president, struck this chord in a paper written for the Stanford community: "We are asking young people to ignore the habits of comfort, and to seek out others with whom they are unfamiliar and sometimes ill at ease. We are exposing them and ourselves to the risk of misunderstanding and, even when sensitivities are violated as they occasionally will be, hostility. But we think it is nevertheless worth the risk, because we are among the few places in this country in which it may be possible to test the workability of the multicultural existence that will, ready or not, be the life of Californians and eventually all Americans in the twenty-first century."

The dynamics of this next chapter in our social history will be trying and difficult. The energies and commitment of those in student affairs will be especially taxed, for they are the ones who historically have assumed the most responsibility for creating caring and supportive student communities, for helping students develop self-worth and dignity, and for mediating and ministering to tensions within student groups. Because faculties have yet to become diverse in any significant way, and will not for at least two decades, the burdens on student affairs will be even heavier in the immediate future. The belief in human worth and dignity will be central to student affairs work in the decades to come; it grows rather than diminishes in importance.

Personal Circumstances Affect Learning. Physical disability, financial handicap, family distress, medical and psychological problems, and inadequate academic skills are examples of conditions that often hamper learning. Colleges and universities should assist students when such circumstances interfere with learning. Many institutions offer medical and counseling services, financial aid, medical insurance, help for the physically disabled, child care, academic advising, and assistance in improving learning skills. Institutions may also offer special summer programs or regular term programs to help students who are underprepared for the educational demands of the school.

Not all assistance is in the form of services and programs. Some schools intentionally develop flexible policies and mores that recognize most students will encounter situations that intrude upon their learning but that nevertheless merit sensible, thoughtful, and caring responses. Examples include ways to make up lost work, to negotiate incomplete grades, to extend deadlines with cause, to be flexible about access to food and housing just before, just after, and during vacations, and to provide special help in meeting standards of normal progress when there are extenuating circumstances. This kind of flexibility mitigates personal situations that, if not responded to, could adversely affect a student's learning and academic progress. It is the fortunate student who encounters policies that are flexible and teachers who use those policies to respond helpfully to an individual. Clearly, an institution can make unusual responses without compromising its mission and fundamental standards.

The reality, however, is that no school is willing to allocate all the resources that could help students face adversity. Hence, the ever-present challenge is to decide how and how much to help. Student affairs can be helpful in this process by analyzing the costs and consequences of various policies and services and can thereby inform institutional decisions about how much is enough. After all, those in student affairs are the ones who most often deal with students who are in trouble, are troubled, or are troubling; those in student affairs can best assess what it might take to get a student back on track. And, it is those in student affairs who most often make judgments about how to ration services. How much counseling is enough? How much tutoring can we provide? How patient should the institution be with a student's severe or chronic behavior problems? Should the student be expected to work and earn more? To what extent is the student's situation a matter over which he or she has some control; could it have been avoided in the first place?

Once again, we see student affairs professionals working in that tense intersection where the needs of an individual may compete with the limits of the institution and the collective needs of all students.

Student Involvement Enhances Learning. Learning is not a passive process. Students learn most effectively when they are actively engaged with their work in and out of the classroom. This assumption, like many of the others, is almost axiomatic. Few would dispute it, yet it is often overlooked. How often do we ask ourselves whether our pedagogy encourages students to take responsibility for their experience? A learning opportunity is missed every time a teacher (be it a professor, activities adviser, orientation director, or resident assistant) does something for students that students could do for themselves. Teachers constantly face the question of whether to help students or to help them help themselves.

In the academic domain, seminars are more likely than lectures to involve and engage students. Within the world of seminars, those in which students share responsibility for choosing topics and making presentations are more engaging than those in which the choosing and presenting is done for them. Relating theory to practice is more likely to engage students than theory alone. Studying government is immeasurably enriched by doing a governmental internship. Learning Chinese is enhanced by practicing it in China, at a language table, or in a language or theme residence.

Opportunities abound in student life to involve students significantly. Student leaders can be given real responsibility—allowed to err and fail and to make significant changes in the institution's traditional fabric. Are quiet hours established for students, or are students first given a chance to experience life without them before being encouraged to address the subject? Students can accept real responsibility for conduct rules, their enforcement and their adjudication, and they can assume significant roles in establishing and reviewing policies, especially those pertaining to student life.

When we think of such matters, some familiar trade-offs appear. The benefit from following the more difficult and messier course is increased genuine student involvement in the management of their collective and individual lives. After all, many college students see the collegiate years as a sort of internship in growing up, learning to negotiate human settings and organizations, and taking charge of themselves. On the other hand, the more difficult route has familiar and often troublesome consequences for the institution and its teachers. Everything takes longer. Student actions are less neat and organized, are more prone to mistakes, and generally tax the patience and even goodwill of many within the institution. "Let me take care of that" is far easier for the club adviser to say than is "I'd suggest starting with office x and going from there. Let me know how you are doing." Or the instructor says, "I'll choose the topics for papers and research projects" rather than "Why don't you come up with a few ideas for us to discuss?" And how many institutions offer residential options whereby students can run their own food services and set their own board bills? The point is that it is both possible and, in the minds of many in student affairs, highly desirable to create student environments that are rich with encouragement and opportunities for students to take significant charge of their own lives. They then can give themselves the highest of all compliments: "We did this ourselves!"

Students Are Responsible for Their Own Lives. An important objective of higher education is helping students of any age become independent and interdependent, able to take personal responsibility and to care actively about the welfare of others. Students learn responsibility and independence when they bear the consequences of their actions and inactions. This learning can be encouraged by creating trial-and-error opportunities within a context of caring and support.

How is this best encouraged? Students note, often with exasperation, that their schools sometimes treat them as adults and at other times as children. This kind of treatment is particularly offensive to older students who account for a substantial part of the enrollment in American higher education. It is tempting to do things for students rather than to provide only the information and encouragement they need to act for themselves. If we do things for students, they will know that the school cares, and they will avoid making mistakes. But they will also miss the chance to learn from their mistakes. Treating students as adults is the better role for colleges and universities because in so doing, we help students to fulfill their educational goals.

On the other hand, many students are not yet adults, and institutions should support them when the going gets rough—offering help but not insisting that it be accepted. That does not mean laissez-faire or indifference. When a student seems determined to follow a foolish course of action, caring can mean initiating talks, playing through scenarios, exploring alternatives, and helping the student to clarify values and consequences. Students often do, after all, need assistance in learning to take responsibility for their own affairs. But we should take care not to insulate them from the need to take that responsibility.

Out-of-Class Environments Affect Learning. Out-of-class social and physical environments are rarely neutral; they help or detract from students' social and intellectual development. Interactions between students and their environments shape attitudes, readiness to learn, and the quality of the college experience.

Problems in the physical environment are usually easy to recognize and judge, although they are often costly to solve. Inadequate gymnasium facilities can result in intramurals being played as late as midnight, an obviously bad situation. Noisy and overcrowded residences, inadequate parking, and inadequate security and lighting at night are other common examples of physical environments that undermine students' abilities to engage in their studies. Lack of lounge space for commuters and lack of child-care facilities for student parents provide other examples of the effects of the physical environment on student lives.

Social environments, on the other hand, are less easily recognized and gauged. Nevertheless, they too can profoundly shape the quality of a student's educational experience. Here are two examples: the presence or absence of trust and the presence or absence of symbols that minority students are welcomed members of the college or university community.

Where students are trusted, one generally finds a minimum of rules and regulations. Often there are honor codes. Students are believed: if a deadline is missed because of illness, the student just says so and is not asked for a note from the doctor; applications for special housing (for married couples or disabled persons, for example) do not require proof before processing. Examples abound of practices that signal trust. In these environments, breaches of trust are taken seriously. Students who lie to gain some unwarranted advantage or benefit are likely to find themselves without access to those benefits in the future, or even to find themselves separated from the institution.

Minority students often labor under the weight of self-doubt. They wonder if they can really make it and if their admission was "a gift." They may ask, often to the point of great doubt, if they are really welcome to participate fully in the life of the college. When they encounter difficulty, they may worry that it is because of their skin color. Left unasked and unanswered, such questions can have a crushing effect on the social environment of a campus. And such an environment can chill and detract from, rather than enable and nurture, students' learning.

Colleges and universities are rich with symbols that provide subtle signals to students—signals that they are considered a real and genuine part of the fabric of the institution. Some school mascots, for example, have been seen by some as offensive to their ethnic and cultural heritages, although they may be deeply embedded in institutional traditions. What messages do we send if cheerleaders, student spokespersons, and student orientation advisers all reflect the same ethnic and cultural heritage? Our publications should also be inclusive of the full range of students in our institutions. Powerful messages of noninclusion can be sent just because we do not take time to evaluate the message.

Those in student affairs are often able to view the student experience through a lens that helps them understand how the environment affects students. Hence, they can act as architects who help design and shape the environment to help students achieve.

Now let us turn to certain aspects of the campus environment that have special importance—what they are and how they should deliberately support the learning of students. Included are the importance of community and friends, the absence of bigotry, the freedom to doubt and question, and the challenge to practice effective citizenship.

Students Are Helped by Community and Friends. A campus is usually a collection of small communities such as schools, departments, residences, teams, clubs, and service, religious, social, and friendship groups. Healthy communities are settings where students learn to make and keep friends, work together, care about the welfare of others, balance freedom and responsibility, and appreciate human differences. Communities are of high quality when they encourage friendships, intimacy, and intelligent risk taking, and when they allow values to be freely shared and examined.

Over the years, those in student affairs have worked from the conviction that students grow and learn better if they have friends. When things go wrong in students' lives, they turn first to other students for advice, counsel, and support. When things go really well, it is friends who are the first to learn. When students need information about the university (who the good faculty are, how to register, what the good courses are, what really goes on around here), again they turn to other students. Eventually they may turn to parents, family members, advisers, counselors, doctors, teachers, or deans—but only eventually. They turn to friends first.

It holds, therefore, that if we want a friendly, supportive, and caring environment where advice and counsel are readily available, we need to make certain that students make friends. While it is important to pay some attention to an overall campus community, it is far more important to ensure that there are many smaller, human-scale subcommunities. These are the settings where friendships are formed and nurtured.

The residence is the most common and perhaps the most potent setting within which to foster a student community. But there are other settings too: a class, a department, a college union, a lab, a religious group, a club, a workplace, an ethnic organization, or a team. These are all affinity groups, social organisms, or subcommunities of sorts that can, with very little thought and effort, break down the barriers of anonymity and facilitate and support friendships. They are available to both traditional and nontraditional students.

Such subcommunities are also the outposts of the larger support services of the college or university—outposts where the need for such things as special advising, emergency interventions, or psychological help are quietly recognized. Students can help each other to recognize and seize opportunities, to know about campus resources, and to recognize serious trouble at an early stage.

In this context, it should be noted that strong student affairs organizations provide both centralized and decentralized services, make use of both professional and peer or volunteer staff, and consciously create networks of students who are actively involved in helping each other. The likelihood of students making and keeping friends is much greater when students are part of a supportive and caring community. When that happens, it is likely that students' learning, growth, and life skills will be enriched significantly.

Bigotry Cannot Be Tolerated. Any expression of hatred or prejudice is inconsistent with the purposes of higher education in a free society. So long as bigotry in any form exists beyond the boundaries of the campus, it will remain an issue for colleges and universities as well. There must be an institutional commitment to create conditions that ensure bigotry is forthrightly confronted.

The anathema of bigotry is a good example of a belief that is firmly held by virtually everyone in the collegiate community. Yet, it is the rare campus that is free from acts of bigotry; some are deliberate, but most are results of ignorance, thoughtlessness, or downright rudeness. Nevertheless, each incident is a cruel reminder that changing attitudes is very difficult, certainly much more difficult than changing institutional policies and customs.

Most acts of bigotry occur in the domains of student affairs: residences, student media, student organizations, and public places like plazas, bulletin boards, and unions. Hence, it usually falls to student affairs to provide the leadership to try to prevent acts of bigotry and to marshal responses to them when they occur.

These tasks are formidable and call upon many of the professional skills common to student affairs staff. Staff members are able to clarify and articulate relevant institutional values in policies and handbooks. For example, the introduction to the code of student conduct on a campus might indicate that all students must be free to pursue scholarship untrammeled by intrusive harassment because of their race, ethnicity, sex, religion, or sexual preference. Student affairs professionals have responsibility for orientation programs, advising, residential life, and other activities that can increase students' sensitivities to difference. They are in prime positions to confront and to teach others to confront bigotry directly, to model the language and behaviors of respect, to counter those of offense and denigration, and to be influential in shaping institutional policies about student conduct and responses to transgressions.

One of the biggest challenges schools face is locating the proper boundary between unwanted, offensive, intrusive, and harassing words and conduct on the one hand and protected expression on the other. There are almost always major difficulties when campuses depend heavily upon laws and judicial responses to regulate and shape behavior. This is especially so when one encounters the tensions between protected and deeply offensive speech. As a result, teaching students and others to address and resolve conflict by dialogue and mediation rather than by avoidance or appeals to authority has become an especially important part of the student affairs agenda.

Effective Citizenship Should Be Taught. A democracy requires the informed involvement of citizens. Citizenship is complex, and students can learn from practical as well as academic approaches to civic responsibilities. Active participation in institutional governance, community service, and collective management of their own affairs contributes significantly to students' understanding and appreciation of civic responsibilities.

There are many settings on a typical campus where students can learn to govern and be governed, to shape and negotiate bureaucracies, to regulate and be regulated, and to judge and be judged. Student governments and judicial systems are obvious examples. Less obvious and probably more important are clubs, organizations, teams, and residences. These are the settings where the most students are likely to be personally engaged and to experience the inevitable and often vexing challenges of governance. These settings are also small enough so that students avoid the sense of powerlessness that comes with large organizations. In these smaller settings, they can make a difference if they try.

Student affairs, while not likely to overlook the importance of institution-wide governance arrangements, recognizes that the lessons of governance are really confronted and learned in small groups or organizations. Opportunities for service and volunteer experiences also create opportunities for work on effective citizenship. Work in the community or in the institution can help students of all ages understand their greater responsibilities to the community. Both those helping and those being helped benefit. Further, students learn that service is an essential component of effective citizenship both on and off the campus.

The Freedom to Doubt and Question Must Be Guaranteed. Students need to be encouraged and free to explore ideas, test values and assumptions in experience, face dilemmas of doubt and perplexity, question their society, and give and receive criticism. Hence, the doctrines of academic freedom and free speech, which are central to the classroom, must extend to other areas of campus life.

Colleges and universities must protect and encourage ideological exploration and avoid policies or practices that bind the inquiring minds and spirits of students, faculty, and staff.

This approach means, among other things, protecting debate, ensuring fair and objective discussion, insisting on truthfulness, and resisting one-sided, emotional, and exaggerated presentations. It also means ensuring that policies about student organizations and activities are written for educational reasons and not to discourage or prohibit activities that are unpopular or even offensive or that might result in bad press or external complaints.

The ideological and social experimentation of students can be a painful process, and the participation of student affairs staff in it, as educators, is very important. As students test the strength of their convictions and their advocacy skills, student affairs staff and their colleagues must be willing to do the same with theirs. Student affairs professionals should not be ethically neutral, but neither should they be ethically prescriptive. Their honest participation in the exchange and examination of values, beliefs, conflicts, and dilemmas helps to create an atmosphere that is supportive without being uncritical. Who cannot recognize the importance of keeping the proabortion and antiabortion debates open and civil or the importance of ensuring that students may freely advocate their solutions to the problems of acquired immune deficiency syndrome (AIDS) and other sexually transmitted diseases, whether by promoting safer sex or promoting abstinence?

Some students, however, will test their emerging views by imposing them on others. Hence, the concern for a supportive atmosphere extends naturally to discouraging actions that infringe on the rights of others and that are educationally counterproductive for all concerned. One thinks here of the frequent requests to schools to ban recruiters because they are from firms that pollute or from the military or the CIA or because they do business with South Africa or because they discriminate against gays and lesbians. These are powerful and legitimate issues that merit thought and choices by individual students. Banning such recruiters may be justified in the minds of some; but is that justification sufficient to deprive individual students of choices that are rightfully theirs?

Student affairs staff may even lean toward the side of ensuring that their campus does not become too comfortable or lacking in ideological debate and conflict. They will worry less about the public relations concerns of the institution and more about the importance such conflict plays in the education of students.

Conclusion. In this chapter, I have discussed some assumptions and beliefs that are rooted in the history of student affairs. Many are clearly part of the general idealistic fabric of higher education; no one of them is unique to student affairs. Yet taken as a set, they anchor the work of those in student affairs and make what they do, and how they do it, distinctive and valued. Just as they have served student affairs and their institutions well for a long time, these assumptions and beliefs are likely to serve equally well in the future. They are concepts that do stand the test of time and are equally applicable to diverse students. The task for student affairs is to translate these assumptions and beliefs into practice. When this is accomplished effectively, both students and institutions prosper.

References

American Council on Education. "The Student Personnel Point of View, 1937." In *Points of View*. Washington, D.C.: National Association of Student Personnel Administrators, 1989. (Originally published 1937.)

American Council on Education. "The Student Personnel Point of View, 1949." In *Points of View*. Washington, D.C.: National Association of Student Personnel Administrators, 1989. (Originally published 1949.)

National Association of Student Personnel Administrators. "A Perspective on Student Affairs, 1987." In *Point of View*. Washington, D.C.: National Association of Student Personnel Administrators, 1989. (Originally published 1987.)

Kennedy, D. "Reflections on Racial Understanding." Office of the President, Stanford University, Stanford, Calif., Jan. 1989.

Chapter 3

Evolving Theoretical Perspectives of Student Development

M. Lee Upcraft
Leila V. Moore

The student affairs profession has always used theoretical perspectives about students to guide its practice. Our original theory of student development, in loco parentis, served us for more than 300 years. Since 1960, our theories, as reflected in the writings of our scholars and as reported in our journals, have been clarified, tested, and modified. In the eighties, we have become increasingly conscious of the inadequacies and gaps in our theories. For example, African American student development is not adequately explained by theories based on white students. Gender differences are not adequately explained by theories based on male students. Only recently have we seen the emergence of models and theories that address these and other inadequacies of our traditional student development theories. In this chapter, we will review the history of student development theory and present the challenges remaining in the evolution of such theory.

The Forerunner of Student Development Theory: In Loco Parentis

The first developmental rationale used by institutions of higher education was based on the concept of in loco parentis. The early colonial colleges believed they had a responsibility to act on behalf of parents for the good of their students. Students were considered children, and the institution their "parents." In fact, the average age of seventeenth-century freshmen was about fourteen, so there was some reason for treating them as children.

So much has been made of in loco parentis as the legal relationship between students and their institutions that we forget that it originally had a developmental rationale: the development of Christian moral character. In fact, historian Frederick Rudolph argues that the development of students' character was substantially more important than the development of their intellect. For example, President Lord of Dartmouth once said, "The very cultivation of the mind has frequently a tendency to impair the moral sensibilities . . . of students." President Talbot of Denison agreed: "At college we tend to exaggerate the importance of the intellect." For the most part, the college experience was moralistic, theistic, and rationalistic; and when there was a conflict, morality and theology prevailed (Rudolph, 1962, p. 139).

This original student development theory was implemented through a highly controlled and contained environment governed by extensive rules, which were strictly enforced by the president and the faculty. Rules were very specific and rigidly enforced, and punishments were severe—often including floggings, suspension, and expulsion (Rudolph, 1962). The dimensions of Christian moral character were very well defined, the factors influencing that character were known, and the outcome was not only well defined but also unchallenged by any evidence. Despite the emergence of the social sciences in the late nineteenth century and the development of counseling theories in the first half of the twentieth century, the development of Christian moral character was the predominant developmental theory that guided our relationship with students until the mid-twentieth century.

Twentieth-Century Influences

The first secular influence on our thinking about college students emerged in the late nineteenth century when psychological theorists such as Freud and Jung began to write about humans from a perspective different from theologians and philosophers. As the field of psychology developed, theorists such as B. F. Skinner and others influenced the student affairs profession. Undoubtedly, the most influential psychologist on student affairs was Carl Rogers. For many student affairs professionals trained in the fifties and sixties, before the emergence of what we now call student development theory, Rogers (1951, 1961) provided a very powerful theoretical basis for our work. His *client centered* theory of counseling was a combination of assumptions based on self-psychology, phenomenology, and self-actualization principles. His concept of *unconditional positive regard,* in which the counselor maintains a nonjudgmental attitude toward the client, served as an interpersonal relations principle adopted by many student affairs practitioners in the fifties and sixties.

Initially, however, psychological theorists focused on adults, and it was only later that psychologists such as Erik Erikson began to focus on adolescent development. Erikson (1950, 1968) was the first to look at personality development in a social context and to define the identity development of youth. His often quoted (and frequently misunderstood) concept of identity crisis has become an accepted part of our thinking about student development. Erikson believed that the task of establishing one's identity is especially critical during the college years—a time during which youths must redefine themselves. This period of development can be a time of emotional turmoil, or even massive personality disorientation.

Another psychologist of influence was Jean Piaget (1964). Although Piaget is known primarily as a child-development theorist, two aspects of his work have particular relevance to student development. One is that mental structures gradually become more complex through the process of problem solving and analysis. The second is Piaget's description of equilibrium and disequilibrium. When current mental structures fail to be useful in problem-solving activities, a period of confusion, discomfort, or disequilibrium occurs. In this confused and sometimes painful state, the person begins the process of restoring equilibrium by developing more complex mental processes. Students may be seen as moving from more simple to more complex mental processes and through equilibrium/disequilibrium stages.

A second influence of the early twentieth century was the emergence of the vocational guidance movement, introduced by Frank Parsons in 1909. In his book *Choosing a Vocation,* he described the activities involved in choosing an occupation. This early description advanced the theory of matching self-understanding (interests, abilities, and opportunities) with the requirements of a particular occupation. Over the next forty years, vocational guidance turned on this principle. The "best fit" was the outcome sought, and research in this area focused on assessment of interests and abilities. Since college graduation marked a time for placement in the work force, the need for additional theory was heavily influenced by the extent to which college graduates experienced certainty of choice and success in finding meaningful employment. Work emerged in the 1950s as a primary source of satisfaction, to the extent that it rapidly became the "organizing focus for one's identity" (Tyler, 1969, p. 132).

Theories of career development proliferated during the fifties and early sixties. Notable among the group of career theorists was Donald Super (1957), who hypothesized that career choice includes continuous updating of knowledge about self and knowledge about the world of work. Super's work was followed by several other theorists who added to our theory base about decision making, life planning, and the special considerations of returning adults regarding career choice, vocational development, and vocational maturity.

Also in the sixties, John Holland (1966) developed a personality typology that investigated the determinants of occupational choice. He identified six distinct personality types: realistic, intellectual, social, conventional, enterprising, and artistic. He then related these types to a classification of corresponding model environments to produce his theory of vocational choice. "For Holland, the typology described both students and subcultures (environments) and the theory predicts that students of a given type will choose an occupation located in an environment matching that type" (Katchadourian and Boli, 1985, p. 40).

A third major influence on the emergence of theory was the development of the student personnel profession, beginning with the appointment of Thomas Arkle Clark as the first dean of men at the University of Illinois in 1909. The landmark publication *The*

Student Personnel Point of View (American Council on Education, 1937), although not a student development theory, did offer some basic assumptions about how students grow and develop in the collegiate environment, including the following:

- Intellectual development is just one aspect of the growth of a student; others include social, emotional, interpersonal, moral, and vocational development.
- Theories about college students are not meant to be used to treat all students as though they had the same characteristics. These theories describe the relationships between and among different characteristics.
- The education process is interactive, not linear.
- The education process involves not only knowledge but also skills and attitudes.

Later, writers such as Gilbert Wrenn (1951), Esther Lloyd-Jones and M. R. Smith (1954), Kate Hevner Mueller (1961), E. G. Williamson (1961), and others began to focus on college students and higher education as a legitimate field of study.

Student Development Theory in the Mid-Twentieth Century

Our assumptions about students and their development suffered a serious challenge with the popularization of college going. Up until World War II, college was really for the elite, upper-class, white male. Only about 10 percent of high school graduates actually went on to college. The first significant expansion and diversification of the college student population came just after World War II when veterans attended colleges in droves as a result of the first federal financial aid effort, the GI Bill. These veterans, who had fought for their country all over the world, had little tolerance for the rigid rules by which colleges attempted to regulate their lives. They were the first to challenge in loco parentis as a practical basis for defining the relationship between students and their institutions. They were not to be the last.

Psychological Theories. In the early sixties, for the first time, social scientists began to theorize more specifically about college students. During this period, theories emerged about student growth and change, about those aspects of growth that most affect college students, about clusters of personality types and college environments represented in American higher education, and about influences in campus environment that most often influence growth and change.

The landmark book by Nevitt Sanford (1962), *The American College,* contained may postulates about students that are still relevant today. For example, he believed that student development is expressed in a high degree of *differentiation*—that is, a large number of different parts having different and specialized functions—and in a high degree of *integration*—that is, a state of affairs in which communication among parts is great enough so that the different parts may, without losing their essential identity, become organized into large wholes in order to serve the larger purposes of the person.

Sanford (1967) also later postulated the concepts of *support* and *challenge.* He argued that students attempt to reduce the tension or challenge of the collegiate environment by striving to restore equilibrium. The extent to which students are successful depends on the degree of support that exists in the collegiate environment. Too much challenge is overwhelming; too much support is debilitating. The challenge-support cycle results in growth and change.

Sanford's writings were followed by Arthur Chickering's publication of *Education and Identity* in 1969. He expanded Sanford's integration/differentiation concept to include what Chickering called seven *vectors of development,* including developing competence, becoming autonomous, managing emotions, establishing identity, freeing interpersonal relationships, clarifying purposes, and developing integrity.

About the same time, personality typology theorists came on board, including Roy Heath (1964) with his description of the college male as the "reasonable adventurer" and Clark and Trow (1966) with their description of various student subcultures including academics, nonconformists, collegiates, and vocationals. Other theorists included Peter Madison (1969), who postulated a student development theory based on psychoanalytic concepts; Douglas Heath (1968), who combined five developmental trends that define maturing with four structures that define the person; and Florence Brawer (1973), who developed the concept of *functional autonomy*.

In the seventies, the work of other theorists emerged. Jane Loevinger's (1976) concepts about ego development provided particularly useful ways of understanding the relationships between ego development and individual interactions with others, areas of particular growth or concern, and cognitive style. She defined eight growth stages of ego development that closely parallel the work of Erikson and other psychological theorists.

Theories of Reasoning and Cognitive Development. In the seventies, another trend in theory emerged. Other theorists, instead of developing generalized theories of student development, began to look at specific aspects of student development. For example, William Perry (1970) developed a theory of intellectual and ethical development. He saw students moving from a simplistic, categorical view of the world to a more relativistic, committed view through nine stages. According to Perry, freshmen progress from an unquestioning, dualistic framework to the realization of the contingent nature of knowledge, values, and truth. As they move through these stages, they integrate their intellects with their identities, resulting in better understanding of their own value systems and related value commitments.

Similarly, Lawrence Kohlberg (1971) developed a cognitive stage theory of the development of moral judgment. In his view, moral judgment is a progression through various stages of modes of thought. He is concerned with how and why judgments are made, not with their content. The structure of moral thought includes the decision-making system, the problem-solving strategy, the social perspective, and the underlying logic in making a moral choice. His stages include the preconventional level, the conventional level, and the autonomous or principled level.

Sociological Theorists. Psychology was not the only discipline to affect our thinking about students. Also in the late sixties, several sociologists argued that to have a complete understanding of college student development, one had to look not only at the student but also at the environment in which that student lived.

They focused on the interpersonal aspect of the campus environment, with a special emphasis on the powerful influence of the peer group. The first notions about peer group influence were established in 1966, when Theodore Newcomb and Everett Wilson, in their book *College Peer Groups,* introduced the idea of the peer group's powerful effects on students in the first six weeks of college. Feldman and Newcomb (1969), in their book *The Impact of College on Students,* summarized the peer group influence in more specific terms:

- Helps students achieve independence from home and family
- Supports or impedes the institution's academic goals
- Offers students general emotional support, and fulfills needs not met by the curriculum, classroom, or faculty
- Gives students practice in getting along with people, particularly those whose backgrounds, interests, and orientations differ from their own
- Provides students support for changing, or not changing
- Affects staying in or leaving college

This study of the students' environment then expanded beyond the peer group to the more generalized concept of campus ecology. In the mid seventies, we began to look at the influence of campus environments on student development, focusing on the relationship between the student and his or her environment. Several theorists contributed to the ecological perspective, including Barker's (1968) behavioral-setting theory; Clark and Trow's (1966) subculture approach; Holland's (1973) personality types and model environments; Stern's (1970) need-press culture theory; and Pervin's (1968) transactions model. Readers who want more detailed information about these theories should consult Walsh (1978).

In 1973, the Western Interstate Commission for Higher Education outlined some basic assumptions of the ecological perspective based on these theories and research about college students:

- Students enter college with their own personalities, attitudes, values, skills, and needs based on their prior experiences in their homes, families, communities, and peer groups.

- Students enter into an environment they have never before encountered, physically different from anything they have experienced before, more homogeneous and intense.
- The collegiate environment can have a powerful impact on students, depending on the institution's history, composition, size, collective attitudes, values, and needs.
- Students, particularly freshmen, have a high need to identify and affiliate with other students; campus facilities, faculty, staff, and students provide this opportunity.
- Students affect environments, and environments affect students.
- Some students are very susceptible to the press of the environment, while others seem immune.
- Some environments are weak, unstable, and rapidly changing, while others are strong, stable, and less likely to change.
- When there is congruence between the student and his or her environment, the student is happier, better adjusted, and more likely to achieve personal and educational goals.
- Collegiate environments can be described, influenced, and channeled by the institution for the betterment of students.

These basic assumptions were reinforced by the research of Astin (1973) and Chickering (1974), both of whom confirmed the powerful influence of the residential environment. They found that freshmen who live in collegiate residence halls, compared with those who live elsewhere, are more likely to earn higher grades, stay in college and graduate, and experience more positive personal development.

More Recent Student Development Theory in the Eighties

In the eighties, we diverted our attention away from the foundation work of the psychological and social theorists of the two preceding decades. The eighties became a decade of filling in the theoretical gaps that were missed by earlier theorists. At the same time, however, the increasing diversity of students led to serious challenges of existing student development theories, because these theories failed to explain fully the development of student subpopulations such as women, racial and ethnic groups, older students, international students, homosexual and bisexual students, student athletes, honors students, and commuters, just to name a few. Models of student development specifically addressing these students proliferated in the eighties. In responding to these theory gaps, theorists turned to other fields of study, such as medicine, theology, and anthropology. The exploration of specific aspects of student development has continued, including spiritual development, ethical development, learning styles, values development, family backgrounds and dynamics, life experience prior to college, involvement, and so-called mattering.

Involvement Theory. Currently, the most often quoted student development theory is Alexander Astin's involvement theory. Basing his theory on the extensive body of retention literature, Astin believes that students learn best in the collegiate setting by becoming involved. Astin defines student involvement as the amount of physical and psychological energy the student devotes to the academic experience. He believes involvement theory has five basic postulates:

1. Involvement refers to the investment of physical and psychological energy in various "objects." The objects may be highly generalized (the student experience) or highly specific (preparing for a chemistry exam).
2. Regardless of its object, involvement occurs along a continuum. Different students manifest different degrees of involvement in a given object, and the same student manifests different degrees of involvement in different objects at different times.
3. Involvement has both quantitative and qualitative features. The extent of a student's involvement in academic work can be measured quantitatively (how many hours the student spends studying) and qualitatively (does the student review and comprehend reading assignments, or does the student simply stare at the textbook and daydream?).

4. The amount of student learning and personal development associated with any educational program is directly proportional to the quality and quantity of student involvement in that program.
5. The effectiveness of any educational policy or practice is directly related to the capacity of that policy or practice to increase student involvement [Astin, 1985, pp. 135–136].

Mattering/Marginality Theory. According to Schlossberg, Lynch, and Chickering (1989), student success is dependent upon the degree to which students feel they matter. *Mattering* refers to the beliefs people have, whether right or wrong, that they matter to someone else, that they are the object of someone else's attention, and that others care about them and appreciate them. In the collegiate environment, students must believe that they matter and that others (peers, faculty, staff, and family) care about them. They must feel that they belong if they are to succeed. They must feel appreciated for who they are and what they do if they are to grow, develop, and succeed in college. On the other hand, students who feel out of things, ignored by the mainstream, and not accepted will feel marginal, and, therefore, are much less likely to succeed in college. Minority students in predominantly white institutions are often most susceptible to these feelings of marginality.

Freshman Development. Another more recent general theory of student development is Vincent Tinto's theory of freshman development. Tinto (1987) reflects on the stages of freshman integration into college life and suggests that, by extension, the process of student departure may be conceptualized as three distinct stages: separation, transition, and incorporation.

In this *separation* stage, freshmen disassociate themselves from membership in past communities, homes, schools, and work. For students just out of high school, this means breaking away from family and reaching closure on relationships with high school friends. Separation begins during the last year of high school as going off to college is anticipated. New students in the separation stage reject the values of family and community in order to adopt those values thought appropriate to college.

The *transition* stage bridges the old and the new. New students have not yet acquired the norms or established the personal bonds needed for full integration into the college community. Freshmen from different backgrounds will probably encounter more difficulties in learning the new norms, values, and behaviors. For example, the transition can be expected to be more difficult for ethnic minorities, older adults, and those from very poor or rural backgrounds.

To negotiate the *incorporation* stage successfully, freshmen must establish full membership in both the social and academic communities of college life. Social interactions are the primary vehicle through which such integrative associations occur. Individuals need to establish contact with other members of the institution—students and faculty alike. Failure to do so may lead to dropping out. Experiences important to freshmen success in this stage include participation in orientation seminars, good peer support, knowledge of student and academic services, and at least one caring relationship with a faculty or staff member.

Chickering Revisited. The work of Arthur Chickering, mentioned earlier in this chapter, has been consistently among the most widely applied theories about students. Since 1969, with a substantial base of research to support this theory, Chickering has made some adjustments to his original seven vectors (Thomas and Chickering, 1984). If he were revising his vectors today, he would add or change the following.

The *developing competence* vector was originally defined as students' ability to develop intellectual competence, physical and manual skills, and social and interpersonal competence. With respect to intellectual competence, Chickering would take into account recent advances in what is known about reflective thought, brain dominance, and learning theory. With respect to physical and manual skills, he would take into account our more complete understanding of nutrition, exercise, and other wellness concepts. And with respect to interpersonal competence, he would include the competencies needed for the world of work, including active listening, giving constructive feedback, speaking in public, and other interpersonal skills.

The *managing emotions* vector was originally defined as students' ability to manage the key emotions of agression and sex and to broaden their range of emotions. Chickering sees an increasing urgency for managing emotions because of the increase in campus violence, substance abuse, date rape, and sexual harassment. And because of an increase in prolonged depression, suicide gestures, and completed suicides among students, he would emphasize anxiety and depression as other emotions to be managed.

The *developing autonomy* vector was originally defined as students' ability to become emotionally and instrumentally independent, primarily from parents and the peer group. Today, Chickering would change this vector to *developing interdependence,* moving from individualism to a greater emphasis on social responsibility and global interdependence. He would recognize interdependence as the capstone of development.

The *establishing identity* vector was originally defined as students' ability to develop sense of self by clarifying physical needs, characteristics, and personal appearance by establishing appropriate sexual identification, roles, and behaviors. Chickering would add recent concepts about gender role development, including sexual orientation. He would dissolve age norms linked to career and family.

The *freeing interpersonal relationships* vector was originally defined as students' ability to develop increased tolerance of others, capacity for intimacy, and relationships based on trust, independence, and individuality. Because of increasing cultural pluralism in America and increasing global interdependence, Chickering would now increase the importance of developing high levels of tolerance and acceptance. He would recognize the changing conditions under which one learns about intimacy, since marriage is now not the only context for sustained intimate relationships. And he would focus on students learning more about single parenthood, dual-career couples, unmarried couples living together, and homosexual couples.

The *clarifying purposes* vector was originally defined as students' ability to develop sense of purpose in their lives, leading to plans and priorities for careers, avocations, and life-styles. Chickering would now move from the "one life, one job pattern" assumption to a multiple-career perspective. He acknowledges that stress in the workplace makes the integration of family, leisure, and work more difficult. Work in service of the self seems to be ascending over work in service to others.

The *developing integrity* vector was originally defined as students' ability to develop personally valid sets of beliefs that have internal consistency and that guide behavior. Chickering now includes developing a sense of social responsibility as well as personal responsibility. He believes we must educate students about environmental pollution, toxic wastes, exploitation of the powerless, and the increasing gap between the haves and have-nots. He believes knowledge implies a responsibility to act.

More Specialized Theories of Student Development

Other theories of student development deal with more specialized areas, such as the spiritual and the cognitive.

Spiritual Development. Some critics have argued that most developmental theories are exclusively secular and that they ignore students' spiritual development. Theorists such as Westerhoff (1976) and Parks (1986) have written about the spiritual development of young adults. J. W. Fowler (1981, 1987) proposes six stages of faith development, which may help us understand the spiritual development of college students.

Stage 1 is *intuitive-projective faith* (early childhood). Fantasy and limitation are powerful influences in the young child, who is unable at this early age to be controlled by logical thinking. Thus, the child is profoundly influenced by moods, actions, and language of the visible adults around him or her. As conceptual thinking emerges, the child becomes concerned with knowing how things are and the difference between what is real and what only appears to be real.

Stage 2 is *mythic-literal faith* (childhood and beyond). Persons in this stage adopt the stories, beliefs, and observances that symbolize being part of a community. Moral rules, attitudes, and beliefs are interpreted literally. If the person begins to see that stories contradict one another, literalism breaks down, and the conflicts between authoritative stories must be faced. Mutual interpersonal perspective taking emerges.

Stage 3 is *synthetic-conventional faith* (adolescence and beyond). The world now extends beyond the immediate family. New cognitive abilities allow for mutual perspective taking. Faith must now provide a basis for one's personal identity and outlook, as well as synthesize personal and family-based values and information. Transition to the next stage can occur when there are serious contradictions between valued authority sources, marked changes by recognized leaders of previously deemed sacred and immutable practices, or challenges made by the individual who is cognitively able to see the world from a relativistic point of view.

Stage 4 is *intuitive-reflective faith* (young adulthood and beyond). This individual recognizes the need to take responsibility for his or her commitments, life-style, beliefs, and attitudes. Certain tensions emerge: individuality versus definition by group membership, self-fulfillment versus service to others, relativity versus absoluteness. Transition to the next stage can occur when disturbing inner voices and disillusionment with one's compromises press on toward a multidimensional approach to life and truth.

Stage 5 is *conjunctive faith* (mid-life and beyond). One is open to the voices of one's deeper self. One comes to recognize the prejudices, ideal images, and myths that are part of self-esteem by virtue of one's experiences, social class, religious tradition, or ethnic group. In this stage, one strives to unify opposites in mind and experience. Transition to the next stage can occur when the individual becomes increasingly uncomfortable living and acting in the in-between of an untransformed world and his or her transforming vision of the ultimate environment.

Stage 6 is *universalizing faith* (mid-life and beyond). In this stage, one moves beyond the paradox and polarities and becomes grounded in a oneness with the power of being or, more specifically, a sovereign god. Their visions and commitments free them for a passionate, yet detached, spending of the self in love, devoted to overcoming division, oppression, and brutality. People in this stage include Ghandi, Martin Luther King, Jr., and Mother Teresa.

Cognitive Development. Another domain of theory that has been historically neglected by student development theorists and practitioners is cognitive development. Perhaps they have neglected it because student affairs practitioners tend to see their role as fostering the psychosocial development of students outside the classroom as opposed to the cognitive development of students inside the classroom. Nevertheless, cognitive development is important and should be included in our student development theory base.

David Kolb (1984) believes learning is a cycle, and he has developed a four-stage model of learning: reflective observation, concrete experience, abstract conceptualization, and active experimentation. He believes that in order for learning to take place, one passes through all four stages, perhaps several times, and not necessarily in the same order.

In the *reflective observation* stage, one understands ideas from differing views and forms opinions from the process of taking in many ideas and forming one's own opinion. The *abstract conceptualization* stage involves looking at the logic of an idea and systematically using ideas or theories to solve problems. This is the thinking stage of learning.

The other two stages, *concrete experience* and *active experimentation,* involve learning from one's feelings and by doing. In the concrete experience stage, learning includes becoming personally involved in daily situations and personal experiences. In the active experimentation stage, one learns by solving real problems and carrying out real projects. Kolb believes a person enters the learning cycle at a stage determined by his or her habits and preferences, but all learning involves passing through all four stages of the cycle.

Student Development for Persons of Color

Student development theorists have been criticized for not fully explaining the development of persons of color. Most critics would acknowledge that students of color are in many ways similar to other students in their development. However, these same critics would argue that existing developmental theories make certain assumptions about the commonality of environment, culture, and backgrounds of students that simply are not valid. They would also argue that being raised in a minority culture in a majority society creates different developmental outcomes for youth of that minority culture. Parental roles, child-rearing practices, cultural values, community commitments and obligations, and other culturally related factors may combine to produce different developmental dynamics for minority students. Many developmental theories assume that culturally related factors are constant, and they ignore cultural differences in explaining minority student development. These cultural differences are too strong to be ignored (Wright, 1987).

W. E. Cross, Jr. (1978) sees persons of color moving through four stages that reflect their development. The first is the *preencounter stage,* which is characterized by a limited self-awareness about difference and dependence upon majority group for sense of worth and by an attitude toward the world and self that is determined by the majority group.

Next is the *encounter stage,* which is characterized by an awareness of differences between majority and minority groups—an awareness that is usually precipitated by a significant event. Minority group members search for their own group's history, reinterpret all events from their own group's perspective, and experience the deepening trauma of discrimination.

The third stage is the *immersion stage,* which is characterized by the destruction of the old identity and the glorification of the new identity as a minority group member. Minority group members discard majority group values and stereotypes, behave as though the majority group were not human, feel a very strong attachment to the minority group, confront the system, and participate in political action on behalf of their group.

Last is the *internalization stage,* which is characterized by the internalization of the new identity, meaning that the minority individual can renegotiate with the majority. Minority group members at this stage have inner security and compassion for all minorities. They demonstrate commitment to their principles and participate actively in making social change.

Other theorists who have developed models to help us understand the development of persons of color include Atkinson, Morten, and Sue (1983), and Ho (1987). For African Americans, see

Asante (1988). For Hispanics, see Martinez (1988). For Asian Americans, see Sue and Sue (1971). And for American Indians, see Johnson and Lashley (1988).

Identity Development for Majority Students

Janet Helms (1984) has developed a theory of majority member cultural awareness that helps explain how the majority group, by virtue of its control of the economic and cultural dimensions of our society, directly and adversely affects minority groups—and itself indirectly. Majority member cultural awareness proceeds through five stages beginning with the *contact stage,* in which majority group members are aware of the existence of minority group members, but they do not perceive themselves as racial beings; they tend to assume that racial and cultural differences are unimportant. Next is the *disintegration stage,* in which majority group members acknowledge that prejudice and discrimination exist. Guilt may emerge as racial and cultural differences become more apparent, and majority group members may either retreat to the contact stage or overidentify with the minority. In the *reintegration stage,* majority group members blame the victim (minority members) for creating their own problems. They denigrate minority groups and believe majority group members are victims of reverse discrimination. In the fourth, the *pseudoindependent stage,* Helms believes majority group members accept minority group members at a conceptual level and become interested in understanding racial and cultural differences. Interactions will tend to be with minority group members who are perceived to be similar to oneself. Finally, in the *autonomy stage,* majority group members become knowledgeable about racial and cultural similarities while accepting, respecting, and appreciating both minority and majority group members.

Student Development and Gender

Carol Gilligan's landmark work *In a Different Voice* (1982) argues that contemporary theories of human development fail to take into account possible differences in male and female development. She believes that Freud, Erikson, Piaget, Kohlberg, and others have mistakenly based their concepts of human development on male development and, in the process, totally misrepresented female development. Gilligan believes that the concepts of *autonomy* and *separation* are indicative of male development and that female development is better explained by the concepts of *connectedness* and *relationships.* She believes that Erickson's fifth stage (youth) stresses separateness rather than connectedness, "with the result that development itself comes to be identified with separation, and attachments appear to be development impediments, as is repeatedly the case in the assessment of women" (pp. 12–13).

Gilligan also believes Kohlberg's theory mistakenly portrays women to be deficient in moral development because helping and pleasing others (stage three) are not ends in themselves, but necessary steps on the way to higher stages where relationships are subordinated to rules (stage four), and rules to universal principles of justice (stages five and six). She believes that advanced stages of moral development for women may well be their care for and sensitivity to the needs of others and that Kohlberg's later stages should include the concepts of connectedness so that his theory is valid for women.

Mary Belenky, B. M. Clinchy, N. R. Goldberger, and J. M. Tarule (1986) have extended Gilligan's work to include stages through which women advance their cognitive development, comparing this with William Perry's theory, which they believe is male based. These stages are (1) *silence,* in which women are powerless and rely totally on others for their sense of well-being; (2) *received knowledge: listening to the voices of others,* in which women rely on the knowledge of others and learn by listening to "those who know"; (3) *subjective knowledge: the inner voice,* in which women for the first time become aware of inner resources for knowing and valuing and find inner sources of strength; (4) *subjective knowledge: the quest for self,* in which women start shaping and directing their own lives and begin to choose self over others; (5) *procedural knowledge: the voice of reason,* in which women begin to abandon subjectivism and absolutism in favor of reasoned reflection; (6) *procedural knowledge: separate and connected knowing,* in which women experience themselves as both essentially autonomous (separate from others) and in relationships (connected to others); and (7) *constructed knowledge: integrating the voices,* in which women find a place in themselves for their own reason and intuition as well as for the expertise of others.

Another related approach to gender identity is O'Neil and Roberts-Carroll's phases of the gender role journey (1988). The first phase is *acceptance of traditional gender roles,* in which one accepts stereotypical notions of masculinity and femininity and endorses restrictive views of gender roles such as strength, control, power, and restrictive emotionality for men, and warmth, expressiveness, nurturance, and passivity for women.

The second phase is *ambivalence about gender roles,* in which, because of exposure to new ideas and other people's views of gender roles, one experiences dissatisfaction with stereotypical notions of gender roles and questions their restrictiveness. One vacillates between the safety of stereotypical gender roles and the excitement and anxiety of possible gender role change.

The third phase is *anger,* in which one experiences and expresses negative emotions about prevailing social norms, about individuals and institutions that reinforce stereotypes and sexism, and about stereotypical socialization of males and females. One also experiences limited outlets for negative emotions, resulting in isolation and personal pain about sexism, as well as conflict, anxiety, and depression.

The fourth phase is *activism,* in which one makes in one's own life gender role changes that are less restrictive and conflictual and uses anger about sexism in positive ways. One commits oneself to social, political, and educational plans and undertakes personal, professional, and political courses of action to increase awareness of restrictive gender roles and sexism.

The last phase is *celebration and integration of gender roles,* in which one experiences new awareness and satisfaction of viewing self and the world in a less restrictive and stereotypic way and integrates anger about sexism regularly with efficiency and effectiveness. One understands other people's gender role journeys and experiences gender role freedom in personal and professional relationships. For other theoretical writings on gender development, see Josselson (1987) and Downing and Roush (1985), among others.

Student Development and Adult Learners

Patricia Cross, in her landmark publication *Adults As Learners* (1981), was one of the first to challenge the age bias of our student development theories. She interpreted adult student development in the light of adult developmental learning theories, including force field analysis (Miller, 1967), expectancy-valence paradigm (Rubenson, 1977), congruence model (Boshier, 1973), and anticipated benefits theory (Tough, 1979). Cross developed her own *chain of response* adult learning model, in which she asserts that adult learners start with a self-evaluation that leads them to desire more education if their prior experiences with education were positive. They establish appropriate goals and expectations that may be based on life transitions—either gradual or related to traumatic events such as loss of a job, divorce, or the death of a friend or family member. They then gather information about potential learning activities while they consider special opportunities and overcome barriers. Finally, they participate in some learning activity.

Schlossberg, Lynch, and Chickering (1989) view adult learning as a transition process that extends from the first moment one thinks about returning to college to the time when the experience is complete and integrated into one's life. They break down the transition process for adult learners into three main parts: *moving into* the learning environment, *moving through* it and preparing to leave, and *moving on*. For adult learners, the transition process may extend over many years—generally much longer than for eighteen- to twenty-one-year-olds. Also, the longer the transition, the more it will pervade an individual's life.

Student Development Theory and Sexual Orientation

Until recently, gay, lesbian, and bisexual development was almost totally ignored by development theorists. While gay, lesbian, and bisexual students have a great deal in common with their heterosexual colleagues, they are faced with somewhat different developmental issues because of their sexual orientation.

Cass (1979, 1984) identifies six stages of homosexual identity formation that are differentiated on the basis of a person's perceptions of his or her own behavior and actions that arise as a consequence of this perception as a homosexual. The first stage is *identity confusion,* in which individuals realize that their feelings, thoughts, and behaviors can be defined as homosexual. They ask the question "Who am I?" and accept the possibility that they may be homosexual. Confusion and turmoil characterize this stage as the individual lets go of an identity as a heterosexual.

The second stage is *identity comparison,* in which individuals become aware of the differences between their own perceptions of behavior and self and their perceptions of how others view that behavior and self. They feel alienation from all others and a sense of not belonging to society at large.

The third stage is *identity tolerance,* in which individuals seek out homosexuals and the homosexual subculture to counter feelings of isolation and alienation from others. They begin to tolerate, but not accept, a homosexual identity. By the end of this stage, the individual's self-image has increased to the point where he or she can say, "I am a homosexual."

The next stage is *identity acceptance,* in which individuals continue to increase contacts with other homosexuals—contacts that validate and normalize homosexuality as an identity and way of life. They accept rather than tolerate a homosexual self-image.

The fifth stage is *identity pride,* in which individuals tend to devalue the importance of heterosexual others to themselves and revalue homosexual others more positively. They are proud to be homosexual and no longer conceal their homosexual identity.

The last stage, according to Cass, is *identity synthesis,* in which individuals realize that the them-and-us attitude of stage five, in which all heterosexuals are viewed negatively and all homosexuals are viewed positively, no longer holds true. Supportive heterosexuals are valued, and unsupportive heterosexuals are further devalued. The individual's personal and public sexual identities become synthesized into one identity, and the individual is able to integrate his or her homosexual identity with all other aspects of self.

Summary

In this chapter, we have reviewed the history of student development theory, and we have presented, in a very cursory way, several student development theories. The decade of the nineties will bring exciting new challenges to the continuing discovery and revision of student development theory. These challenges include being able to answer yes to the following questions:

1. Can we develop theories that explain the unique development of students by gender, race, ethnic membership, age, and culture and at the same time develop theories that generalize to students regardless of these factors?
2. Can we adapt our many individual and group developmental theories to the many different campus environments and environmental factors that affect student development? Can we learn as much or more about environmental theories as we know about individual student developmental theories?
3. Can we develop a better theoretical basis for describing and explaining how the backgrounds of students—including race, ethnicity, family history, and life experiences—affect student development?
4. Can we persuade practitioners to apply existing and evolving theories to the practice of the student affairs profession? Can we develop better assessment models to validate and verify existing and evolving theories?

There is no doubt that as we enter the 1990s, student affairs professionals will have an even greater responsibility to know and understand student development theories, given the increased diversity of American college students and the collegiate environments in which they develop. We can no longer rely on one or two theories to guide our work. We must not only familiarize ourselves with emerging theory, but we must also contribute to that theory base through our literature and research.

References

American Council on Education. *The Student Personnel Point of View.* Washington, D.C.: American Council on Education, 1937.

Asante, M. K. *Afrocentricity.* Trenton, N.J.: Africa World Press, 1988.

Astin, A. "The Impact of Dormitory Living on Students." *Educational Record,* 1973, *54,* 204–210.

Astin, A. *Achieving Educational Excellence: A Critical Assessment of Priorities and Practices in Higher Education.* San Francisco: Jossey-Bass, 1985.

Atkinson, D. R., Morten, G., and Sue, D. W. *Counseling American Minorities: A Cross-Cultural Perspective.* (2nd ed.) Dubuque, Iowa: Brown, 1983.

Barker, R. G. *Ecological Psychology: Concepts and Methods for Studying the Environment.* Stanford, Calif.: Stanford University Press, 1968.

Belenky, M. F., Clinchy, B. M., Goldberger, N. R., and Tarule, J. M. *Women's Ways of Knowing: The Development of Self, Voice, and Mind.* New York: Basic Books, 1986.

Boshier, R. "Educational Participation and Dropout: A Theoretical Model." *Adult Education.* 1973, *23* (4), 255–282.

Brawer, F. *New Perspectives on Personality Development in College Students.* San Francisco: Jossey-Bass, 1973.

Cass, C. V. "Homosexual Identity Formation: A Theoretical Model." *Journal of Homosexuality,* 1979, *4,* 219–235.

Cass, C. V. "Homosexual Identity Formation: Testing a Theoretical Model." *Journal of Sex Research,* 1984, *20* (2), 143–167.

Chickering, A. *Education and Identity.* San Francisco: Jossey-Bass, 1969.

Chickering, A. *Commuting Versus Resident Students: Overcoming the Educational Inequities of Living Off Campus.* San Francisco: Jossey-Bass, 1974.

Clark, B. R., and Trow, M. "The Organizational Context." In T. M. Newcomb and E. K. Wilson (eds.), *College Peer Groups: Problems and Prospects for Research.* Hawthorne, N.Y.: Aldine, 1966.

Cross, P. *Adults as Learners.* San Francisco: Jossey-Bass, 1981.

Cross, W. E., Jr. "The Thomas and Cross Models of Psychological Negrescence: A Review." *Journal of Black Psychology,* 1978, *5,* 13–31.

Downing, N. E., and Roush, K. L. "From Passive Acceptance to Active Commitment: A Model of Feminist Identity Development for Women." *The Counseling Psychologist,* 1985, *13* (4), 695–709.

Erikson, E. H. *Childhood and Society.* New York: Norton, 1950.

Erikson, E. H. *Identity: Youth and Crisis.* New York: Norton, 1968.

Feldman, K. A., and Newcomb, T. M. *The Impact of College on Students.* San Francisco: Jossey-Bass, 1969.

Fowler, J. W. *Stages in Faith: The Psychology of Human Development and the Quest for Meaning.* New York: Harper & Row, 1981.

Fowler, J. W. *Faith Development and Pastoral Care.* Philadelphia: Fortress Press, 1987.

Gilligan, C. *In a Different Voice.* Cambridge, Mass.: Harvard University Press, 1982.

Heath, D. *Growing Up in College.* San Francisco: Jossey-Bass, 1968.

Heath, R. *The Reasonable Adventurer.* Pittsburgh, Pa.: University of Pittsburgh Press, 1964.

Helms, J. E. "Towards a Theoretical Explanation of the Effects of Race on Counseling: A Black and White Model." *The Counseling Psychologist,* 1984, *12* (4), 153–164.

Ho, M. K. *Family Therapy with Ethnic Minorities.* Beverly Hills, Calif.: Sage, 1987.

Holland, J. *The Psychology of Vocational Choice.* Waltham, Mass.: Blaisdell, 1966.

Holland, J. *Making Vocational Choices: A Theory of Careers.* Englewood Cliffs, N.J.: Prentice-Hall, 1973.

Johnson, M. E., and Lashley, K. H. "Influence of Native-Americans' Cultural Commitment on Preferences for Counselor Ethnicity." *Journal of Multicultural Counseling and Development,* 1988, *17* (30), 115–122.

Josselson, R. *Finding Herself: Pathways to Identity Development in Women.* San Francisco: Jossey-Bass, 1987.

Katchadourian, H. A., and Boli, J. *Careerism and Intellectualism Among College Students: Patterns of Academic and Career Choice in the Undergraduate Years.* San Francisco: Jossey-Bass, 1985.

Kohlberg, L. "Stages of Moral Development." In C. M. Beck, B. S.

Crittenden, and E. V. Sullivan (eds.), *Moral Education.* Toronto: University of Toronto Press, 1971.

Kolb, D. *Experiential Learning: Experiences as the Source of Learning and Development.* Englewood Cliffs, N.J.: Prentice-Hall, 1984.

Lloyd-Jones, E. L., and Smith, M. R. *Student Personnel Work as Deeper Teaching.* New York: Harper & Row, 1954.

Loevinger, J. *Ego Development: Conceptions and Theories.* San Francisco: Jossey-Bass, 1976.

Madison, P. *Personality Development in College.* Reading, Mass.: Addison-Wesley, 1969.

Martinez, C. "Mexican Americans." In L. Comas-Diaz and E.E.H. Griffith (eds.), *Cross-Cultural Mental Health.* New York: Wiley, 1988.

Miller, H. L. *Participation of Adults in Education: A Force Field Analysis.* Boston: Center for the Student of Liberal Education for Adults, Boston University, 1967.

Mueller, K. H. *Student Personnel Work in Higher Education.* Boston: Houghton Mifflin, 1961.

Newcomb, T. M., and Wilson, E. K. (eds.). *College Peer Groups: Problems and Prospects for Research.* Hawthorne, N. Y.: Aldine, 1966.

O'Neil, J. M., and Roberts-Carroll, M. "A Gender Role Workshop Focused on Sexism, Gender Role Conflict, and Gender Role Journey." *Journal of Counseling and Development,* 1988, *67,* 193–197.

Parks, S. *The Critical Years: Young Adult Search for Faith to Live By.* New York: Harper & Row, 1986.

Parsons, F. *Choosing a Vocation.* Boston: Houghton Mifflin, 1909.

Perry, W. G., Jr., *Forms of Intellectual and Ethical Development in College.* New York: Holt, Rinehart & Winston, 1970.

Pervin, L. A. "Performance and Satisfaction as a Function of Individual-Environment Fit." *Psychological Bulletin,* 1968, *69,* 56–68.

Piaget, J. *Judgment and Reasoning in the Child.* Patterson, N.J.: Littlefield Adams, 1964.

Rogers, C. *Client Centered Therapy: Its Current Practice, Implications, and Theory.* Boston: Houghton Mifflin, 1951.

Rogers, C. *On Becoming a Person.* Boston: Houghton Mifflin, 1961.

Rubenson, K. "Participation in Recurrent Education: A Research Review." Paper presented at meeting of National Delegates on Developments in Recurrent Education, Paris, Mar. 1977.

Rudolph, F. *The American College and University.* New York: Vintage Books, 1962.

Sanford, N. (ed.). *The American College.* New York: Wiley, 1962.

Sanford, N. *Where Colleges Fail.* San Francisco: Jossey-Bass, 1967.

Schlossberg, N. K., Lynch, A., and Chickering, A. W. *Improving Higher Education Environments for Adults.* San Francisco: Jossey-Bass, 1989.

Stern, G. G. *People in Context.* New York: Wiley, 1970.

Sue, S., and Sue, D. W. "Chinese-American Personality and Mental Health." *Amerasia Journal,* 1971, *1,* 36–49.

Super, D. E. *The Psychology of Careers.* New York: Harper & Row, 1957.

Thomas, R., and Chickering, A. W. "Education and Identity Revisited." *Journal of College Student Personnel,* 1984, *25* (5), 392–399.

Tinto, V. *Leaving College: Rethinking the Causes and Cures of Student Attrition.* Chicago: University of Chicago Press, 1987.

Tough, A. "Choosing to Learn." In G. M. Healy and W. L. Ziegler (eds.), *The Learning Stance: Essays in Celebration of Human Learning.* Washington, D.C.: National Institute of Education, 1979.

Tyler, L. *The Work of the Counselor.* (2nd ed.) East Norwalk, Conn.: Appleton-Century-Crofts, 1969.

Walsh, W. B. "Person/Environment Interaction." In J. Banning (ed.), *Campus Ecology: A Perspective for Student Affairs.* Cincinnati, Ohio: National Association of Student Personnel Administrators, 1978.

Westerhoff, J. *Will Our Children Have Faith?* New York: Seabury Press, 1976.

Western Interstate Commission for Higher Education. *The Ecosystem Model: Designing Campus Environments.* Boulder, Colo.: Western Interstate Commission for Higher Education, 1973.

Williamson, E. G. *Student Personnel Services in Colleges and Universities.* New York: McGraw-Hill, 1961.

Wrenn, G. *Student Personnel Work in Colleges and Universities.* New York: Ronald Press, 1951.

Wright, D. (ed.). *Responding to the Needs of Today's Minority Students.* New Directions for Student Services, no. 38. San Francisco: Jossey-Bass, 1987.

PART TWO

Forces for Change and Implications for the Profession

A major purpose of this volume is to assist the profession in identifying the major forces that will influence higher education and student affairs. We believe that we must understand and plan for five broad areas as we prepare for the future: changing students, a rapidly evolving social agenda, the legal and regulatory environment, technology, and changed staff characteristics. Each of these areas will have a profound influence on higher education and student affairs in the future. Our students will change, and in Chapter Four, George Kuh provides a comprehensive view of the changing characteristics of our students, including age, gender, and ethnicity. His thoughtful review points out geographic differences and the trend to part-time enrollment for certain groups. Kuh also provides an analysis of the latest data on expectations of students as they come to college. His section on implications provides food for thought for each of us.

In Chapter Five, Arthur Sandeen and James Rhatigan provide a broad overview of selected social issues that will influence campus life in the future. Ethnicity, gender, safety, security, health issues, and national events will all influence our practice. The authors propose some strategies and alternatives to confront these issues, and they can challenge us to provide leadership on our campuses.

We are all very aware of the changes that statutes, judicial decisions, and rulings of administrative agencies have made in our professional practice. In Chapter Six, Robert Fenske and Edward Johnson examine these trends and provide suggestions to aid student affairs professionals in gaining control, or at least in maintaining a sense of direction in a rapidly changing legal and regulatory environment.

Technology will influence not only how students learn, live, and work but also how student affairs professionals approach their responsibilities. The implications of the technological revolution are enormous for higher education and have particular relevance for student affairs. Don Mills explores these questions in Chapter Seven and provides suggestions regarding how we can gain a sense of mastery of the implications of technological changes—both possibilities and problems.

Changes in staff are already with us. In Chapter Eight, these changes in academic preparation, career paths, and professional development needs are examined. New and creative approaches are needed if we are to embrace the diversity that is student affairs and still find common ground as we face the future.

Others may identify other major forces that will influence our future. But we believe that the forces discussed here are the most important and that careful analysis and planning can help all of us be better prepared to face our shared tomorrow.

Chapter 4

The Demographic Juggernaut

George D. Kuh

"Remember Joe College? The young man who, after working hard and succeeding in high school, arrived in Berkeley, where he found a place to live and set out to sample the rich and incredibly varied intellectual feast at the University of California. Joe was independent, strongly self motivated, and academically well prepared; he was able not only to sample the intellectual wares but also to settle down, about junior year, to a major field of study, which he pursued with diligence and increasing confidence in order to graduate a neat four years after his arrival.

"Joe doesn't live here anymore. Perhaps, in truth, he never did. But now he can't. Times have changed, things have changed, Berkeley has changed" (Schoch, 1980, p. 1, cited in Thelin, 1986).

The University of California, Berkeley has changed indeed! The 1987 freshman class was 56 percent nonwhite, 2 percent American Indian, 25 percent Asian American, 12 percent black, 17 percent Hispanic, 40 percent white, and 4 percent who declined to state their ethnic backgrounds (Bunzel, 1989).

Through the 1960s, Joe College was the dominant, and in many respects, the accurate characterization of the typical undergraduate in American colleges and universities. Today, the so-called typical college student defies succinct description. On some campuses, students reflect the ethnic and racial diversity of the United States. Fewer than half of undergraduates are eighteen to twenty-two years old. Enrollment patterns vary; some students take one or two classes a term while others are enrolled full-time. Many work full-time while taking classes; others alternate between work and study. Most students take five or more years to obtain the baccalaureate degree (National Association of Student Personnel Administrators, 1987).

Perhaps no group is more aware of the challenge presented to colleges and universities by an increasingly diverse student cohort than student affairs professionals. After all, student affairs staff members are considered experts on students and campus environments (National Association of Student Personnel Administrators, 1987). To prepare for the effects of demographic shifts in the United States on institutions of higher education, student affairs professionals must understand the proximate causes of these changes in order appropriately to adapt existing programs and services—or to develop new ones.

The purposes of this chapter are to summarize trends in student characteristics, attitudes, and values and to discuss some implications of these changes for student affairs. First, I will review the factors contributing to stable college enrollments in the 1980s, and I will summarize the demographic shifts produced by differential birth rates of racial and ethnic groups in various parts of the country. Then, I will discuss the values, attitudes, and aspirations of the current college-age cohort. Finally, I will consider the implications for student affairs professionals.

Factors Contributing to Stable College Enrollments

Despite the gloomy projections of declining college enrollments in the eighties (Frances, 1985), the decline failed to materialize. The reasons for continued growth in enrollments are now well known: the decrease in the number of traditionally aged students was offset primarily by an increase in the number of women and adult students, many of whom attended college part-time (Carnegie Foundation for the Advancement of Teaching, 1989a).

Women. The ten-year period between 1976 and 1986 produced a reversal in the male-female composition of higher education enrollments. In 1976, total enrollment was 53 percent male, 47 percent female; by 1986, it was 47 percent male, 53 percent female. Since 1978, women have outnumbered men among first-time freshmen (Astin and Green, 1987). Between 1972 and 1983, the percentage of women over the age of twenty-four in college rose by 13 percent compared with an increase of only 4 percent in the number of males of the same age (National Center for Educational Statistics, 1985).

Part-Time Students. Part-time students have been a major factor in maintaining enrollments, accounting for 39 percent of all students in 1976. In 1988, the figure rose to 43 percent (*Chronicle of Higher Education,* Sept. 1, 1988). Fewer than half of all community college students were part-time in 1970, but more than 60 percent of community college students in 1980 were part-time (Warren, 1985). The increase in the number of women attending college was due primarily to the large number of older female part-time students. Women made up about half of the part-time enrollment in 1976, but close to 58 percent in 1986. Between 1980 and 1987, average part-time enrollment increased 13.6 percent at two-year institutions and 6.1 percent at four-year schools, while the number of full-time freshmen decreased (College Board, 1988).

The increase in part-time students was almost 50 percent greater than the overall growth in the college-age population, but current projections estimate only a 4 percent increase between 1987 and 1992 in the number of students twenty-five years or older who will attend a college or university. Thus, the adult student population has apparently peaked and will not be a significant source of new students (Frances, 1985). Nevertheless, by the turn of the century, part-time students will likely be the majority on college campuses.

The Demographic Juggernaut

Between 1964, the end of the baby boom, and 1979, birth rates in the United States declined. Hodgkinson (1983) likened the effects of this decline on the educational system to a mouse passing through a snake—decreasing school enrollments, diminishing numbers of high school graduates, and smaller cohorts of traditionally college-age youth. In addition to the increase in women and part-time students, four other factors account for the shift in the biographical characteristics of college students: differential fertility rates of ethnic groups, immigration rates, high school graduation rates, and college participation rates of ethnic groups.

Fertility Rates. From an all-time high of approximately 30.4 million in 1982 (Spencer, 1984), the population aged eighteen to twenty-four years was projected to decrease by more than 7.0 million (or almost one-quarter) by the turn of the century. This age group will rebound to 24.6 million in the year 2000 and will be about 27.7 million in 2010. Thereafter, census bureau projections show the eighteen- to twenty-four-year-old group fluctuating between 24.0 and 28.0 million people, unlikely again to reach the 1982 zenith of 30.4 million. More important, the number of eighteen- and nineteen-year-olds will bottom out to 6.6 million in 1995 from a peak of 8.8 million in 1980. By the year 2000, the number of eighteen- to nineteen-year-olds will return to a level of about 7.5 million but will not increase significantly above that level in succeeding years.

Even though population growth in the United States was at a historically low point in the 1980s, and with approximately twenty-one million women in the prime child-bearing ages of twenty to twenty-nine (three million more than in 1975), the rate of child bearing remained constant at about 1.8 births per woman (contrasted with nearly 3.7 births per woman in the late 1950s). Minority groups, however, exhibited a growth rate of two to fourteen times greater than those of the nonminority population (Estrada, 1988). By tracking the average number of children produced by various racial and ethnic groups, changing proportions of whites, blacks, Hispanics, and Asian Americans in the college age cohort can be anticipated. For example, whites tend to bear 1.7 children per female; blacks and Hispanics outproduce whites on average (2.4 and 2.9 children respectively). The higher growth rate of minority populations is due largely to their youthful age structure; the more youthful the population, the higher proportion of women in the child-bearing ages.

The ethnic birth rate differential also partially explains geographical differences in the numbers of people of color in the traditionally college-age cohort. For example, the percentage of black enrollment in public elementary and secondary schools tends to be greatest in southern states (Alabama, Georgia, Florida, Mississippi, Louisiana), while the percentage of Hispanic enrollments is highest in New Mexico, Texas, California, and Arizona (Hodgkinson, 1985). In California and Texas, Hispanics represented over 40 percent of all students enrolled in public schools in 1980 (Hodgkinson, 1983); by 2000, over half of all youth in California will be members of minority groups. In seventeen states, the percentage of minority enrollments is at least 25 percent. All of the twenty-five largest city school systems have "minority majorities" (Hodgkinson, 1985, p. 3). Five regions of the United States will be particularly influenced by the escalating Hispanic birth rate: the Southwest; the Northeast, particularly New York City and the Boston to Washington corridor; south Florida, which is heavily influenced by the flow of refugees from Cuba; the Chicago metropolitan area; and the Pacific Northwest, an area where Hispanics are small in number but growing very rapidly (Estrada, 1988).

Immigration. The ethnic backgrounds of immigrants have also shifted dramatically over the past three decades. Prior to 1960, immigrants were more likely to be from eastern Europe and Canada. Since 1970, immigrants have been more likely to be from Asia, Mexico, or Cuba. Indeed, half of all the immigrants now living in the United States are from Mexico, Latin America, or an Asian country, and most of them entered since 1975.

The Asian population in the United States grew by a startling 142 percent between 1970 and 1980, a rate of growth not likely to be repeated because of the swell of immigration in the 1970s attributed in part to post-Vietnam events. The number of Hispanics grew by 61 percent between 1970 and 1980. The number of persons of Mexican origin grew by 93 percent over the same period, reflecting the geographical proximity of Mexico and ease of immigration. If the influx of Hispanic immigrants continues at current rates, the United States will experience the second largest wave of immigrants in the nation's history (Wilson and Justiz, 1987–88).

High School Graduation Rates. The number of students participating in higher education is, in part, a function of high school graduation rates. The "High School and Beyond" study of the high school class of 1980 and its subsequent follow-ups in 1982 and 1984 (Carroll, cited in Mingle, 1987) revealed that about 50 percent of high school seniors enrolled in some form of postsecondary education (including short occupational programs) in the fall following graduation. Within two years of graduation, more than two-thirds attended some type of postsecondary institution (Mingle, 1987).

About 85 percent of first-time college students attend a college or university in their home states (*Chronicle of Higher Education,* Sept. 1, 1988). Ninety percent of the students in public institutions are residents of the states in which the institutions are located, while 67 percent of the students in private institutions are residents of the state. However, between 1979 and 1986, freshmen were increasingly more likely to leave their states of residence to go to college. This shift was due primarily to changes in eight states. In four states—New Mexico, Nevada, Hawaii, and Washington—students were less likely to leave their home states. But in four other states—Arkansas, Tennessee, South Dakota, and Oregon—freshmen in 1986 were more likely to go out of state to college than were their counterparts of 1979 (Carnegie Foundation for the Advancement of Teaching, 1989b). The states with the highest percentages of out-of-state migration include Connecticut (32 percent), Nevada (21 percent), New Hampshire (43 percent), New Jersey (36 percent), New Mexico (21 percent), and Vermont (36 percent) (*Chronicle of Higher Education,* Sept. 6, 1989, p. 9).

The geographical redistribution of high school graduates resulting from immigration and differential fertility rates of ethnic groups will have a dramatic influence on characteristics of college students in some regions of the country. For example, although all states will experience declines in high school graduates, many states in the Southwest and the Far West will see the number of graduates bottom out earlier and then experience increases over previously established highs. At the same time, other states will experience declines over longer periods and recoveries that may never again approach the numbers of high school graduates in the late 1970s.

For example, the numbers of high school graduates in the West (Alaska, Arizona, California, Colorado, Hawaii, Idaho, Montana, Nevada, New Mexico, Oregon, Utah, Washington, and Wyoming) and in the southwestern and south-central regions (Alabama, Arkansas, Florida, Georgia, Kentucky, Louisiana, Mississippi, North Carolina, Oklahoma, South Carolina, Tennessee, Texas, Virginia, and West Virginia) are projected to exceed the number of high school graduates from those regions in 1981, while the northeastern and north-central regions will fall far below their earlier levels. By 1994, Connecticut, Delaware, Maine, Maryland, Massachusetts, New Hampshire, New Jersey, New York, Pennsylvania, Rhode Island, and Vermont will have high school graduating classes about 35 percent smaller than those of 1981. States in the north-central region (Illinois, Indiana, Iowa, Kansas, Michigan, Minnesota, Missouri, Nebraska, North Dakota, Ohio, South Dakota, Wisconsin) will have high school graduating classes, on average, 22 percent below their 1981 levels (Kaufman, 1986; McConnell and Kaufman, 1984).

Nationally, more than 77 percent of ninth graders complete high school. But graduation rates vary by state. In Minnesota, more than 90 percent of high school students graduate (the rest of the top ten states are within a day's drive of Minneapolis!); in New York, only about two-thirds of ninth graders eventually graduate from high school. Black students have a lower rate of high school graduation than whites, although the percentage of blacks completing high school increased from about 68 percent to almost 76 percent between 1976 and 1985 (Wilson and Justiz, 1987). Hispanics are more than twice as likely as whites to drop out of high school (Fields, 1988). Astin (1982) and Dolman and Kaufman (1984) also found that lower percentages of black and Hispanic ninth graders, compared with white ninth graders, persisted to high school graduation. For example, the Hispanic dropout rate in New York City has been as high as 80 percent, compared with 32 percent in Miami and 50 percent in Los Angeles. In Alaska, 54 percent of Alaskan natives and about 40 percent of American Indians do not graduate from high school (Rendon, 1989).

More important, many minority high school students may not be well prepared for the demands of higher education. For example, in Florida in 1986, the percentage of white high school seniors who passed the state-mandated competency test required for graduation was almost three times as large as the percentage of black students (Hossler, Buffington, and Coomes, 1988).

College Participation Rates of Ethnic Groups. In 1975, the college participation rates of black students and white students were almost identical (Mingle, 1987). However, the disparity in college-going rates between whites and blacks has increased so that proportionately fewer black high school graduates are now entering a college or university. College enrollment rates for blacks dropped from 33.5 percent of high school graduates in 1976 to 26 percent in 1985. The participation rate for eighteen- to twenty-four-year-old Hispanic high school graduates declined from a high of about 36 percent in 1976 to about 27 percent in 1985 (Fields, 1988).

Asian American high school graduates continue to attend college in large numbers and to perform better academically than other minority and white students (Gardener, Robey, and Smith, 1985). They represent a smaller segment of the high-school-age population than do either blacks or Hispanics, with growth rates projected at about 3 percent for the remainder of this century. In 1988, two-year public institutions enrolled about 35 percent of all students but 53 percent of all American Indians and Hispanics and 40 percent of all blacks (*Chronicle of Higher Education,* Sept. 1, 1988). The overrepresentation of minority students in community colleges is related to, but not wholly accounted for by, their overrepresentation in courses typically taken by first-year college students. As educational level increases, the percentages of minority students in the college population declines steadily (Warren, 1985). Further exacerbating this disconcerting trend, very few students—white or minority—transfer from community colleges to four-year institutions. For example, in Texas, only 19.3 percent of community college students transfer (Fields, 1988); in Los Angeles, only 5 percent continue their educations in four-year institutions.

Because relatively few minority students start college, only minuscule numbers of minority students receive baccalaureate degrees. In the 1984–85 academic year, Hispanics earned only 2.7 percent of all bachelor's degrees, blacks 5.9 percent, American Indians 4.0 percent, and Asian Americans 2.6 percent. In that same year, whites earned 85 percent of all bachelor's degrees (Mingle, 1987). Thus, colleges and universities face problems retaining, as well as attracting, minority students.

Summary. Twenty years ago, the typical college student was Joe College—male, white, and between eighteen and twenty-two years of age. By 1988, 18 percent of all college students were minorities. Even though the traditionally college-age population has declined by 6.0 million since 1970, college enrollments rose from 8.6 million in 1970 to 12.6 million in 1988. About 65 percent of the enrollment increase can be attributed to people older than twenty-four years of age. Since 1975, the number of college students older than twenty-four grew by only 8 percent, while the number of students from twenty-five to thirty-four years of age grew by 24 percent and the number thirty-five years old and over jumped by 40 percent. Today, about 40 percent of all college students (4.8 million) are twenty-five years of age or over, and 43 percent enrolled are part-time, compared with 32 percent in 1965. Women outnumber men; the 6.6 million female college students make up more than half (53 percent) of all students, compared with 3.5 million who made up 40 percent of all college students just fifteen years ago (Kuh, Bean, Hossler, and Stage, 1989; *Chronicle of Higher Education,* Sept. 1, 1988).

Ironically, while the proportion of people of color in the traditionally college-age population continues to increase, their participation in higher education peaked in the 1970s (Mingle, 1987). The lone exception is the number of Asian Americans who doubled their college enrollment from 1976 to 1984. Despite the increase of minority students in high school, fewer blacks and Hispanics are going to college. Conversely, more whites are attending despite an actual decrease in white student high school enrollments. Thus, higher education remains an unrealized dream for most minority students.

Changing Aspirations and Values

The Cooperative Institutional Research Program (CIRP) at the University of California, Los Angeles has tracked college student attitudes, values, and aspirations for more than two decades. Some of the most pronounced changes are reflected in students' preferred major fields of study. Since 1966, the fields of business, computer science, and engineering have increased in popularity, while the traditional liberal arts fields have declined. The sharpest declines have been in the humanities (English, literature, foreign language, philosophy, and theology), the fine and performing arts (art, music, speech, and theater), and the social sciences (anthropology, economics, geography, history, political science, psychology, social work, and sociology). Taken together, these three broad disciplinary areas accounted for about one in three freshmen in 1966, but only about one in five in 1988 (Astin and others, 1988).

CIRP data also reinforced the widely publicized decline of college admission test scores. Fewer entering students intend to major in areas that test their academic skills, especially their verbal skills. English, foreign language, literature, history, and philosophy are areas that demand critical and analytical reading, writing, and thinking skills. More than two-fifths of freshmen report that a "very important" factor in their decision to go to college was a desire to improve their reading and study skills (*Chronicle of Higher Education,* Sept. 6, 1989, p. 9), a figure nearly twice that of 1975. Also, between 1975 and 1985, the proportion of freshmen reporting that they will need tutoring nearly doubled (Astin, 1985). Astin concluded that an unprecedented number of underprepared students with deficiencies in basic learning skills are pursuing higher education.

Majors leading to careers in school and college teaching have declined by almost 75 percent since the 1960s but now are on the rebound. In 1988, 8.8 percent of first-year students said they planned to pursue teaching, compared with the low point of 4.7 percent in 1982. Other career choices reflecting greater than 50 percent decline include clergy, research scientist, and law enforcement. Astin (1985) observed that none of the career choices reflecting increases in popularity, such as business, computer science, and engineering, requires more than a baccalaureate degree. The sharpest drops occurred in areas that usually require graduate training but do not pay well—teaching, nursing, social work, law enforcement, and the ministry.

A desire to make money seems to be an important factor in explaining shifts in majors. "Being very well off financially" has become steadily more popular as a life goal, increasing from 40 percent in 1975 to 73 percent in 1989 (*Chronicle of Higher Education,* Sept. 6, 1989, p. 9). In contrast, the life goal of "developing a meaningful philosophy of life" has dropped precipitously. The most valued goal in 1970, it was endorsed by 83 percent of entering freshmen. It was eighth on the list in 1989, endorsed by about 50 percent (*Chronicle of Higher Education,* Sept. 6, 1989, p. 9), a slight increase from a low point of 45 percent in 1983. Thus, "Today's students are much more inclined than earlier generations to believe that learning is for earning" (Astin, 1985, p. 220).

Conversely, attitudes reflecting altruism and social concern—helping others in difficulty, promoting racial understanding, and concern for the environment—have declined in popularity along with creative and artistic goals. However, in recent years there seems to have been a resurgence of interest in public service. For example, 56 percent of the entering freshmen in 1988 said it was essential or very important for them to help others who are in difficulty. The difference between men (46 percent) and women (65 percent) on this item is noteworthy (Astin and others, 1988).

Substantial proportions of first-year students say that it is "very important" or "essential" that they become an authority in their field (72 percent), are recognized by colleagues (55 percent), have administrative responsibility over others (40 percent), are very well-off financially (73 percent), and succeed in their own business (52 percent) (*Chronicle of Higher Education,* Sept. 6, 1989, p. 9). Since 1972, these status and achievement goals have become more popular among women, with the result that the sex differential has narrowed (Astin and Kent, 1983).

Student Attitudes: A Product of the Times. Certainly, there is some continuity as well as change over time in the aspirations and attitudes of undergraduate cohorts (Moffatt, 1989). However, we tend to emphasize change more than continuity when we consider biographical characteristics of students. When differences are noted, for example, in the values of students, the implication is often that the values of the current student cohort are not as worthwhile as those of earlier generations. Some phrases used to describe the current cohort of undergraduate students include self-concerned, nonideological, disenchanted with the political process, and politically moderate but liberal in social attitudes (75 percent favor a woman's right to abortion). Students are friendly but in a pragmatic sort of way (Levine, 1983). Consider Moffatt's (1989) description of friendship among undergraduates at Rutgers: "Friendliness was the fundamental code of etiquette among the students in the 1980's, the one courtesy that they expected of each other in daily life. It had its rules. You were not friendly to everyone, but you ought to be friendly to anyone you had met more than once or twice. . . . To violate 'friendly' in an apparently deliberate way was to arouse some of the strongest sentiments of distrust and dislike" (pp. 44–45).

Students are optimistic about their own individual futures but much less optimistic about the future of society—resulting in what Levine (1983) called a "Titanic Ethic." That is, students sense that the ship (the United States or the world) is going to sink. Forced to ride on a doomed vessel, students have decided to go first-class, attempting to acquire as many of the symbols of affluence as possible, such as televisions, stereos, cars, and condominiums, while the ship is still afloat.

Much of our knowledge about undergraduate student attitudes in the 1980s is based on Cooperative Institutional Research Program data. However, these data primarily reflect the attitudes of traditional-age first-year students. Another perspective is offered by upper-class students. For example, a *Newsweek* campus poll conducted in December 1985 indicated that only 7 percent of college students reported that the most important reason for attending college is to make a substantial amount of money. Almost three times that many said the most important reason for attending college is to learn about important ideas and thoughts. Four times as many, almost one-third (31 percent), said the most important reason for going to college is to obtain a fulfilling job after graduation.

While 10 percent of the *Newsweek* poll respondents said that the most important factor to consider in seeking a job after graduation is a good salary, 39 percent said they were more concerned about whether the work would be interesting. Twelve percent thought the most important factor for them would be whether the job would allow them to make a contribution to society. This hardly sounds like a generation riveted on promoting their own careers or exclusively interested in financial security—the needs of society be damned!

Nevertheless, college students are more materialistic and less altruistic than their counterparts of previous decades. The attitudes and values of the current college student cohort have been heavily influenced by world events and by the attitudes and values of the larger society in which they have been socialized. "They had grown up in much more uncertain cynical-making times . . . the Vietnam collapse, Watergate, and the pallid years of Jimmy Carter's America" (Moffatt, 1989, p. 27). The class of 1990 did not know Lyndon Johnson's Great Society or the works and deeds of Martin Luther King, Jr. or Robert Kennedy. Both parents of a college student of the current generation are likely to be working outside the home. As the class of 1990 was experiencing puberty, the world became a global village: China was opened, and then closed, to trade and tourism; major powers intervened in the Falkland Islands and Grenada; and television provided coverage of the Iranian hostage crisis, Lee Iaccoca's marketing strategy, the Three Mile Island and Chernobyl debacles, and the 1989 bloodbath in Beijing's Tiananmen Square (Komives, 1986; Levine, 1983; Moffatt, 1989).

The Relation Between Attitudes and Values. Many social psychologists consider attitudes to be at the fringe or outer layer of personality. Stronger than preferences, but not as deeply integrated as values, attitudes are changeable, sometimes within a relatively short period of time. For example, attitudes toward persons of color may change over time. While surveys of student attitudes are interesting, such barometers do not capture the core of values that drive human behavior.

Values, on the other hand, are basic building blocks of the human experience, the very core of one's personality. Values reflect the essence of life, the nature and quality of our relationships with others and with the spiritual world, and individual beliefs regarding charity, goodness, and morality. For example, respect for the dignity and fundamental worth of every human being may not change much over the life span. Those who hold such a value may not think about it often, but it is there nonetheless.

By the time students go to college, their values are fairly well set, perhaps not well clarified, but nonetheless integral parts of their personalities. The college experience profoundly influences the values of only a small proportion of students; about 7 percent of college students seem to undergo significant personality reorganization during college (Clark and others, 1972).

In *Habits of the Heart,* Robert Bellah and his colleagues (1985) examined the underlying values of contemporary American society. Bellah underscored two competing or contradictory themes that characterize life in the United States: individualism and commitment. Individualism reflects a desire to be autonomous and economically independent from others, able to take care of oneself and not reliant on others. For example, current college students seem to be willing to overlook the foibles in others, and they do not expect others to conform to their expectations as long as, in return, they do not have to conform to expectations of others. On the other hand, commitment reflects a need for connectedness to others, a sense of belonging that a community provides.

Bellah and others (1985, p. 84) explain it this way: "We find ourselves not independently of other people and institutions but through them. We never get to the bottom of our selves on our own. We discover who we are face to face and side by side with others in work, love, and learning. All of our activity goes on in relationships, groups, associations, and communities ordered by institutional structures and interpreted by cultural patterns of meaning. Our individualism, our sense of the dignity, worth, and moral autonomy of the individual, is dependent in a thousand ways on a social, cultural, and institutional context that keeps us afloat even when we cannot very well describe it."

Yankelovich's (1981) research also supports the thesis that the dominant social ethic is in the midst of a transformation from the ethic of self-denial that prevailed through the 1960s and 1970s, to an ethic of self-fulfillment in the 1980s, and now to a new ethic of commitment. Commitment reflects a shift from an emphasis on self toward a need for connectedness with the world. In 1973, the so-called search for community trend was important to about one-third of Americans. In the 1980s, the percentage increased to 47 percent, a clear signal of a countertrend away from the self. The attitudes of the current college cohort are consistent with these trends and suggest that considerable caution should be exercised when drawing conclusions about what students value based on surveys of entering students.

Implications of Shifting Demographics for Student Affairs

Shifts in students' biographical characteristics, attitudes, and values present unprecedented challenges to institutions of higher education in general and to student affairs professionals in particular. The degree to which these changes characterize students at any given institution varies greatly. For example, national colleges, such as Grinnell, Carleton, Yale, and Williams, are not likely to witness marked shifts in the age and academic preparation of first-year students because they are established colleges with salient liberal arts missions. Other types of institutions, such as state-supported institutions with regional reputations, urban institutions, and community colleges, will continue to attract disproportionately high numbers of part-time, older, and commuting students, and students of color. The number of ethnic minority students an institution will enroll will be influenced by the region of the country in which the institution is located.

Further, the attitudes and values of students may be less materialistic and more allocentric than the national trend in institutions such as Berry College or Earlham College. Thus, the degree to which the implications of shifting demographics are relevant for student affairs will depend on the institution's mission, geographical location, and commitment to the egalitarian ethic that undergirds mass higher education in the United States. No matter where an institution is located, the sine qua non for student affairs professionals remains constant—to be (and not merely assert to be) experts on students and the campus environment. Student affairs professionals must know their students and how changing characteristics of students shape the environments in which students live and learn: How many students are part-time, commuting, traditional age, adult learners, or from various cultural, ethnic, and racial heritages? How do these qualities influence what their attitudes and values are, what they need to learn, where and how they live (on or off campus), their academic and career goals, and how they can best attain these goals?

The Pluralism Imperative. Inexorable demographic trends promise an increasingly diverse (in terms of age and ethnic heritage) student body at most institutions. *Diversity* accurately describes changing student characteristics. Colleges and universities must not only respond to disparate needs of an increasingly heterogenous student body but also develop strategies that will acknowledge and celebrate differences in cultural heritage, life goals, and expectations of students of color and other underrepresented groups. Thus, while diversity reflects student characteristics, the pluralism imperative demands that campus communities establish meaningful patterns of interaction that encourage understanding, respect, and appreciation of these differences. Multiple voices are necessary to create the conditions for a better world.

Recipes do not exist for moving institutions beyond mere tolerance of diversity (a major achievement at some institutions) to forming genuine pluralistic learning communities that can serve as models for society. The reports of racial incidents on college campuses are harbingers of significant challenges ahead. There are places to look, however, for examples of institutional commitments to the pluralism imperative—Berea, Grinnell, Stanford, and the University of California, Davis. At present, however, no institution of higher education can be satisfied with the degree to which a pluralistic learning community has been achieved.

The implications for student affairs are legion and systemic. Nothing less than institutional transformations are needed. Virtually every institution of higher education committed to personal development must become engaged in a cultural transformation process that embraces cultural mores binding certain groups to some ideas and ideals while excluding other groups. Tierney (1989) argues that "we need to understand which ideas bind and which exclude" and how curricular and out-of-class experiences of students communicate the importance of this understanding to all participants—faculty, students, administrators, and others. Before students can become concerned about and committed to equity and social justice, they must hear people talking about and acting on these issues. How student affairs professionals and faculty members interact and spend their time provides strong signals to students about the nature of academic life, about the nature of knowledge, and ultimately about the nature and quality of tomorrow's society. Certainly such concerns should not be addressed only in the classroom. How students spend their time out of class, with whom, and toward what ends are equally powerful influences in the creation of a pluralistic world view.

Richardson and Bender (1987), Steele (1988, 1989), and others (Nettles and Thoeny, 1988; Richardson, Simmons, and de los Santos, 1987; Thomas, 1981) have described with greater specificity the challenges to higher education presented above. Richardson (1989) described the educational "ladder" that must be established to attract and graduate Hispanic, black, and American Indian students. The ladder warrants attention for two reasons. First, Richardson's recommendations are based on research conducted at institutions with successful track records in graduating students of color; and second, responsibility for campus-level implementation of the rungs of the ladder will fall squarely on the shoulders of student affairs professionals. The "rungs" identified by Richardson (1989, p. A48) are the following:

- early intervention of the public schools to strengthen preparation and improve students' educational planning
- summer "bridge" programs to accustom minority students to college-level course work and the campus atmosphere before they begin college
- special orientation programs and help with choice of courses in registration
- tailored financial aid programs
- strong academic-assessment programs, coupled with courses designed to offset gaps in preparation
- adequate tutoring services, learning laboratories, and organized mentorship programs
- intrusive academic advising to guide selection of courses and to intervene before small problems become major

- career guidance to translate nonspecific educational goals into programs of study in which course work and desired outcomes are clearly linked

Few of the rungs of Richardson's ladder can be put into place without "a complex interplay of state policies, community settings, administrative strategies, and student preparation and motivation" (p. A48). However, the absence of these conditions should not inhibit student affairs professionals on any campus from committing themselves to acknowledging and working tirelessly toward realizing the pluralism imperative.

For example, additional resources are not necessary for student affairs staff to develop further the capacity for closer personal relationships with members of different cultures. To be successful, minority and first-generation college students need more information about college than do most white students (Rendon, 1989). Student affairs professionals must become involved in articulation and transition initiatives with local elementary and high schools, community agencies, and churches. The Western Interstate Commission for Higher Education (Halcon, 1988) has compiled a set of successful outreach practices. One example of an outreach initiative is the "Just Do It" program, recently instituted by the University of Louisville, in which a team of institutional agents, made up of an admissions representative, another student affairs professional, and a faculty member, visit the homes of minority students to answer questions about the university.

In the future, the nature of the college experience (both curricular and extracurricular) for an increasing number of students will be different from what many student affairs staff today fondly remember from their undergraduate days. Certainly the college experiences will be, in the eyes of graduates from the 1960s and 1970s, less traditional for commuter students, older students, and minority students who do not find residential campuses particularly inviting or accommodating. The ceremonies and traditions usually associated with an involving undergraduate experience—events such as homecoming, mother-daughter or parents weekends, athletic events, concerts, and so forth (Kuh and Whitt, 1988)—are not viewed as particularly attractive or worthwhile activities. According to

Moffatt (1989), college life has become more like the private lives of students, no longer centered on the organized extracurriculum such as student government and clubs.

The assumptions that student affairs staff and faculty members use to make meaning of the institutional context will be challenged in the 1990s and beyond. Given the increasingly nontraditional nature of students, engendering a sense of campus community (Jacoby, 1989) will be increasingly difficult. Campus events and traditions, once powerful mechanisms for maintaining a sense of community, may become less influential because fewer people will participate. As more part-time and older students matriculate and as more people move on and off the campus daily, campus boundaries become more porous. Even traditional-age-student rooms, replete with compact-disc players, televisions, videocassette recorders, refrigerators, personal computers, and other accoutrements, provide evidence that many students do not leave their former lives behind when they go to college. As the college experience becomes less well distinguished from other aspects of one's life, clarifying what should happen during college (intellectual risk taking and expanding understanding of cultural and ethnic differences, for example), how the college experience differs from other life experiences, and what behaviors are considered appropriate in the college setting will take on added importance.

A caveat is necessary, however. Too great an emphasis on cultural differences may lead to inappropriate ends; not giving equal time to what students have in common invites preoccupation with differences. Many students (perhaps not enough, however) are ultrasensitive to charges of racism, ethnocentrism, and xenophobia. The desire to avoid doing injury in forging new relationships may have a dampening effect on willingness to take risks to get to know someone different from oneself; students, student affairs professionals, and others may become fearful of blundering, of making mistakes.

Understanding persons from different cultural backgrounds requires risk taking. The exploration of differences is more likely to be successful when based on friendship and remembering that similarities really are more important than differences. Student affairs professionals must hold fast to the best, not the worst, assumptions about human motivations. Sensitivity and sensibility will not be improved by hasty or thoughtless charges that one incident or behavior is, for example, racially motivated. For all inappropriate behaviors, innocence is usually a better hypothesis than malevolence, particularly when dealing with often naive traditional-age college students from single-culture backgrounds. Even for situations in which this assumption is erroneous, it will move people closer to understanding and resolving problems (Gardner, 1988).

Student affairs professionals must be prepared for frustration and occasional disappointment. As with other social transformations, the pluralism imperative will take hold in fits and starts. Cultural differences are readily manifested in misunderstandings and other communication problems. The language with which white staff members and students are familiar and that used by students of color are often different. Even the very best efforts will not always be successful in resolving differences in understanding. Ironically, perhaps, those institutions and individuals that try the hardest will be most susceptible to public scrutiny. Failures will be widely publicized and will be temporarily devastating for those personally involved. There is no acceptable alternative, however.

Student Development. Encouraging students' intellectual, social, and emotional development, long a goal of the student affairs profession, will become increasingly more complicated and challenging. Certainly, programs and activities are needed to encourage students' intellectual and personal development to levels that enable them to be academically and socially successful. Yet this challenge may place student affairs professionals, and their institutions, in awkward situations. For example, some learning skills programs, such as remedial reading, in which many new students must participate to be successful academically, have stigmas associated with them.

Inherent in the developmental philosophy are challenges presented to students to encourage growth. Often these challenges, as presented through programming and small group work, will elicit short-term discomfort or frustration in students. Creating dissonance, often a precursor of developmental change, may unwittingly contribute to dissatisfaction and, perhaps, attrition—

particularly if such efforts are not carefully adapted for use with students from nonwhite cultural and ethnic backgrounds. In addition, few students will recognize the value of academic and personal development programs; many of those most in need of such programs will be most reluctant to participate (Kuh, 1980). Finally, the research on which most developmental theories are based was conducted on white populations and may be misleading when used to design programs and interventions for minority students. (See Chapter Three.)

Assessment. The assessment bandwagon (Ewell and Boyer, 1988), rolling full steam across the national landscape of higher education, may be a vehicle to leverage additional resources to support more sophisticated and usable data collection about student characteristics and behaviors. Student affairs professionals must collaborate in the design of each institution's assessment strategy. Although assessment tends to emphasize outcome measures, the potential exists for collecting relevant information to illuminate aspects of students' out-of-class experiences that contribute to, or detract from, attainment of an institution's educational purposes (Kuh, Bean, Hossler, and Stage, 1989). "The Involving College Inventory: A Guide for Assessing Campus Environments" (Kuh and others, 1989) is an example of a formative assessment tool that can be used by student affairs staff to guide institutional audits in determining the degree to which students take advantage of out-of-class learning opportunities.

Through the use of the Involving College Inventory and other assessment tools (Hanson, 1989), student affairs professionals can become aware of the ways in which an institution alienates certain groups of students, such as people of color or commuters. And they can identify those programs, services, and functions that do not adequately meet student needs—for example, failure to provide well-lighted parking areas, adequate study and eating facilities, and convenient office hours for commuting, older, and part-time students. By becoming active collaborators, student affairs can play a significant role in assessment by sharing knowledge about the college student experience, by influencing what is measured and how it is measured, and by ensuring that many of the most important developmental changes associated with college attendance are monitored.

Student Affairs Staffing. Recruitment and retention efforts of historically underrepresented students, many of whom will be first-generation college students, will require additional resources. As more so-called high-risk or dropout-prone students matriculate, student affairs staff will be expected to ameliorate conditions associated with attrition by, for example, providing additional support services during high-stress periods in the academic year (Conyne, 1978) and substantial front-loading of resources during the critical first few weeks and months of the college experience (Upcraft, Gardner, and Associates, 1989). The importance of transition programs, including summer and fall orientation and continuing orientation (Dannells and Kuh, 1977), is obvious. What is not obvious is how these programs can be modified to speak more directly and persuasively to students of color and their families.

Inequities often exist between full-time, part-time, and evening students with regard to access to health centers and recreational facilities. In some instances, participation in social activities by certain groups of students, such as adult learners, is effectively precluded because of scheduling during evening hours when students must be with their families or at work. At most institutions, approximately three part-time students are needed to equal the same amount of tuition revenue produced by one full-time student (Frances, 1985). Although the number of part-time students will continue to increase, resources available to student affairs are not likely to follow suit. Thus, student affairs will likely be very thinly stretched in the coming decade.

Conclusion

Demographic trends present significant challenges to colleges and universities in general, and to student affairs in particular. The size of the traditional-age college cohort is shrinking while becoming more ethnically diverse. Second, because Hispanics, blacks, and American Indians have lower high school completion rates, the size of the traditional college-age cohort that attends college may become even smaller. Extrapolation of enrollment trends from the status quo and historical trends is risky. Further, blacks and Hispanics and other racial and ethnic minorities tend to cluster in various regions of the country and within metropolitan areas—most often in the central cities—so that even if their higher education participation rates do increase significantly, not all institutions, regions, or states can expect to see increased enrollments. Thus, student affairs professionals must be cognizant of regional variations in the size of the traditional college-age population and its racial and ethnic mix, cognizant of the educational and economic aspirations of their clientele, and cognizant of public policy influencing access to postsecondary education, especially student financial aid and tuition pricing.

Realization of the pluralism imperative is the most significant challenge ever faced by American higher education. Removing obstacles in the college environment to academic and social integration, satisfaction, achievement, and ultimately graduation is not the sole responsibility of student affairs professionals. Cooperation and participation from all groups of institutional agents will be required. Thus, student affairs professionals must create partnerships with faculty and others to foster conditions on campus that ensure the community will acknowledge, respect, and celebrate differences. Student affairs professionals working in concert with other administrators, faculty, alumni, and currently enrolled students can do much to keep an institution of higher education vibrant and viable in the twenty-first century.

Several years ago, a magazine advertisement proclaimed, "The future isn't what it used to be." The ad also stated that "there is no future in believing something can't be done. The future is in making it happen." With that in mind, student affairs professionals must visualize a future that acknowledges, respects, values, and celebrates pluralism and work purposefully toward this end.

References

Astin, A. W. *Minorities in American Higher Education.* San Francisco: Jossey-Bass, 1982.

Astin, A. W. *Achieving Educational Excellence.* San Francisco: Jossey-Bass, 1985.

Astin, A. W., and Green, K. C. *The American Freshman: Twenty Year Trends.* Los Angeles: University of California, Los Angeles, Higher Education Research Institute, 1987.

Astin, A. W., and others. *The American Freshman: National Norms for 1988.* Los Angeles: American Council on Education and University of California, Los Angeles, Higher Education Research Institute, 1988.

Astin, H. S., and Kent, L. "Gender Roles in Transition: Research and Policy Implications for Higher Education." *Journal of Higher Education,* 1983, *54,* 309–324.

Bellah, R. N., and others. *Habits of the Heart.* New York: Harper & Row, 1985.

Bunzel, J. H. "Affirmative Action Must Not Result in Lower Standards or Discrimination Against the Most Competent Students." *Chronicle of Higher Education,* March 1, 1989, pp. 131–132.

Carnegie Foundation for the Advancement of Teaching. "New Strategies Keep Enrollments Growing." *Change,* 1989a, *21* (1), 39–42.

Carnegie Foundation for the Advancement of Teaching. "Student Migration Patterns: What They Mean for States." *Change,* 1989b, *21* (3), 29–34.

Chronicle of Higher Education. Almanac. Sept. 1, 1988.

Clark, B. R., and others. *Students and Colleges: Interactions and Change.* Berkeley: University of California, Berkeley, Center for Research and Development in Higher Education, 1972.

College Board. *Summary Statistics: Annual Survey of Colleges, 1989–90.* New York: College Board, 1988.

Conyne, R. K. "An Analysis of Student-Environment Mismatches." *Journal of College Student Personnel,* 1978, *19,* 461–465.

Dannells, M. D., and Kuh, G. D. "Orientation." In W. Packwood (ed.), *College Student Personnel Services.* Springfield, Ill.: Thomas, 1977.

Dolman, G., Jr., and Kaufman, N. S. *Minorities in Higher Education: The Changing Southwest— Texas.* Boulder, Colo.: Western Interstate Commission for Higher Education, 1984.

Estrada, L. F. "Anticipating the Demographic Future." *Change,* 1988, *20* (3), 14–19.

Ewell, P. T., and Boyer, C. M. "Acting Out State-Mandated Assessment: Evidence From Five States." *Change,* 1988, *20* (4), 40–47.

Fields, C. "The Hispanic Pipeline: Narrow, Leaking, and Needing Repair." *Change,* 1988, *20* (3), 20–27.

Frances, C. "1986: Major Trends Shaping the Outlook for Higher Education." *AAHE Bulletin,* 1985, *38* (4), 3–7.

Gardener, R. W., Robey, B., and Smith, P. C. *Asian Americans: Growth, Change, Diversity.* Washington, D.C.: U.S. Bureau of the Census, 1985.

Gardner, J. W. *Constituents and Followers.* Leadership Papers, no. 8. Washington, D.C.: Independent Sector, 1988.

Halcon, J. J. *Exemplary Programs for College Bound Minority Students.* Boulder, Colo.: Western Interstate Commission for Higher Education, 1988.

Hanson, G. R. *The Assessment of Student Development Outcomes: A Review and Critique of Assessment Instruments.* Trenton: College Outcomes Evaluation Project, New Jersey Department of Higher Education, 1989.

Hodgkinson, H. L. *Guess Who's Coming to College: Your Students in 1990.* Washington, D.C.: National Institute of Independent Colleges and Universities, 1983.

Hodgkinson, H. L. *All One System: Demographics of Education, Kindergarten Through Graduate School.* Washington, D.C.: Institute of Educational Leadership, 1985.

Hossler, D., Buffington, S., and Coomes, M. D. *College Enrollments Through the 1990s: Untangling the Implications of Demographic and Public Policy Trends.* Bloomington: Indiana University, School of Education, Institute for Postsecondary Research and Planning, 1988.

Jacoby, B. "Colleges Must Do More to Enhance the Education of Commuting Students." *Chronicle of Higher Education,* Jan. 18, 1989, p. A44.

Kaufman, N. S. "Shifts in Postsecondary Clientele." In P. Callan (ed.), *Environmental Scanning for Strategic Leadership.* New Directions for Institutional Research, no. 52. San Francisco: Jossey-Bass, 1986.

Komives, S. "Keynote Address to the 1986 Undergraduate Life Symposium." Indiana University, Bloomington, July 1986.

Kuh, G. D. "Student Affairs Administration in the Enigmatic Eighties." *Viewpoints in Teaching and Learning,* 1980, *56* (2), 23–34.

Kuh, G. D., Bean, J. P., Hossler, D., and Stage, F. K. (eds.). *ASHE Reader on College Students.* Needham Heights, Mass.: Ginn, 1989.

Kuh, G. D., and Whitt, E. J. *The Invisible Tapestry: Culture in American Colleges and Universities.* ASHE-ERIC Higher Education Report No. 1. Washington, D.C.: Association for the Study of Higher Education, 1988.

Kuh, G. D., and others. "The Involving College Inventory: A Guide For Assessing Campus Environments." Paper presented at the 4th National American Association of Higher Education Conference on Assessment, Atlanta, Ga., June 1989.

Levine, A. "Riding First Class on the Titanic: A Portrait of Today's College Student." *National Association of Student Personnel Administrators Journal,* 1983, *20* (4), 3–9.

McConnell, W. R., and Kaufman, N. S. *High School Graduates: Projections for the 50 States (1982–2000).* Boulder, Colo.: Western Interstate Commission for Higher Education, 1984.

Mingle, J. R. *Focus on Minorities: Trends in Higher Education Participation and Success.* Denver, Colo.: Education Commission of the States and the State Higher Education Executive Officers, 1987.

Moffatt, M. *Coming of Age in New Jersey: College and American Culture.* New Brunswick, N.J.: Rutgers University Press, 1989.

National Association of Student Personnel Administrators. *A Perspective on Student Affairs.* Washington, D.C.: National Association for Student Personnel Administrators, 1987.

National Center for Educational Statistics. *Trends in Adult Student Enrollments.* Washington, D.C.: U.S. Department of Education, 1985.

Nettles, M. T., and Thoeny, A. R. *Toward Black Undergraduate Student Equality.* Westport, Conn.: Greenwood, 1988.

"*Newsweek* On Campus Poll." *Newsweek,* Jan. 1986.

Rendon, L. I. "The Lie and the Hope: Making Higher Education a Reality for At-Risk Students." *AAHE Bulletin,* 1989, *41* (9), 4-7.

Richardson, R. C., Jr. "If Minority Students Are To Succeed in Higher Education, Every Rung of the Educational Ladder Must Be in Place." *Chronicle of Higher Education,* Jan. 11, 1989, p. A48.

Richardson, R. C., Jr., and Bender, L. W. *Fostering Minority Access and Achievement in Higher Education.* San Francisco: Jossey-Bass, 1987.

Richardson, R. C., Jr., Simmons, H., and de los Santos, A. "Graduating Minority Students." *Change,* 1987, *19* (3), 20-27.

Spencer, G. *Projections of the Population of the United States, by Age, Sex, and Race: 1983 to 2080.* Current Populations Reports, series P-25, no. 952. Washington, D.C.: U.S. Bureau of the Census, 1984.

Steele, S. "I'm Black and You're White, Who's Innocent?" *Harper's,* June 1988, pp. 45-53.

Steele, S. "The Recoloring of the Campus." *Harper's,* Feb. 1989, pp. 47-55.

Thelin, J. R. "The Search for Good Research." *The Review of Higher Education,* 1986, *10,* 151-158.

Thomas, G. E. (ed.). *Black Students in Higher Education: Conditions and Experiences of the 1970s.* Westport, Conn.: Greenwood, 1981.

Tierney, W. G. *Curricular Landscapes, Democratic Vistas: Transformative Leadership in Higher Education.* New York: Praeger, 1989.

Upcraft, M. L., Gardner, J., and Associates. *The Freshman Year Experience.* San Francisco: Jossey-Bass, 1989.

Warren, J. R. "The Changing Characteristics of College Students." In W. Deegan, D. Tillery, and Associates, *Renewing the American Community College.* San Francisco: Jossey-Bass, 1985.

Wilson, R., and Justiz, M. J. "Minorities in Higher Education: Confronting a Time Bomb." *Educational Record,* 1987-88, *68* (4) / *69* (1), 8-14.

Yankelovich, D. *New Rules: Search For Self-Fulfillment in a World Turned Upside Down.* New York: Random House, 1981.

Chapter 5

New Pressures for Social Responsiveness and Accountability

Arthur Sandeen
James J. Rhatigan

The difficulty of accurate forecasting has never deterred people from the effort. We live in a society required to respond to bits of communication from across the world, nearly simultaneously with their actual occurrence. While inundated by data, people nonetheless must ponder what it all means.

What are the implications of what we have learned? What lies ahead? We are intrigued by these questions because they help reduce the uncertainty of future events. The better one can anticipate, the better control of events one will have. This is the essence of planning.

It is from this point of view that a look forward to the 1990s seems worthwhile. From an array of social issues that will require attention in the coming decade, we have selected for discussion in this chapter a few that may have particular influence on higher education and student affairs. We do not claim that the issues selected for review are the only ones that will influence student affairs. These selected issues, however, rank among the most critical to attend to as we confront the future. We hope that an introduction to new issues and a reminder of the importance of long-standing issues will help student affairs administrators focus their energies to solve the problems we will face as a profession.

If the recounting of social issues seems to highlight the foibles, frustrations, and failures of American society, it seems appropriate to point out that every society in every decade of human history has had its list. Yet, there is no reason why a society has to be a captive of its present social agenda. The ability to resolve issues and to move on would seem to be a great ambition for any nation.

We will discuss six major social agendas in this chapter: ethnic issues, women's issues, questions of safety and security, health issues, substance abuse, and national political and economic forces. We will present implications for student affairs and higher education, and we will offer strategies to deal with the dilemmas of these social agenda items. We do not claim to have definitive answers to resolve the inevitable tensions these agenda items will bring. However, through examination, we may find the means to move beyond these items as we develop our academic communities.

Ethnic Issues

Concerns regarding ethnic identity and ethnic differences will continue to occupy a prominent place in American society in the coming decade and will require significant attention on the college campus. The complicated set of issues involved in ethnicity presents both simple and complex dilemmas—dilemmas that invite discussion and concern and that thus far have defied definitive solutions. The issue of resolving concerns related to ethnicity is elusive because factors combine in different ways, at different times, and with different groups; this seems to be true across the spectrum of races.

It would be difficult to imagine how much space on printed pages has been devoted to ethnic issues. Culture, religion, history, geography, education, politics, and economics, whether considered singularly or in combination, have occupied the attention of scholars and of nearly every living person with an opinion.

Both currently and historically, race (loosely defined) has

been at the center of controversy. There are problems among races, between races, and within races. Today, the Russians and national groups are contending for influence in the Soviet Union. Within the non-Russian population, the Georgians and Abkhazians maintain a historical enmity that is ethnic in nature. Some Japanese disparage Koreans. Northern Europeans have been known to treat southern Europeans poorly, skin color being a factor. Asians on the African continent are victims of discriminatory treatment, as are Africans on the Asian continent. While South Africa occupies the world's attention, the treatment of Australian aborigines is also recognized as harsh. Many Guatemalans of Spanish ancestry are antagonistic toward the native population.

The United State is multiethnic, so issues are plentiful, as are explanations as to why progress toward their resolution is so slow. It would be understandable if one were to conclude that, in matters of race in the United States, there are no clear answers; but this would be an incorrect conclusion. The fact is that only a small percentage of Americans would argue the nation has made no racial progress. But regrettably, the record of progress seems fragile, lacking a permanence that would give people confidence that one part of the journey toward equality had, once and for all, been completed.

People of goodwill among all of the ethnic groups in the United States need to continue the struggle, even while knowing that within existing lifetimes, much will remain to be done. One problem is that many citizens will not participate in these efforts; ethnocentrism abounds, as do self-interests of many kinds. So it is imperative that American college campuses be places where students can both study these issues and seek experiences and relationships that endure beyond perceived racial and ethnic barriers.

Indeed, the changing demographic characteristics (see Chapter Four) alone will mandate creative and innovative responses for the good of all students. Recent theoretical models (see Chapter Three) may aid us in increasing our understanding of the complex questions involved in resolving ethnic differences.

Strategies. Solutions to ethnic problems in American society need to be addressed from the bottom up and the top down. First, prejudice and discriminatory practices begin and end with the individual. It probably will be of minimal use to propose solutions to others until we confront our own limitations. Any person in a position of responsibility on almost any campus will have to face the issues of race. These matters are often encountered in private, but they need not be. Sharing concerns, frustrations, and fears may be helpful steps toward an individual's personal resolution.

Second, individuals are connected to one or more institutions in the course of doing business. These institutions maintain and convey values that eventuate in behavior. It is essential that university and college leaders possess values that are consistent with democratic principles. When these values are lacking, the institution will be less likely to achieve equality of opportunity or to be seen as a place where diversity is welcome. In higher education, one first must look to governing boards and presidents for leadership. Within student affairs, leadership toward humane values begins with the chief student affairs officer (Welch, McHugh, and others, 1988).

Third, progress has been made through some institutions' approaches to multicultural and ethnic diversity using cocurricular programs and other interventions. While the experiences of one institution do not always generalize, it is possible to learn from those that have successfully met issues. Practitioners have an obligation to share successful practices with colleagues at conferences and through the written word.

Finally, a democratic society does not exist in the abstract. The way any society behaves is a product of its values. The United States owes a debt to humanism, which has as a principal tenet a belief in progress. The idea of an enlightened society carries with it the notion that good citizenship can be taught (National Association of Student Personnel Administrators, 1987). Progress toward humane values has been made in the United States. Regrettably, the process has been slow and appears at times to be reversible.

Women's Concerns

Issues of particular importance to women will continue to occupy attention in the coming decade. Some issues are unresolved from the 1980s, and some new issues are surfacing. Women with different needs may be coming to college, and this change will create a campus climate that may be different from that of the previous decade.

Among the primary goals of women will be a focus on fairness in the workplace; there will be continuing pressure to achieve hiring, pay, and promotion standards that do not disadvantage women. Women will be looking for a positive work environment and for the application of simple principles of justice, which thus far are not found in every office on every campus.

The passage of the Equal Rights Amendment in the 1980s was an important goal, but it was not achieved during that decade. This failure has caused the fight for equality to be waged in local jurisdictions. It could be argued that conservative political currents have given a sense of urgency to activists, and they will likely seek to involve a greater number of women and men who are interested in halting what some activists see as an erosion of gains already achieved. The college campus may very well be an important focus of attention for persons seeking to influence issues such as this.

A centerpiece of the struggle is the reproductive rights of women. State interest in this matter is of growing concern to those whose positions are familiarly known as "prochoice." In *Roe* v. *Wade* (1973), the Supreme Court established a woman's constitutional right to have an abortion. A recent Supreme Court case, *Reproductive Health Services* v. *Webster* (1989), appears to have weakened that decision and likely will invite other challenges. It is expected that the reproductive rights of women will be a prominent issue on college campuses; it is an issue that will evoke strong responses from those holding different views.

Increasing demand for child-care services on campus will be an issue in the 1990s. Although child care certainly is not an issue solely important to women, they have been its most important advocates. Faculty, staff, and students with children will be requesting on-campus services, and funding of these services will be an issue on some campuses.

The sexual harassment of women students, faculty, and staff presents a set of concerns that will persist into the next decades. While statistics, policies, and administrative rulings have prohibited sexual harassment, the problem persists. Physical harassment, as well as verbal harassment including inappropriate language or creating an intimidating or offensive environment, poses situations that must be confronted. Whether sexual harassment is deliberately intended or is a result of insensitivity, campuses will be called on to correct the offensive behavior.

An increasing amount of literature in the past decade has focused on physical violence directed at women. Perhaps the most common version of this on the campus is *acquaintance rape*. This new phrase describes an old behavior, previously hidden from public awareness. It is now clear that the vast majority of college women subjected to physical abuse know their assailants. While many campuses are implementing programs and other approaches to resolve the issue, the problem persists. Acquaintance rape has emerged as a problem of greater magnitude than anyone would have suspected.

Another gender-related issue is the "chilly" classroom climate discussed by Hall and Sandler (1985). In the classroom, women are often subjected to subtle and sometimes direct messages that devalue their intellectual and scholarly abilities. For example, women are often less likely to be called upon directly than are men students, are more often interrupted, and are more likely to be subjected to sexist humor. In many institutions, they lack female faculty role models, and they may be discouraged from enrolling or staying in majors that are traditionally male.

Strategies. Steps to improve the climate of higher education for women are possible and must be pursued. First, efforts to reduce stereotypes about women and women's roles must be increased. Progress has been made, but it falls far short of what is needed. (One could argue as a corollary that the role of men also needs attention.) Campuses will need to decide whether these issues belong in the curriculum. If they do, then a series of negotiations will be required as to where and how offerings will be made. Campuses that elect not to integrate these issues into the curriculum must decide how they will address them.

Second, the changing nature of work and family responsibilities will require the campus to be more flexible in meeting the needs of employees with families and the needs of women students.

Third, policies and programs intended to provide an environment free of verbal, physical, or psychological abuse must be put into place. Timely enforcement and firm application of policies will be needed to counter the behavior of those who violate the rights of others, and programs that educate men and women about harassment will need to be offered in a variety of campus settings.

Fourth, women and men on the campus in the coming decade will need to talk about power—its uses and abuses, and the elements it comprises. So long as power is seen almost exclusively in terms of control, one group will seek to get it while another group will seek to keep it. The efficacy of different kinds of power (for example, the power to influence) must be examined. Authoritative models will need to coexist with bureaucratic models if permanent progress in women's issues is going to occur.

Fifth, the "chilly" classroom climate must be addressed. More female faculty must be hired; women must be supported and assisted when they choose a traditionally male major or career; faculty must be made more aware of behaviors that negatively affect women students; and forceful action must be taken against faculty, staff, or students who exhibit sexist or harassing behavior.

Safety and Security

Personal safety and security are issues that clearly pertain to the college campus for the coming decade. Many people are willing to offer explanations about the tendency toward violence in American society, but a summary of those arguments is beyond the scope of these few paragraphs. It is fair to say that a so-called breakdown in values frequently is cited, though there is less agreement as to the precise sources of that breakdown. But there can be little doubt that respect for others is a matter in need of attention in the United States.

One recent survey (Werner, 1989) revealed that many grade school and high school students are concerned about violence in their schools. Drugs, alcohol, broken homes, physical abuse, and psychological abuse are among the issues students bring to school. The behavioral and psychological manifestations of these factors in students are always serious, and sometimes violent.

We expect, then, that the coming decade will see issues of

violence increasing on the campus. Even now, there are national workshops on campus violence. One comprehensive book on the subject has been offered (Smith, 1988). A relatively new monograph, *Responding to Violence on Campus* (Sherrill and Siegel, 1989) also provides specific suggestions for reducing campus violence. The national professional associations are including articles in their journals, and members are making presentations at regional and national meetings.

College students are vulnerable because campuses have been built largely on the basis of trust. Security measures on campuses tend to be modest; preventive education programs on safety and security are not part of many campuses. It is clear criminals understand that college students possess assets and that students tend to be casual about protecting those assets. Theft is growing as a campus crime; and when a thief is detected, violence is close at hand. There are many explanations for violence but the result is clear: campuses are not as safe as they used to be.

It is also necessary to note that campuses may receive students who are victims of violence elsewhere. Apart from students who will come from violent homes, there will be victims of crime from settings off the campus. These student casualties of violence have been present and will be present, inviting a more strategic response from the campus.

Elsewhere in this chapter, we indicated that treatment of some citizens is prejudicial, mean spirited, and destructive to the spirit—both of the perpetrator and of the victim. Violence to the spirit is more crippling and deserves the fullest attention that citizens can give to it in the coming decade.

Strategies. Student affairs administrators will need to face the issues of safety and security on campus. Potential liability will encourage this, but our own values should demand it. First, where large percentages of the student population live in campus housing, major attention to security will be necessary. Concern about safety has always been felt, but new pressures are emerging due to legislation and organized crime-victim groups. We expect that liberal housing policies from the past two decades may be revisited on the basis of safety and security rather than on morality; this position should be carefully examined.

Second, the informal education of students about safety and security is in need of development. Current approaches are haphazard or may not exist at all. Crime prevention education must become a priority for student affairs.

Third, technology may contribute to a program of campus security. Administrators from all segments of the campus need to continue communicating about how to employ technical improvements to reduce campus violence. Fourth, prevention of violence may be enhanced if all campus citizens insist on respect between and among persons and constituent groups. When this respect is abridged, a campus must respond quickly and decisively.

Substance Abuse

The widespread abuse of alcohol and other drugs in American society is reflected on most college and university campuses. In the past ten years, there has been a very encouraging educational effort with alcohol abuse education, conducted primarily by student affairs staff. These programs have been geared mainly to prevention by raising the level of awareness about alcohol and its impact. But despite these efforts, most institutions report that alcohol continues to be abused widely, more so than any other drug (Goodale, 1986).

Institutions are increasingly concerned about the liability they may incur as a result of alcohol-related activities and incidents. There is a growing list of legal cases in this area, and considerable professional literature concerning it (Barr and Associates, 1988).

Public pressure to confront substance abuse is growing, and student affairs administrators frequently find themselves in the middle of substance abuse issues. They are expected to conduct effective education and prevention programs on the one hand and, on the other, to administer disciplinary sanctions against offenders of the law and campus policies. In addition, the student affairs division usually includes the counseling program, student health programs, and alcohol and drug education programs for the campus, which provide psychological and medical treatment to students with substance abuse problems.

A recent Gallup Poll (1988) indicated that the American public views drug abuse as the most serious problem facing schools at all levels. With this kind of concern, it is obvious that colleges and universities have a responsibility to respond. Effective programs are usually the results of joint efforts among students, faculty, health professionals, law enforcement personnel, and community service providers.

Although there is no single or easy explanation as to why so many young people abuse alcohol and other drugs, it is clear that doing so provides some form of temporary relief from feelings or personal circumstances that are bothersome. Thus, if substance abuse programs focus only on the alcohol and other drugs themselves, then only the symptoms will be addressed. Certainly not all substance abusers have serious mental health problems, but many will need professional assistance in confronting honestly the personal issues that led to their substance abuse.

Strategies. With the increasing pace of life, the emphasis upon individual competition, the presence of stress, and the easy availability of alcohol and other drugs, it is unlikely that substance abuse problems will decrease in future years. With that in mind, we offer the following suggestions to student affairs administrators working with the issue of substance abuse. First, we must recognize significant differences among colleges and universities regarding the amount and type of substance abuse. Prevention and treatment programs should be based upon realistic evaluations of the particular needs of individual campuses. These assessments may also help administrators avoid interference from those who would determine a college's priorities on the basis of politics.

Second, if substance abuse continues to be as pervasive as it currently is, public institutions may face increasing external pressure to control the behavior of students, to take severe disciplinary sanctions against abusers, and to conduct drug tests as part of the admissions and graduation processes. Federal legislation related to prevention programs and policies on substance abuse already exists and is linked to funding for financial aid and some grants. These pressures will require administrators to communicate honestly and frequently with governing board members and legislators to convince them that the institution is addressing the highly volatile issue of substance abuse through education and prevention efforts.

Both education and prevention are essential. During the decade of the eighties, education became a funding priority for federal and state governments as well as for the private sector. That priority must continue if colleges and universities are to meet the challenges of substance abuse. If external decision makers are not confident that colleges are vigorously confronting campus substance abuse problems, then it is likely that additional restrictions and requirements may be externally imposed.

Third, while most colleges cannot provide long-term psychological therapy to large numbers of students, the need for additional psychological services on most campuses will continue to increase in the coming decade. To meet this need, chief student affairs officers may have to shift existing resources to psychological services. After an assessment is made, other changes in the campus environment may also be called for, such as more flexible academic policies, additional recreational facilities, or more opportunities for students and faculty to meet one another informally. Efforts to decrease the amount of stress students experience may reduce substance abuse.

AIDS

The former surgeon general of the United States has stated that acquired immune deficiency syndrome (AIDS) is one of the most serious health problems that has ever faced the American public (Koop, 1988). The impact of this disease has already been felt on college campuses and will increase in the next decade because the number of people infected with the virus continues to grow.

Due in large part to the assistance provided by the American College Health Association, many colleges and universities now have policies in place regarding AIDS, and educational programs for their students and employees as well. The American College Health Association publication *AIDS on the College Campus* (Keeling, 1986) has been widely distributed and includes excellent guidelines for institutions on policies, educational programs, housing, testing, confidentiality of information, and other subjects.

Extensive resources on AIDS and other sexually transmitted

diseases are available to student affairs staff through the American College Health Association, the U.S. Public Health Service, the Center for Disease Control, and other health-related organizations. Many colleges and universities have appointed policy and program committees to address AIDS education on their campuses and have produced written materials to inform their students about AIDS and other sexually transmitted diseases.

Most student affairs staff who have become active in AIDS education have discovered quickly that it is relatively easy to disseminate information about the disease but extremely difficult to change the sexual behavior of students. There is very little evidence at this point to indicate that relevant information alone has resulted in any significant change in the sexual behavior of college students. In some college communities, there is still misinformation about the disease, moral rejection of homosexuals, and an unwillingness to discuss sexual practices and condom use in an open manner. However, these obstacles to an effective AIDS education program are not as serious as the need to convince students to alter their actual sexual behavior.

As the disease becomes more widespread, it will be necessary for student affairs administrators to allocate additional resources for programs and support. Student health services will certainly become more outreach oriented in their work. Coordination among counseling centers, medical staff, housing, student life, and local agencies will be necessary for effective AIDS education programs.

Among the most useful efforts student affairs staff can make in AIDS education programs is to involve students and student organizations in planning and implementation. Dealing frankly and openly with one's sexual behavior is often embarrassing for a nineteen-year-old college student. Creative, nonthreatening ways must be found, or educational programs will probably not result in changes in sexual behavior. Many men and women aged eighteen to twenty-four are active sexually; and with the AIDS epidemic growing, colleges and universities have a major responsibility to teach their students how to avoid contracting the disease.

Strategies. As concern about AIDS increases in future years, institutions may want to consider the following suggestions. First, there could be no clearer indication of an institution's commitment than to include AIDS education and other health issues as part of the general education requirements for an undergraduate degree. Such a policy would ensure that each student is presented with accurate, up-to-date information about AIDS and other diseases and would provide an excellent forum for extended discussions about behavioral change.

Second, despite vigorous educational efforts, it is clear that fear and prejudice concerning AIDS can result in blatant discrimination against persons with the disease. Institutions should have policies that make such discrimination unacceptable, and they will have to work hard to educate their students, faculty, and employees about attitudes toward persons with AIDS.

Third, few colleges and universities are adequately equipped to deal on their own with persons with AIDS. Liaisons with public health associations, religious groups, legal societies, hospitals, and other organizations should be established to expand the institution's ability to provide support for their students, faculty, and employees.

National Political and Economic Issues

No one is able to predict precisely what economic, political, or social issues will dominate the future. But one principle does remain clear: the general society plays a major role in setting the agenda in higher education.

Major events of the last sixty years in the United States (for example, the Great Depression, World War II, the civil rights movement, and the Vietnam War) each had a tremendous impact upon colleges and universities and changed the nature of student life and the priorities of student affairs administrators. These external events brought new students to the campuses, introduced new programs and services, changed social and behavioral norms, and made college the major vehicle in our society for upward social mobility. Colleges and universities scrambled to respond to these changes. The success of institutions has been uneven, but virtually all institutions have tried to respond.

It is perhaps unnerving that what we do in higher education is so vulnerable to national and international events. However, higher education is a reflection of the major values of the country, and thus will always have to respond to changes in the political, economic, and social landscape. Student affairs staff will have to anticipate as best they can and respond to what finally occurs.

The outline of issues is always emerging. At the time of this writing, it would seem that the coming decade might include an accelerated agenda of issues brought to the campus by persons with physical handicaps and learning disabilities. Program availability issues will be added to the existing focus on accessibility problems, and this special population will be more assertive.

Violence will continue to be a national problem, as noted earlier, and there appears to be no relief from the trend. The entire nation will be required to deal with the problems of violence, but the greatest burden and the most volatile circumstances will be found in the largest cities. Civil liberties may well be tested if violence escalates. Campuses will not be immune, nor will constituent campus groups be neutral on how to deal with the problem.

If the large middle class continues to shrink in the United States, economic issues might well claim center stage in the coming decade. Companion economic issues—such as underemployment of college graduates, diminished opportunities for women and minorities, unemployment due to the shift in the economy from an industrial to a service and information base—will influence both society and higher education. Costs for higher education, having grown enormously in the past two decades, will certainly continue to be an issue of concern.

The multiethnic balance will shift more noticeably in absolute numbers to races other than white. Part of this shift will be because of differential birth rates, and part of it will be due to immigration to the United States; many concerns will develop from this demographic shift. (See Chapter Four.) Certainly the onset of any major international crisis involving the United States could dominate the national psyche for any part of or all of the coming decade. Where, what, and how this might occur is unknown, but every thoughtful person recognizes the possibility.

Strategies. While no one can control the future, one need not be powerless in approaching it. To feel powerless is to abdicate the potential for influence. Few of us will be on center stage in the events of the world, but we can prepare to live in the future whatever our circumstances First, to the extent that student affairs staff members understand their own fundamental values, they will be as prepared as anyone can be for the changes that the future will bring. These values will provide a durable foundation for a productive life and are essential for anyone working in an educational setting. Resisting momentary currents of inappropriate enthusiasm or despair is a necessary obligation for anyone hoping to teach students.

Second, student affairs staff should be clearly aware of the mission of their institution and should only remain at the institution if they feel comfortable and committed to its mission. Fundamental differences in perspective between the institution and student affairs staff will not serve either well. A college or university that understands its unique educational role will be best equipped to respond effectively to major changes caused by external events.

Third, certainly the worst way to prepare for inevitable but unpredictable change in our society would be for student affairs staff to isolate themselves from the rest of the campus and the surrounding community. Strength in student affairs is related clearly to cooperation and collaboration with faculty, academic departments, students, and community agencies.

Summary

Social issues will have a real and direct influence on higher education and on student affairs. Despite the complexity of these issues and the unpredictability of some events, a number of steps can be taken to reduce the negative impact of these social trends and to use them as opportunities to help all students—regardless of age, gender, ethnicity, disability, or political conviction—to learn, grow, and develop. Student affairs staff must take leadership in that effort, and the leadership must begin at the top of the organization. Such leadership requires that student affairs staff demonstrate values of humane conduct and continually work at the process of open dialogue and debate on issues. Student affairs staff will need to review policies and to take actions to respond to changing needs. They must devise methods to respond to students who come to institutions with long-term problems and to students who encounter difficulties while enrolled, and they may need to reallocate resources and to make difficult decisions. But in any case, they will have to deal with the social issues that will influence the practice of student affairs in the future.

References

Barr, M. J., and Associates. *Student Services and the Law.* San Francisco: Jossey-Bass, 1988.

Gallup, G. "Twentieth Annual Gallup Poll of the Public's Attitudes Toward the Public Schools." *Gallup Opinion Index,* 1988, 276.

Goodale, T. (ed.). *Alcohol and the College Student.* New Directions for Student Services, no. 35. San Francisco: Jossey-Bass, 1986

Hall, R. M., and Sandler, B. R. *The Classroom Climate: A Chilly One for Women?* Washington, D.C.: Project on the Status and Education of Women, Association of American Colleges, 1985.

Keeling, R. P. *AIDS on the College Campus.* Rockville, Md.: American College Health Association, 1986.

Koop, C. E. *Understanding AIDS.* Rockville, Md.: U.S. Department of Health and Human Services, 1988.

National Association of Student Personnel Administrators. *A Perspective on Student Affairs.* Washington, D.C.: National Association of Student Personnel Administrators, 1987.

Reproductive Health Services v. *Webster,* 109 S. Ct. 3040 (1989). *Roe v. Wade,* 410 U.S. 113 (1973).

Sherrill, J. M., and Siegel, D. G. (eds.). *Responding to Violence on Campus.* New Directions for Student Services, no. 47. San Francisco: Jossey-Bass, 1989.

Smith, M. C. *Coping with Crime on Campus.* New York: American Council on Education and MacMillan, 1988.

Welch, H., McHugh, B., and others. *Racial Discrimination on Campus.* Washington, D.C.: National Association of Student Personnel Administrators, 1988.

Werner, L. "School Today." *USA Weekend,* Aug. 18, 1989, pp. 4–5.

Chapter 6

Changing Regulatory and Legal Environments

Robert H. Fenske

Edward A. Johnson

In the United States, both the federal and state levels of government historically have been reluctant to develop laws, policies, or regulations that directly affect the day-to-day academic or student affairs operations of colleges or universities. In regard to student affairs, government has tacitly recognized higher education's in loco parentis responsibilities. This laissez-faire relationship is partly due to the early traditions that developed during the first two centuries of American higher education when, beginning with the founding of Harvard in 1636, colleges and universities were almost entirely private, church-controlled institutions. The beginning of significant growth in the public sector is usually dated from the establishment of the University of Virginia in 1825. The public sector, however, did not achieve equality in enrollment with the private sector until 1950. Since that time, growth in the public sector has been rapid, and the current ratio of

Note: The authors gratefully acknowledge the comments made by Paul G. Barberini, Gary H. Knock, and John H. Schuh on the final draft of this chapter.

about four students enrolled in public colleges for every private college student has held since the mid 1970s. As would be expected from this shift to predominance of public institutions, government has become more closely involved with higher education. Such involvement has resulted in laws and regulations that directly affect student affairs.

Rapidly changing political, social, and economic forces are affecting higher education as it moves into the final decade of the twentieth century. These forces significantly influence the way in which the federal and state levels of government shape and regulate campus operations. Because of different funding and legal relationships with colleges and universities, the states now create a more immediate and widespread "environmental press" on higher education, especially on the public sector. The private sector historically has been insulated much more from government influence than have public institutions; however, increased government funding, especially through student financial assistance, has significantly eroded the traditional insularity.

Scope and Limitations

Within the narrow confines of this brief chapter, it is not possible to discuss all levels of relationship between government and higher education, such as laws regulating mandatory retirement or the immigration status of foreign citizens. The focus of this chapter will be on selected recent federal and state laws and regulations aimed specifically at colleges and universities, especially those that affect students. The chapter is organized into three main sections. In the first two sections on regulatory environments, the federal level of government is considered first, then the state. The section on legal environments follows. The final section considers how student affairs in particular is affected by these changing environments and concludes with a brief discussion of possible future trends.

The Federal Regulatory Environment

Today, federal involvement in higher education includes three roles. The first, funding of basic and applied research, began at a significant level in the 1950s and still continues, although at a somewhat reduced rate (in inflation-adjusted terms) over the last decade. Because this role affects student affairs only indirectly and focuses exclusively on a relatively small number of research universities, it will be discussed only incidentally in the remainder of this chapter. The other two current roles are often described by the terms *access* and *quality*.

Access as the focal point for promoting equal education opportunity—part of the federal government's concern for social justice since the late nineteenth century—was given great impetus by the massive legislative initiatives of the Great Society of the mid 1960s, especially the Higher Education Act of 1965. Ensuring access is currently carried out through large-scale funding of student financial aid and provides the main opportunity for the federal government to affect campus operations in general, and student affairs in particular.

Quality in higher education has been expressed as an increasingly urgent concern of the federal government since 1980, with particular reference to improving the U.S. position in international economic competition. Thus far, this concern has not been expressed through funding, but rather through the recommendations of so-called reform task forces (National Commission on Excellence in Education, 1983; National Institute of Education, 1984) and exhortation and criticism by government officials (Gladieux and Lewis, 1987).

Only one of the three federal roles, promotion of equal educational access, seems to affect student affairs directly through regulatory channels. The other two roles in research and quality do not, for differing reasons. Federal research funding has become increasingly burdensome to faculty researchers in colleges and universities because of accountability and auditing requirements of research contracts, but these regulatory burdens do not affect campus student affairs operations. Federal concerns about improving academic quality have been expressed through criticism and exhortations for reform rather than through program funding; hence, there have been no significant regulatory effects on higher education.

Student Financial Aid. Federal promotion of equal educational opportunity continues to be focused on access and is expressed as funding of student financial aid. Student aid has been called "the very lifeblood of the institution" (Atwell, 1981). Federal student aid exists on virtually every campus and is awarded in one form or another to a majority of all full-time students sometime during their undergraduate careers (accurate statistical estimates are not available because participants are not cross-tabulated among all aid programs).

The scale of federal aid is large by any measure, currently comprising about three-fourths of total student aid from all sources. In 1987–88, $17.09 billion of federal aid was awarded, compared with $1.503 billion from states and $4.36 billion from private or institutional sources (College Board, 1989, p. 6).

All of the current forms of student aid (grants, loans, work-study) came about after the monumental Higher Education Act of 1965. But all of these programs began, by current standards, on a relatively small scale. The federal commitment to student aid mushroomed in the 1975 amendments to the act. These amendments created the program now called *Pell Grants* for the purpose of providing a floor of support to all needy students.

Congress continued heavy funding of student aid through the 1980s, over the strenuous objections of the Reagan administration, by awarding at least ten billion dollars annually. This level of funding carries with it heavy fiduciary responsibilities—governmental expectations of careful stewardship of funds and awards. The Pell Grant program and the huge guaranteed student loan programs (the largest of which was renamed *Stafford Loans* in 1988) were originally intended to be administered by national data processing organizations under contract to the government. However, administration of eligibility and need levels now mainly occurs on campuses, and awards for both are made by campus student aid offices. All other student aid programs are administered entirely by the institutions. The fiduciary responsibilities of campus-based programs are burdensome, but the institutions really do not have the option of dropping the programs because student aid is vital to the initial enrollment and retention of so many students.

The federal regulations call for annual audits, and failure to meet required standards for any reason can result in discontinuance of federal aid funds until the noncompliance is remedied. In some cases, the institutions have been required to find and contribute funds from their own or other sources to replace missing federal funds not accounted for under the institution's fiduciary process.

Burdensome though compliance with the fiduciary requirements may be, such requirements are no more than would be expected under the principle of good stewardship of public funds. However, in the 1970s, campus administrators became more concerned because federal officials seemed increasingly eager to use enforcement of student financial aid regulations as an opportunity to enlarge the federal presence on campus. For example, the administrative regulations for the 1976 amendments included the provision that continued institutional eligibility for participation in federal aid programs would be contingent on such measures of institutional quality as the percentage of students completing programs and the percentage of students finding employment in a field directly related to the academic major. These and other potential intrusions into campus affairs that were traditionally sacrosanct were—to the relief of campus officials—largely abandoned when the Reagan administration inaugurated its programs intended to curtail federal involvement and ultimately shift all responsibility to the states, parents, and students. Congress, however, continued to fund aid programs at relatively high levels.

Student Loans. Beginning in the mid 1980s, the federal regulatory environment began to take on a new and more ominous dimension. The government's concern focused on the rapidly escalating cost of the Stafford Loan (formerly *Guaranteed Student Loan*) program and on the persistent and seemingly intractable problem of loan defaults. Concern of both the federal government and the higher education community grew along with the expenditures, because loans became, contrary to the original goals for federal student aid voiced in the late 1960s and early 1970s, the dominant form of student aid by 1987–88 (Lewis, 1988). The higher education community has been concerned that loans may be overburdening the future of too many students (Hansen, 1987) and possibly distorting their career and academic major choices (Mohrman, 1987).

Both Congress and the administration have been increasingly concerned over the persistently high loan default rate, an apparently uncontrollable flow that has driven program expenditures to new heights year after year, with no end in sight. Loan defaults are directly under the purview of federal regulations. Therefore, the government can, and is, using direct action rather than simple criticism and exhortation. The highest default rates have been, and continue to be, primarily in proprietary schools and community colleges—the two postsecondary sectors that focus on serving the minority and low-income students. These students are at highest risk for dropping out early and defaulting on loans.

New Uses of Regulation. In 1988 under the leadership of former Secretary William Bennett, the Department of Education finally moved vigorously to stem the default rate through new regulations withdrawing eligibility for federal student aid from those institutions with an unacceptably high default rate. Consequently, the *Chronicle of Higher Education* noted in late June 1989 that "more than 700 institutions had been notified by the Department of Education that funds for certain student aid programs would be cut off at the end of this week because they had yet to comply with the regulations" (Deloughrey, 1989, p. 1). Clearly, this enforcement represented a new dimension of regulation, shifting from a focus on the mere fiduciary responsibilities of the institution to punishing the institution for behavioral failures on the part of its former students. (Loans do not go into repayment status until after the student graduates or drops out.) It should be noted that institutions cannot determine who borrows; once need is established, the institution cannot prevent a student from borrowing.

Other key regulations were initiated and enforced in the 1980s—regulations intended to link academic performance of students with eligibility for student financial aid necessary to continue their programs of study. Standards for satisfactory progress and good standing were established by the federal government under consultation with the higher education community. Student performance in meeting these academic standards is monitored, however, entirely by the institutions.

The federal student aid delivery system has, from its very

inception, been extremely complex and subject to continual change. Often, bureaucratic changes were not coordinated with the institutional schedules of periodic application and award processes. Thus, the delivery system has frequently been thrown into disarray. Students frustrated by lack of funds to enroll or to stay in school have vented their displeasure at campus officials and have not been mollified by explanations of bureaucratic foul-ups in far-off Washington, D.C.

A consequence of the overregulation of federal student aid is that "the procedures students and families face in applying for assistance have become far too complex. The system itself seems to have become a barrier to educational opportunity for the very students, low-income and disadvantaged, that Pell Grants and other federal aid were originally intended to reach. Yet federal requirements . . . continue to balloon the application forms students and parents must fill out" (College Board, 1989, p. 9).

Another new and even more ominous (and, to the higher education community, odious) dimension of the federal regulatory environment has recently emerged. The federal government is now willing to use the threat of withdrawal of student aid as a club to enforce desired student behaviors unrelated to and beyond the direct control of the colleges and universities. Specifically, the target behaviors identified so far include failure to register for the draft, drug and alcohol abuse, and illegal immigration. Draft registration is now, and immigration status will soon be, specified on the aid application forms and are to be verified by the institutions. In the case of drug and alcohol abuse, institutions are required to develop and operate campuswide programs and to withdraw federal student aid from those students who are convicted of alcohol- and drug-related crimes.

These new regulations are not merely recommendatory; they are to be enforced, with stiff penalties for noncompliance. For example, the *Chronicle of Higher Education* reported in July 1989 that "the first person to be prosecuted for fraudulently claiming on a federal student loan form that he had registered for the draft pleaded guilty. [He] was placed on probation for eighteen months, ordered to register and told to repay the government the $5,088 in Pell Grants" (Jaschik, 1989, p. A28). And the same *Chronicle* article that noted the 700 institutions cited for failure to reduce default rates also reported that "about 180 institutions, many of which were also among the 700, were told that they could lose funds for Perkins loans, College Work Study and Supplemental Educational Opportunity Grants because they had not complied with efforts to make campuses 'drug free'" (Deloughrey, 1989, p. 1). The article goes on to quote a college official who said he "resented the increasing number of federal regulations tied to student aid" (p. A18).

The State Regulatory Environment

Since the 1950s, there has been a strong and unmistakable trend toward increasing involvement of state government in the affairs of higher education. The instruments of involvement used by governors and legislators are a bewildering and rapidly proliferating infrastructure of bureaucracies. "In the past 35 years, the no-man's land between the states and the university has been filled by an array of coordinating boards, governing boards and multi-campus systems. It is no longer simple to describe where the state ends and the university begins" (Newman, 1987, pp. 11-12).

The key concern of state involvement in the 1950s and 1960s was accountability, and the purpose of state involvement in higher education was to regulate the growth of expenditures, to bring political pressure to bear in changing the mission of public institutions in order to achieve social goals set by the state, and to control or eliminate duplication of programs (Hines, 1988, p. 40P). A major effort in most states was mounted to move away from the traditional method of incremental budgeting to formula budgeting, which would allow better control of expenditure growth.

The concept of performance budgeting was introduced in the 1970s (actually a revival of earlier attempts in the 1950s, according to Orwig and Caruthers, 1980) to focus on excessive program duplication as enrollment growth slowed. Programs were periodically audited to determine whether they had reached previously specified goals, with discontinuance the implied punishment for failure (Floyd, 1982).

However, discontinuing programs with tenured faculty proved to be a difficult task, and many states turned in the 1980s to some form of incentive budgeting. Some incentive methods use a "stick" approach, others use a "carrot." An example of the first approach is the Tennessee Performance Funding Program, which links "levels of appropriation to measurable outcomes, thus making funding contingent on demonstrated results" (Hines, 1988, p. 54). Obviously, with a fixed amount of state appropriations, some programs that do not measure up will experience no increase in budgets—or even cutbacks or elimination. An example of the "carrot" approach is the Fund for Excellence in Virginia, in which institutions compete for new money that is separate from budget appropriations by submitting proposals for new programs to improve academic quality. New Jersey and Ohio, among others, have similar plans (Hines, 1988, pp. 54-55).

All of these coordinating, planning, and budgeting activities require resources, and the states have responded by developing large staffs in a wide variety of agencies. "Today the states and territories have more than 16,000 full-time and 9,000 part-time legislative employees, including staff for bill drafting, fiscal and budget matters, information services, legal services, program evaluation and research . . . . States today have sophisticated computer capacity, not just for the legislature but for the administration, including the budget officer, the personnel office, the state auditor, etc. . . . In many states, for the first time, state government is equipped with the capacity to understand what is actually happening on campus, including the details of campus expenditure" (Newman, 1987, pp. 40-41).

In recent years, the role of the governor has moved to the forefront, and he or she has been referred to as the single most important person in higher education (Kerr, 1985, p. 47). A primary focus of governors' attention to higher education has been the area of economic development. "In 1985, 38 state-of-the-state addresses by governors cited economic development as a top state priority. In every case, this was linked directly to a recognized dependence on higher education" (Newman, 1987, p. 3).

The fixation on the instrumental use of higher education for economic development and competitiveness inevitably raises concerns about partisan involvement and excessive intrusion of politics into the previously insular academic environment. "Supposedly, the U.S. Supreme Court decision in the 1819 Dartmouth College Case had permanently established a buffer between state politics and institutions of higher education. Daniel Webster had successfully argued before Chief Justice Marshall that not only must there be an inviolable sanctuary for criticism of the social order, there should also be recognition that colleges and universities involved *long-term* processes . . . that should be protected from the vagaries of two- and four-year state partisan political cycles" (Fenske, 1980, p. 182). The long-term processes of student degree programs, professional careers of faculty, and terms of campus presidents can be jeopardized by excessive intrusions of zealous governors who are in office for much shorter terms than any implied in these academic processes. Brevity of gubernatorial terms is exemplified in an extreme case (involving an impeached governor) in which one state (Arizona) had three different governors in one recent fourteen-month period.

In the push for improving quality of academic programs for the purpose of improving state economic competitiveness, what happens to the maintenance of wide access to higher education for a given state's burgeoning minority population? Which is winning in the arena of competition for state monies, social justice or economic development? In Florida, for example, the state has mandated the so-called rising junior plan, which requires that all public-college students must pass the College Level Academic Skills Test before getting a two-year associate degree or enrolling in an upper-division university course (Blumenstyk, 1989, p. A22). This requirement "would have a particularly severe impact on otherwise qualified minority students and on those for whom English is not the native tongue" (p. A22). Beginning in 1989, higher scores required to pass the test will probably result in lower percentages of minority students allowed to rise to junior status. It is estimated that 70 percent of Hispanic students and nearly 80 percent of black students who take the test will not be allowed to continue progress toward the baccalaureate beyond the sophomore year (Blumenstyk, p. A22).

Federal and state regulatory and legal influences on higher education since the 1950s reflect alternating emphases on concerns for equal educational opportunity and academic programs. As

Hansen and Stampen (1987) point out, these two concerns ideally should be complementary, yet in practice they are often in conflict. Their research has demonstrated that during alternating emphases between these two concerns, gains in either goal were won at the expense of the other.

The Reagan years, beginning in 1981, clearly saw a swing to improvement of academic quality as an overriding emphasis. But implementation efforts at achieving this goal were just as clearly delegated to the states by the Reagan administration. "The Educational Consolidation and Improvement Act of 1981 (ECIA) reversed the flow of educational policy development that had characterized the previous quarter century. The enthusiasm exhibited by the states in filling the power vacuum left by ECIA probably exceeded the Administration's expectations. Like it or not, the focus of action on educational policy is in the state capitols where it will remain for an indefinite time period" (Clark and Astuto, 1988, p. 13). The states also will carry forward the emphasis on academic quality rather than access for the foreseeable future. "No war on poverty is likely to capture the imagination of the public in this decade stacked up against a war on the trade deficit" (p. 15).

In summary, state involvement in higher education is increasing rapidly in many ways (budgeting, program assessment, political intrusion) and for many purposes (improvement of academic quality, economic competitiveness, access and degree attainment for minorities). Public colleges and universities—and, to a lesser but still significant extent, private institutions—are just beginning to sense the dimensions and long-term impact of state governors, legislatures, and statewide higher education agencies.

The Legal Environment

The legal environment of student affairs practice has been in continuous ferment during the past three decades, and no apparent relief is in sight. The environment is, on the one hand, illustrated by the recent editorial cartoon of a client seated in his attorney's office asking, "I would like to sue someone for something; any ideas whom and for what?" On the other hand, a somewhat more objective perspective of the environment is that students are probably a relatively small proportion of litigants in higher-education-related court actions (Helms, 1987; Lam, 1988). A third perspective recognizes simply that three decades of litigation, legislation, and regulation have permanently impacted the decision-making processes of student affairs professionals. In spite of the fact that students are relatively unsuccessful as plaintiffs, there are now few actions taken without an evaluation of legal parameters and implications. Formal notions such as *fundamental fairness, equal protection,* and *time, place, and manner* are now a part of the everyday working lexicon of student affairs professionals.

This section is intended to synthesize recent trends and speculate on future legal issues impacting selected areas of student affairs practice. Specifically, the focus will be upon constitutional, tort, and contract issues affecting areas such as academic and disciplinary dismissals, First Amendment regulation, student organizations, and health advising and counseling. Additional background information can be found on these issues in *Student Services and the Law: A Handbook for Practitioners* (Barr and Associates, 1988).

Constitutional Relationships. In retrospect, the changing nature of student enrollments following World War II and the enrollment expansion of the 1960s had a significant impact upon both student-administrator relationships and the use of legal means to seek relief when those relationships became increasingly confrontational in nature. Claims centering on deprivations of U.S. constitutional rights under the First Amendment (freedom of speech and association) and the Fourteenth Amendment (due process and equal protection) had little success from the 1930s through the 1950s. Attendance was considered a privilege subject to the discretion of the institution; proceedings relating to continued attendance were not constitutionally protected. In loco parentis reigned, and institutional autonomy was protected.

Beginning in the 1960s, certain constitutional rights of students began to be recognized, but the courts remained wary of challenging the traditional control of faculty and academic administrators over teaching and the curriculum. That is, on the one hand, the academic environment was viewed as retaining the special characteristics worthy of judicial deference, but on the other, student discipline was increasingly accorded constitutional protections such as notice, hearing, and an impartial decision maker—as well as a nonarbitrary and noncapricious decision based upon the evidence presented.

Following the U.S. Supreme Court's recognition of student constitutional rights in the 1960s (*Dixon* v. *Alabama State Board of Education,* 1961; *Tinker* v. *Des Moines School District,* 1969), and its extension of procedural rights in the 1970s (*Goss* v. *Lopez,* 1975), many predicted that an inexorable process of expanding student academic and disciplinary rights would continue through the remainder of this century. During the 1980s, that concern abated somewhat. The Supreme Court has declined to consider the issue of whether students at public universities have property or liberty interests in education, even though lower courts had so ruled and continue to rule (*Regents of the University of Michigan* v. *Ewing,* 1985; *Board of Curators of University of Missouri* v. *Horowtiz,* 1978). A Supreme Court decision similar to that of the lower courts would have triggered the full due process requirements of the Fourteenth Amendment in academic dismissal procedures and placed public university students squarely within the dictates of *Goss* v. *Lopez,* 1975. Instead, what has been established is a "some due process" requirement and codictum that a "careful and deliberate" decision be rendered.

Nothing suggests at this point that the Supreme Court will expand student procedural due process rights in disciplinary proceedings, absent a new wave of student protests to create situations that might cause the Supreme Court to revisit this area of the law. Public and private colleges and universities have so institutionalized due process procedures that it is less and less likely that they will be subject to a major appellate review. An issue for the 1990s will be whether institutions can continue to fine-tune their procedures to protect recognized interests of students without further burdening university administrators to the point that they cannot carry out their professional responsibilities.

A review of recent case law on academic dismissals indicates that unless there is evidence of extremely unclear institutional policies or procedures, or unusual circumstances of professorial misconduct or institutional negligence, universities win academic dismissal cases. It is likely that in the coming decade, the Supreme

Court will be asked to reexamine the application of due process principles to academic dismissals. If the Court accepts such a case, it will likely find a liberty interest in pursuing a degree program or a property interest in a degree itself. The fact situation for the case will probably relate to academic dishonesty in an area where the distinction between an academic decision and a disciplinary decision has not been articulated clearly by the Court. Should the Court find the liberty or property interest, it will formally extend elements of procedural due process to the academic setting, including the requirement of a formal, adversary hearing in such disputes.

It is likely that the 1990s will see another round of First Amendment challenges on college and university campuses if another cycle of student activism occurs—for example, over abortion debates or regulations prohibiting racial harassment. Case law from the 1960s and 1970s made it clear that the First Amendment applies with full vigor on our public university campuses, that students are "persons" under the U.S. Constitution, inside and outside of the classroom, and that state universities may regulate conduct that materially and substantially interferes with the educational process (*Healy* v. *James,* 1972; *Tinker* v. *Des Moines School District,* 1969). Four competing interests must continuously be balanced: possible threat to campus security, preservation of the academic character of the campus, protection of the rights of others, and the physical maintenance and esthetics of the campus. In the 1980s, the principal case law affirming free expression arose from the erection of shanties as symbolic expressions of students protesting South African apartheid policies and university divestment policies (*Students Against Apartheid* v. *O'Neil,* 1987; *University of Utah Students Against Apartheid* v. *Peterson,* 1986). The legitimacy of individual university restrictions, particularly regarding symbolic expression, will continue to be litigated throughout the next decade.

The use of college admissions and academic assessment tests by colleges and universities and other organizations will likely come under increasing constitutional scrutiny in the 1990s. The use of such tests for admissions, financial aid, and academic advisement purposes has been challenged periodically over the past several decades for its alleged "disparate impact" on females, ethnic minorities, and economically disadvantaged students—possible violation of the equal protection clauses of the Fourteenth Amendment to the U.S. Constitution. The most recent example was the 1989 ruling that the practice of relying only upon Scholastic Aptitude Test scores in awarding New York State Education Department merit scholarships was discriminating because it "deprives young women of the opportunity to compete equally for the prestigious scholarships in violation of both Title IX [of the Education Amendments of 1972] and the Constitution's equal protection clauses" (*Sherif* v. *New York State Department of Education,* 1989). A female high school senior and women's group plaintiffs successfully obtained a preliminary injunction against the New York State Education Department from solely using the test scores in awarding Regents and Empire Program Scholarships; the plaintiffs claimed that the sixty-point average lower scores for females had an unfair impact upon female students. As the case will not be appealed, it is difficult to interpret the precedential value of the case. It is likely, however, that other legal challenges will use equal protection claims to seek to limit the use of tests as sole criteria, particularly in the area of academic assessment. Teacher testing and rising junior tests, for example, have been criticized for this "disparate impact" upon ethnic minority students. The increasing use of such tests by universities, often under state mandates, is likely to lead to similar lawsuits in the coming decade.

Yet another constitutional issue that will gain importance is balancing the constitutionally protected rights of individuals against the responsibility of institutions to create environments free of harassment, racism, and sexism. Many institutions have developed policy statements that prohibit harassing behavior and impose disciplinary sanctions against individuals who harass others on the basis of race, ethnicity, sexual orientation, or gender.

In 1989, just such a policy was constitutionally challenged in Michigan on the basis of the freedom of speech doctrine. The policy of the University of Michigan, which defined discriminatory harassment and established mechanisms for responding to harassing behaviors, included both academic and disciplinary sanctions. The federal district court (*Doe* v. *University of Michigan,* 1989) declared the policy unconstitutional on the grounds of vagueness and being overbroad. The reasoning of the court revolved around the "reasonable person" standard and indicated that for the University of Michigan policy to be constitutional, precision regarding what would "stigmatize" or "victimize" the individual was required.

Other institutions, including the University of California system, have adopted a "fighting words" approach to racial harassment policies, based on *Chaplinsky* v. *New Hampshire* (1942). It should be noted, however, that in the decades since that case, there has not been a single majority opinion that upholds the "fighting words" doctrine. The question remains whether the doctrine would still apply if, in the context of the event, there is no likelihood of violence.

Some institutions have opted for an approach whereby a single incident would not invoke the racial harassment policy. A pattern of harassing behavior would have to be established before action were taken. Institutions following this course believe a pattern of behavior would prove harassment more clearly in the courts. Still other institutions have approached the issue on multiple levels, changing policies while concurrently offering mediation services, educational programs, and intervention. These approaches have not been tested in the courts, but they may have increased the chances that institutional regulations will be upheld.

However it is resolved, the issue of balancing individual rights to freedom of speech against creating climates free of harassing behavior must be confronted. It will be among the pressing legal issues of the future.

Tort Relationships. With the exception of constitutional issues, the area of tort law has been the subject of more litigation than any other during the past thirty years. "A tort is broadly defined as a civil wrong, other than a breach of contract, for which the courts will allow a damage remedy" (Kaplin, 1985, p. 55). In the collegiate setting, tort law has been most often applied in negligence cases relating to personal injuries sustained while on a class field trip, while attending an activity sponsored by the institution or a student group, or while transiting university property.

An institution normally is liable for negligent acts of its employees and, in some cases, of its student organizations. For liability to be found, the institution must have owed a duty to the injured party and must have failed to exercise due care to avoid the injury. In the case of an injury related to a student, courts generally find that the student is classified as an "invitee" and that the institution has the obligation of exercising reasonable care to keep the premises in a safe condition. If, on the other hand, the injury occurs during or is linked to an activity having some relationship with a student organization, a court will determine whether a special relationship exists between the institution and the student and whether that relationship requires the institution to supervise and control student conduct. The doctrine of in loco parentis provided the underlying theory for legally defining that special relationship until its gradual demise during the 1960s. During the 1970s, courts struggled with the definition of that relationship, but in the 1980s, the strong trend of decisions was to affirm that college students are adults—making it unreasonable, impractical, and inconsistent with their rights to require schools to regulate their personal conduct (*Whitlock* v. *University of Denver,* 1985; *Bradshaw* v. *Rawlings,* 1979). Even if social attitudes return in the 1990s to favoring closer supervision of students' behavior, it is likely that universities will continue to distance themselves from organizations, given the impracticality and undesirability of implementing policies reminiscent of in loco parentis attitudes.

Several specific tort issues will continue to impact student affairs administration in the 1990s. Advising on health issues will be a key concern, particularly as it relates to the growing problem of acquired immune deficiency syndrome (AIDS). Institutions have a duty to protect students from known or reasonably foreseeable health dangers. It is unlikely that casual contact transmission of AIDS would be held foreseeable, and no appellate court case has yet so ruled. If it is ruled that universities have a duty, courts will look to the recommendations of health officials, and universities will be judged by whom they listened to and how they responded. The implementation of educational programs and an AIDS policy that follows authoritative medical recommendations likely will be responses that will find judicial support.

Courts will probably not require quarantining or the public identification of students who are infected with AIDS. It is generally believed that AIDS is a handicap subject to the provisions of the

Rehabilitation Act of 1973 (*School Board of Nassau County* v. *Arline,* 1987). Advisers, counselors, and other student affairs personnel will increasingly need to understand the rights of AIDS-infected persons under that act.

The problems associated with alcohol abuse and hazing in Greek-letter societies have been the subject of increasing attention and will continue to be so in the 1990s. The key alcohol-related issue will be the continued probing of tort law limits to find compensation for individuals injured in alcohol-related accidents. Since local chapters of fraternities and sororities are usually "judgment-proof" (that is, less likely to be sued because of their limited assets), there will be a continuing effort to hold national societies liable for failing to oversee their activities properly. Eighty percent of local societies are affiliated with national groups. Those relationships suggest that further precedent-setting cases will have a great impact on legal relationships, particularly if courts rule that serving alcohol to minors in violation of state law is negligence per se.

The fact that all national societies have policies against hazing and that half the states have criminal statutes proscribing hazing has not stopped the practice. The general case law of the 1970s and 1980s finding a responsibility not to cause injury during the initiation process is likely to continue. The issue for the next decade may be whether courts will refuse to impose civil liability on national associations for the negligent conduct of their locals' students, as courts have previously ruled for colleges in similar situations. Should liability be found, the choice for the national societies will be either to withdraw their regulatory and oversight responsibilities or to seek to control locals through strong enforcement.

Contractual Relationships. It is well-established law that the relationship between an institution and a student is contractual in nature. As a result, contract theory continues to be a popular course of action, in addition to constitutional and statutory claims, in part because private college or university students often have no other legal cause of action. Issues relating to admissions, discipline, tuition and fees, program elimination, and degree revocation have all been litigated under contract theory. Early in this century, contract law was being used by universities to justify actions taken against students (*William* v. *Stein,* 1917; *Anthony* v. *Syracuse University,* 1928). It was not until the 1960s and 1970s that courts established express and implied contract theory as being applicable to student-initiated contract claims (*Carr* v. *St. John's University,* 1962; *Healy* v. *Larsson,* 1971). The 1980s proved to be a relatively stable period for contract law litigation. Institutions are winning the vast majority of reported cases. Clear violations of stated policies generally must have occurred for an institution to lose a lawsuit.

Courts continue to struggle, however, with the precise nature of the contractual relationship. Defining the terms and conditions of the contract between a student and an institution is problematic, as is the issue of the implied or inherent authority of the institution to modify its documents or practices. A major issue that may reach an appellate court in the 1990s is the extent to which an academically related contractual claim might give rise to a property right and thus trigger the due process clause of the Fourteenth Amendment to the U.S. Constitution. Two courts have recently reached different conclusions on this issue (*Ikpeazu* v. *University of Nebraska,* 1985; *Bergstrom* v. *Buettner,* 1987). It is also likely that courts will continue to expand their holdings that find an implied covenant of good faith or fair dealing in the contractual relationship (*Johnson* v. *Lincoln Christian College,* 1986; *Banerjee* v. *Roberts,* 1986; *Cosio* v. *Medical College of Wisconsin,* 1987). This implied covenant holding has been applied to both academic and disciplinary proceedings, although judicial deference to academic judgments has limited its success in academically related actions. Because federal constitutional causes of action are generally not applicable to independent institutions, the expansion of the good faith doctrine will have a particularly significant impact upon student affairs administrators at those institutions.

Future Trends

The onerous environmental press of continuing state and federal regulations seems certain to continue. We believe that the Pandora's box opened by the deliberate and unchallenged federal threats to withhold student aid in order to accomplish social goals will not be closed. Instead, we foresee extended use of this effective strategy by the federal government, and parallel strategy being developed by states. The trend of applying governmental sanctions to student aid recipients for issues unrelated to student aid (such as draft registration and drug and alcohol abuse) in effect turns student affairs professionals into law enforcement officers. Nothing could be more detrimental to the traditional role of student affairs.

Legal issues are impinging on higher education more urgently than ever before. Some of the most crucial issues likely to persist well into the 1990s are as follows:

1. Student affairs professionals will be increasingly involved in balancing the constitutional rights of students with the elimination of prejudice and harassment and the promotion of tolerance.
2. Federal and state-mandated AIDS testing and monitoring may have a chilling effect on use of campus health and counseling services and may discourage students from seeking the help they need.
3. Campuses must be in compliance with state-mandated crime and safety requirements, but the reporting of compliance to the state must balance the right of students for accurate information against causing them undue alarm.
4. As competition for students continues into the 1990s, institutions must scrupulously observe truth-in-advertising regulations in the dissemination of admissions information and in all recruiting efforts.
5. Nationwide strengthening and clarifying of date rape and sexual assault laws will increase institutional responsibilities for information and education, as well as for facilities and services for rape-related problems such as medical and psychological treatment and assistance with legal prosecution.
6. State laws against hazing will require closer supervision of all student organizations, but continuing problems with Greek chapters will require special attention and the willingness to deal firmly with violations, including withdrawal of charters if necessary.
7. Court rulings and state laws on liability will require closer monitoring of on-campus and off-campus social events where

alcohol is served, as well as increased willingness to take action against illegal drug and alcohol abuse.

The continuing emphasis on academic quality will place heavy burdens on student affairs professionals to ensure access to, and success in, higher education. In areas such as remedial education, outreach to minorities in recruiting programs, and retention of at-risk students, student affairs must be at the forefront.

The increased pressure from the states for periodic assessment of learning outcomes will provide an opportunity for student affairs professionals to work in tandem with faculty in fostering academic achievement. First, student affairs professionals must make faculty more aware of the strong influence that environmental and affective factors have on cognitive learning. Next, student affairs professionals must develop appropriate skills and knowledge related to assessment of learning. Finally, faculty must be better informed about the assessment expertise available in student affairs divisions.

As the basis for funding academic programs shifts from formulas based on enrollments to incentive funding based on actual learning outcomes, faculty will become more receptive to working in tandem with student affairs professionals. Such collaboration would move higher education toward realization of the student development concept advocated for so many years by the student affairs profession (Fenske and Hughes, 1980).

Cases

Anthony v. *Syracuse University,* 231 N.Y.S. 435 (1928).

Banerjee v. *Roberts,* 641 F. Supp. 1093 (D. Conn. 1986).

Bergstrom v. *Buettner,* 697 F. Supp. 1098 (D.N.D. 1987).

Board of Curators of the University of Missouri v. *Horowitz,* 435 U.S. 78, 90 S. Ct. 948 (1978).

Bradshaw v. *Rawlings,* 612 F.2d 135 (1979), *cert. denied,* 446 U.S. 909 (1979).

Carr v. *St. John's University,* 17 A.D.2d 632, 231 N.Y.S.2d 410, *affirmed* 12 N.Y.2d 802, 187 N.E.2d 18 (1962).

Chaplinsky v. *New Hampshire,* 315 U.S. 568, 62 S. Ct. 766 (1942).

Cosio v. *Medical College of Wisconsin,* 407 M.W.2d 302 (Wis. App. 1987).

Dixon v. *Alabama State Board of Education,* 294 F.2d 150 (5th Cir. 1961).

Doe v. *University of Michigan,* No. 89, 71683 (E.D. Mich. Sept. 7, 1989).

Goss v. *Lopez,* 419 U.S. 565, 95 S. Ct. 729 (1975).

Healy v. *James,* 408 U.S. 169, 92 S. Ct. 2338 (1972).

Healy v. *Larsson,* 323 N.Y.S.2d 625, *affirmed* 35 N.Y.S.2d 653, 318 N.E.2d 608 (1971).

Ikpeazu v. *University of Nebraska,* 775 F.2d 250 (8th Cir. 1985).

Johnson v. *Lincoln Christian College,* 501 N.E.2d 1380 (Ill. App. 1986).

Regents of the University of Michigan v. *Ewing,* 474 U.S. 214 (1985).

School Board of Nassau County v. *Arline,* 489 U.S. 273 (1987).

Sherif v. *New York State Department of Education,* 88 Cir. 8435 (S.D.N.Y. 1989).

Students Against Apartheid v. *O'Neil,* 660 Supp. 333 (W.D. Va. 1987).

Tinker v. *Des Moines Independent School District,* 393 U.S. 503, 89 S.Ct. 733 (1969).

University of Utah Students Against Apartheid v. *Peterson,* 649 F. Supp. 1200 (D. Utah 1986).

Whitlock v. *University of Denver,* 744 P.2d 54 (Colo. 1985).

William v. *Stein,* 166 N.Y.S. 836 (1917).

References

Atwell, R. H. "What Academic Administrators Should Know About Financial Aid." In R. H. Atwell and M. F. Green (eds.), *Academic Leaders As Managers.* New Directions for Higher Education, no. 36. San Francisco: Jossey-Bass, 1981.

Barr, M. J., and Associates. *Student Services and the Law: A Handbook for Practitioners.* San Francisco: Jossey-Bass, 1988.

Blumenstyk, G. "Raising of Standards on Florida's Competency Test for College Students Stirs Controversy." *Chronicle of Higher Education,* July 12, 1989, p. A22.

Clark, D. L., and Astuto, T. A. *Education Policy After Reagan: What Next?* Charlottesville, Va.: University Council for Educational Administration, 1988.

College Board. *Update from Washington,* Feb. 1989.

Deloughrey, T. J. "Colleges Rush to Comply with Rules on Fraud and Drugs After Cavazos Warns of Aid Cut-Off." *Chronicle of Higher Education,* June 28, 1989, pp. 1, A18.

Fenske, R. H. "Setting Institutional Goals and Objectives." In P. Jedamus, M. W. Peterson, and Associates, *Improving Academic Management.* San Francisco: Jossey-Bass, 1980.

Fenske, R. H., and Hughes, M. S. "Current Challenges: Maintaining Quality Amid Increasing Student Diversity." In U. Delworth, G. R. Hanson, and Associates, *Student Services: A Handbook for the Profession.* San Francisco: Jossey-Bass, 1980.

Floyd, C. E. *State Planning, Budgeting and Accountability.* AAHE-ERIC Higher Education Report No. 6. Washington, D.C.: American Association for Higher Education, 1982.

Gladieux, L. E., and Lewis, G. L. *The Federal Government and Higher Education: Traditions, Trends, Stakes, and Issues.* Washington, D.C.: College Board, 1987.

Hansen, J. S. *Student Loans: Are they Overburdening a Generation?* Washington, D.C.: College Board, 1987.

Hansen, W. L., and Stampen, J. O. "Balancing Quality and Access in Higher Education." Unpublished manuscript, Wisconsin Center for Education Research, University of Wisconsin, 1987.

Helms, L. "Patterns of Litigation in Postsecondary Education: A Case Law Study." *Journal of College and University Law,* 1987, *14,* 99–110.

Hines, E. R. *Higher Education and State Governments.* ASHE-ERIC Higher Education Report No. 5. Washington, D.C.: Association for the Study of Higher Education, 1988.

Jaschik, S. "Washington Update." *Chronicle of Higher Education,* July 12, 1989, p. A28.

Kaplin, W. A. *The Law of Higher Education: A Comprehensive Guide to Legal Implications of Administrative Decision Making.* (2nd ed.) San Francisco: Jossey-Bass, 1985.

Kerr, C. "The States and Higher Education: Changes Ahead." *State Government,* 1985, 58 (2), 45–50.

Lam, M. *Patterns of Litigation at Institutions of Higher Education in Texas, 1978–1988.* Monograph 88-8. Houston, Tex.: Institute for Higher Education Law and Governance, 1988.

Lewis, G. *Trends in Student Aid: 1980 to 1988.* Washington, D.C.: College Board, 1988.

Mohrman, K. "Unintended Consequences of Federal Student Aid Policies." *Brookings Review,* Fall 1987, pp. 24–30.

National Commission on Excellence in Education. *A Nation at Risk.* Washington, D.C.: U.S. Government Printing Office, 1983.

National Institute of Education. *Involvement in Learning: Realizing the Potential of American Higher Education.* Washington, D.C.: U.S. Department of Education, 1984.

Newman, F. *Choosing Quality: Reducing Conflict Between the State and the University.* Denver, Colo.: Education Commission of the States, 1987.

Orwig, M. D., and Caruthers, J. K. "Selecting Budget Strategies and Priorities." In P. Jedamus, M. W. Peterson, and Associates, *Improving Academic Management.* San Francisco: Jossey-Bass, 1980.

Chapter 7

The Technological Transformation of Student Services

Donald B. Mills

Student affairs is typically viewed as a professional area that focuses on the person. Indeed, the major philosophical statements of the profession deal primarily with the student and effective interventions with students in higher education (American Council on Education, [1937] 1989a, [1949] 1989b; National Association of Student Personnel Administrators, 1987). There is little mention of technology in the student affairs literature. The 1987 statement maintains the field must adjust to changing conditions and environments of higher education, but the issue of technology is only tangentially discussed. Indeed, student affairs is considered by many to be the "high-touch" counterpart to the "high-tech" aspects of campus life.

Technology, however, is required to increase the efficiency of administrative operations in student affairs. As a profession, we must learn to apply technology in productive ways that will increase both the quality and effectiveness of our work. While doing so, we must also ensure that the use of technology will not endanger the standards that have guided us in the past.

Clearly, technological applications are able to provide more efficient work environments. But the seduction of efficiency should not override the utility of effectiveness. While technological advances have great potential to provide increased communication, data analysis, and speed, they do not solve all of our problems. Introduction of new technology rarely, for example, reduces personnel requirements or saves money. In addition, reliance on technology has the potential to decrease human contact and define relationships more rigidly. Finally, dependence on technology may aggravate a lack of attention to the individual characteristics of students and staff.

The use of technology can create a conundrum for student affairs administrators. As we move toward the future, we will have to manage the paradox of employing technology while maintaining human and personal relationships. (See Chapter Ten.) For example, one decision that has an immediate influence on a student's environment is the assignment of a residence hall and a roommate. The most efficient method of assigning students is to use a computer program to match certain characteristics seen as critical in making successful residence hall and roommate assignments. Yet, this procedure requires reducing a person's personality, and all the complexities that implies, to a series of well-defined behavioral patterns. Humans rarely behave so neatly. How are developmental needs to be ascertained and addressed in such a system? The dilemma of balancing efficiency and human need is clear.

In this chapter, we will discuss the implications of technology for the training and daily activities of student affairs staff. We will examine the effect of technology for students and student uses of technology in addition to technological applications that enhance student development. And, finally, we will consider the management implications for student affairs administrators.

For the purposes of this chapter, the word *technology* will be defined within fairly narrow parameters. It includes computers, video capabilities, and electronic communication. It does not include the engineering and design questions involved in technological advances.

Implications for Professionals

A number of implications for professional practice are related to technology. These include the need to acquire technical literacy, the changed work environment, appropriate application of technology, and expanded communication.

Technical Literacy. Perhaps the most immediate implication of technology is that student affairs professionals must become technically literate. While expert status is not necessary, basic technical literacy is an essential component of effective management. Without such understanding, it will be impossible for managers to make appropriate decisions about both equipment and programs. Technical assistance should certainly be sought, but ultimately the decision regarding kinds and types of technology to employ in a work environment rests with the manager.

Computer literacy can be acquired in a number of ways, all of which require time and effort. Self-help guides are readily available for people who want to develop skills on their own. Most educational institutions also offer courses in computer use. Whatever the method chosen to acquire technical literacy, five requirements must be met. First, student affairs professionals need to master a basic vocabulary of computer terms. Second, they need a general understanding of how the equipment works. Third, professionals must be able to determine data needs for the task at hand. Fourth, they must generally understand programming, personnel, and training needs. And, finally, they must be able to evaluate the capabilities of various types of computers and how a proposed system will relate to other computing systems on campus.

This need for technological literacy will change the training programs in student affairs. Knowledge of the theory, practice, literature, and history of the profession, as well as competence in management and in research and analytical skills, will still be required. But the ability to use a computer and to understand its power will be a central part of being prepared for work in student affairs of the future.

Office Environment. The addition of technology may significantly change the professional working environment. Much of the routine work in an office will remain the same, but technology will enhance access to both information and data. The ability to store information allows greater flexibility in providing standardized responses to individuals while maintaining the ability to personalize correspondence. Paradoxically, while reports and letters may appear to be geared to individual needs, more bureaucratic tendencies may become evident as standardized responses to situations, in the name of efficiency, become the norm. Technology may stimulate the trend in this direction for student affairs agencies by encouraging staff to standardize responses to individual problems.

A second factor that may change the office environment is the search for new ways to use information and for new information to collect. The immense power of computers to store and manipulate data encourages professionals to collect additional information to assist in providing better services to students. Offices may become depositories of data, and staff may focus on the manipulation of data for research purposes. This focus has both positive and negative effects on productivity and meeting student development needs—positive, as more information should result in better decisions, and negative, as a focus on data may cloud the need to respond to the personal growth needs of individuals. The high-tech environment may overshadow the high-touch goals.

Warren Bennis warns against the dangers of focusing on information. When describing the White House during President Nixon's term, Bennis states, "The White House has . . . become a bureaucracy in the same sense that Max Weber meant: It has grown in size; it is characterized by specialization, division of labor, chain of command and hierarchy . . . . If one regards a bureaucracy in its conventional stance as an organization designed to winnow information . . . then the President's office apparatus has all the essential attributes of a bureaucracy" (Bennis, 1976, pp. 104–105). His warning is well-taken for higher education.

While there is a danger of information overload and bureaucratization, there also exists the exciting possibility to use technology to support creative responses. And although standardization of responses may prove negative, it does provide an opportunity for staff members to find the time to attack problems not previously addressed. Technology can be a freeing experience. However, the focus must be on the methodology of solving problems, not on the subtle temptations of immense capabilities. By looking beyond mere efficiency, a manager can use the capabilities of technology to seek and employ new ways of meeting student needs.

Applications. The first uses of computers in higher education were related to areas such as admissions, financial aid, and the registrar. In all of these areas, a complicated record-keeping system was needed; and computer technology allowed large amounts of data to be classified and used effectively. Efficiency in processing records increased, mailing lists and form letters aided in communication with students, and reports could be generated for use in decision making.

The success of the application of computer technology in admissions, financial aid, and the registrar functions provided a model for other areas in student affairs. Housing offices, counseling and testing centers, health centers, and student activities offices also began to employ technology to keep track of important data, to create individual student files, and to provide needed information for both fiscal and facility management. Creation of such student information systems has been a positive way to respond to administrative demands. But whether the computer application is in the registrar's office or the counseling center, planning is essential.

Data fields in the basic system must be defined carefully. If, for example, an administrator wants to know if there is a relationship between academic performance and place of residence, the system must be designed so that place of residence and academic performance can be linked. If you wish to examine the effect of participation in student organizations on retention, the data base must contain the appropriate information.

Decisions must be made about who has access to what information in the data base of an agency. Confidentiality requirements in a counseling center or health service must be defined in advance so that security can be built into the system.

Finally, those designing and accessing the system must understand the use of data. If there is an expectation that personalized letters will be sent to students regarding their status, then connections must be built in during system design to accomplish that goal. Of if categorization of expenditures for budget planning is essential, then appropriate classifications must be designed for data input.

Clear goals and parameters must be established by the using agency and clearly communicated to those responsible for system design. Only then will computer technology prove a useful and effective tool for student affairs agencies.

Communication. Computers are capable of providing incredible amounts of information that can be configured in an almost infinite number of ways, but equally important to student affairs administrators are the communication possibilities of the new technology. Allen Krowe, IBM senior vice-president for finance and planning and the person largely responsible for placing a personal computer on each IBM employee's desk, has said of the power of personal computing, "We realized that the PC could play a significant role in the daily work life of our employees. It has increased productivity, enhanced our ability to communicate with one another, and enriched our jobs" (Ditlea, 1986, p. 194).

Electronic mail, the sending of information from one computer to another, has many benefits. It takes advantage of the computer's ability never to tire, not to attend meetings, not to engage in counseling, not to take lunch breaks, and not to depend on the mail room. The process of electronic mail enables people to work on time schedules using the unique capabilities of the computing technology, and the electronic memory of the computer enables numerous persons to use data bases simultaneously. Electronic mail, in short, has the power to make communication for student affairs more timely and to make data more readily available.

But there are drawbacks to electronic mail. Perhaps most immediate is the cost of establishing an electronic mail system. The size of the system (departmental, divisional, or institutional) will be a significant determinant of the system cost and must be evaluated in the context of service and institutional mission.

A recent entry into the electronic communication field is the facsimile transmission (FAX). The FAX machine has become a staple in many businesses and is increasingly evident on college campuses. At a relatively low cost, documents can be sent and received virtually simultaneously worldwide. FAX technology is relatively inexpensive depending on the requirements. But the important question for the student affairs administrator may not be cost. Policy questions surrounding use of the FAX may be more salient: Will students be able to send admissions and financial aid data by FAX? Will students be able to enter into legal agreements with the institution by facsimile transmission? Will students be permitted to send assignments to faculty by use of FAX or electronic mail? Will faculty respond to students through FAX machines located in residence halls? The importance of these questions lies not in cost or convenience. Rather, the important issue is whether efficiencies gained are worth the potential distance established between people who are communicating by machine rather than by the spoken word.

Any discussion of communication in a technological world must at least mention the telephone. This earlier form of technological communication continues to provide the most common form of technology in the modern workplace, but the phone no longer provides only the opportunity for conversations. By using the power of a computer, existing technology enables a telephone to provide a range of capabilities including message services and data access. Cost controls can be implemented by systems that record the length, time, and location of all calls. Routing of long distance calls can be programmed to use the least expensive or fastest route, depending on criteria established by the user.

Although technology more sophisticated than phones exists, significant benefits can be derived from upgrading phone systems, and costs may be more easily recoverable. Furthermore, the new telephone technology "may cause as dramatic a change in the way we do business as the fax machine has" (Kane and Keeton, 1989).

The developments in communication technology provide expanded opportunities for communication across regional, national, and even international boundaries. Teleconferencing through use of satellite transmission technology enables persons in separate locations to communicate regarding specific issues or a range of issues. At relatively low cost, an office can become part of a computer network for sharing information; and institutional membership in networks reduces the cost for individual participants.

Traditionally, professional development opportunities have been available primarily at conferences, but technology expands the options open to the practitioner. Although conferences will not be replaced, videotapes, teleconferences, and computer conferences are cost-effective methods of sharing information. Staff who may be unable to attend conferences may be able to acquire the same information while remaining on campus. Through technology, the variety of professional development opportunities is expanding.

The discussion of communication systems highlights the issues facing the administrator making decisions about the expenditure of funds for the purchase of technology. There is a gentle seduction surrounding the possibility of instituting new technologies. But there are no inexpensive technologies, and the risk of early obsolescence cannot be overlooked. Since very few student affairs administrators are trained in engineering or technology, most will need to consult with others more knowledgeable. The student affairs staff must articulate the needs of agencies and students; they must not lose sight of the educational goals involved. Their responsibility underscores the need to become technically literate before being faced with technical choice questions.

Technology and Students

For many students, technology and significant technological advances are commonplace. Students in the 1990s will be as comfortable with a rapidly changing technological environment as students were in the 1960s with a rapidly changing social environment. The use of computers is an ordinary and expected part of the educational process, so it is not surprising that one of the most common questions asked of college administrators is what type of computer students should take to the campus. This question raises concerns beyond the mere determination of the most appropriate machine for a student to use.

Cost. Many students have personal computers and can use them for their academic work, but others do not. Lack of access to a personal computer could disadvantage some students in their academic work. How should institutions respond to students who cannot afford personal computers? Should the institution provide them? How should an institution respond if it recommends that a certain computer be used by students and then changes the computing environment on the campus? Instead of suggesting that students buy their own computers, should institutions provide computers for students? Can institutions afford such programs? Should individual computers be available for each student, or should computer labs be established to allow students to share the use of the computers?

Clearly, student affairs staff and the institution should answer these questions only in conjunction with computing experts. Student affairs must be involved, because if the questions were answered by the experts alone, the human element might be lost in the desire to achieve an efficacious decision.

Access to Data. The capabilities of personal computers now make it possible for students to connect directly with data bases stored elsewhere, and an institution may wish to make mainframe computing power available to students. Mainframe access expands not only the depth of opportunity but also the breadth of options available. Data bases are readily available for a variety of academic programs, and specific information of interest to a student can be accessed through a mainframe computer and sent directly to the student's personal computer for further use and manipulation.

One large data base of particular use to higher education institutions relates to libraries. An individual library's entire holdings can be on a data base accessible to students, enabling them to find appropriate resources for academic work and to know what is available in an institution's library and elsewhere. The implications for library administration are significant in terms of both cost and expertise.

Expanded Services. For student affairs administrators, there arises the question of providing computers for students in space reserved for student services. Clearly, the accessibility to computer programs and data bases is a need that must be balanced among other competing student needs. However, as academic programs develop a computer orientation in research and teaching, student learning becomes more dependent on computers. Fairness dictates access must be available for all.

Computer-based writing and other learning skills centers should be available to assist students in self-paced improvement.

Such centers may prove to be of special value for students with learning disabilities. All students, including the physically impaired, can use computers to enhance learning possibilities and to complete writing and research assignments. Some of the readily available software requires only basic computing skills, both for the user and for the instructor. And it should be noted that an additional benefit of computer-based instructional facilities is the partnership that develops between faculty and student affairs professionals when technological services are expanded.

Assessments. SIGI (System of Interactive Guidance and Information) is a career-search self-assessment designed to help students choose potential career paths and appropriate academic programs. The program is self-paced and provides the student options based on answers to questions. The assessment is designed to uncover values, discover skills, and discuss life-style preferences in addition to information about careers. After a student completes the SIGI self-assessment, typically a counselor interprets the results of the exercise. This interpretation can be especially helpful when used in conjunction with an involvement transcript to examine values and indicate resources for additional involvement. (An involvement transcript documents the activities, honors, elected offices, student employment, and memberships of the student.)

Students have been engaged in self-paced career-search activities for some time, but other assessment tools are being developed that allow students to make individual assessments in other areas as well. Perhaps the most encouraging is self-assessment in health areas.

Wellness assessments are now produced in modules that allow individuals to answer standard questions in privacy and that provide printed copies of both positive and negative aspects of the results highlighted for the student. Composite data can be obtained to determine the general wellness knowledge and condition of those taking the assessment (Johnson and Wernig, 1986). This process not only provides data but also releases professional health educators to work directly with student concerns and bypasses the expensive, time-consuming process of individual assessment (National Wellness Institute, 1989). Staff are able to design programs targeted directly to self-reported problem areas.

Assessment techniques are also being developed for persons with alcohol and other drug-related concerns (Cornell University Health Services, 1989). As institutions provide programs to adhere to the requirements of the federal Drug Free Workplace Act of 1988, the cost of staff and programming will undoubtedly escalate. By providing computerized assessment techniques, these costs may be minimized and energies directed to specified program needs.

The future holds opportunities for expanded application of computer assessments. A promising program has been developed at the University of Wisconsin at Stevens Point, namely, the Total Involvement Educational System (Markovich, 1983), which may have possibilities for other campuses. The Total Involvement Educational System is a computer program that identifies the experiential learning involvements of students. Each student is able to access the data base to determine those opportunities that may meet his or her needs and to create a personal involvement record. By establishing such a record, students can assess the full range of skills, knowledge, and competencies they have mastered during their undergraduate years as well as determine deficiencies that need to be remediated. The program includes position descriptions, opportunities for skill development, a menu of potential activities, and referral to particular persons or resources on the campus. The resulting student involvement can then be recorded and used to track participation during a student's career. Used in conjunction with SIGI, the involvement transcript program is used to examine values while indicating resources for additional opportunities.

A difficult decision for student affairs administrators is to determine the location of computers for assessment purposes. Assessments could be located in office areas that correspond to the assessment being conducted, but a more appropriate location might be areas that are considered student turf. Placing computers used for assessment in residence halls, in a student center, or both may be appropriate; providing software programs for student use on personal computers may also be an option.

Video. The technology of video, one of the most important advances in the twentieth century, offers interesting possibilities for students. Students frequently request the entertainment capabilities of cable television, but the video technology also raises a multiplicity of educational opportunities. The choices must be made carefully, however, and in consultation with faculty and technical staff. The decisions relating to video also relate to decisions regarding phone service.

A decision to bring cable video to a campus requires several prior corollary decisions. First, the decision must be made whether to select a commercial cable company, a private cable company developing a campus network, or a campus network using satellite dish technology. Each approach has its advantages, special costs, and disadvantages. But in every case, cable outlets to each desired location on the campus, including residence hall rooms, must be provided. Good fiscal decision making will pair telephone systems and video systems, since cabling requirements are similar.

A major concern regarding cable video systems is control. Obviously, a campus network managed by campus staff controls the content of programming and has the flexibility to change, but campus networks require considerably more time and expertise than does a system operated by a commercial cable television company. Another consideration is the type of programs available. The educational benefits of private channels, dial-up lectures, tutorials, local sports programs, internships for TV majors, and an announcement channel must be weighed against the costs of producing programming.

Video programming offers significant opportunities for the student affairs administrator to be involved with institutional colleagues in creating an environment designed to induce student growth. In fact, student affairs administrators may be the most critical players in this enterprise since the impact of video has been a concern and a constant presence in the student environment for years.

Student Development. The ready availability of technology may serve to enhance or detract from the student learning experience. While the possibility exists to make data available to the students and to make learning opportunities more accessible and easier, there is also the possibility of isolating students from the traditional collegial experience. Technology, by its nature, frequently involves an individual interaction between person and machine. For visual learners, this technology is excellent for academic learning. Easy transmission of student assignments to faculty is a time saver for all. But what is lost?

Student development theories attempt to explain the necessary components for students moving from late adolescence into adulthood (see Chapter Three). The theories further suggest behaviors that students will exhibit as they travel the path to maturity. It is critical that personal interaction be a part of the process. "Student development education is, first and foremost, about integrating knowledge of the world and human life, with issues of meaning and implications of that knowledge. This is critical on the conceptual, the operational, and the political level. What has been divided for purposes of discussion and investigation must be integrated for purposes of living. When wisdom is separated from knowledge, thought from life, students suffer—and so do faculty and staff" (Fried, 1981, p. 54).

Technology allows quick transmission of information and ideas. If interaction between people is eliminated, the possibilities of human growth are stunted. The accumulation of knowledge may occur in isolation and therefore may have no context for application. Institutions could become disseminators of knowledge without the humanizing integration of faculty and students.

The student affairs administrator must continuously develop opportunities for interaction among people so that skills of communication can be developed by both students and staff. The ability to confront problems and to solve them in ways that are ethical remains essential to student growth, so spiritual, physical, and intellectual growth must continue apace with technological expertise. The student affairs administrator must help to create an atmosphere that involves students with the technology but that does not promote academic learning in isolation.

Managing Technology in Student Affairs

The management of technology in student affairs is similar to the management of technology in other areas of the academy. The significant difference is in the mission of student affairs. A manager in student affairs must continuously remember the priority of student development and service to students. The two objectives of student development and increased technological capabilities may not always be compatible.

In order to ensure that a student affairs administrator is managing the system—rather than the system managing the administrator—several safeguards must be present. Ferrante, Hayman, Carlson, and Phillips (1988) have suggested procedures for use in campuswide decisions for computing; they can be adapted for technology in student affairs.

The first procedure is to establish an atmosphere of strategic planning with environmental scanning as an effective planning model for technology. Environmental scanning, as a technique, involves staff in a continuous planning effort. New information is routinely introduced into discussions regarding possible technologies to be adopted. And as technologies are developed, their possible applications are assimilated into the planning process.

The second procedure is to establish a central authority to coordinate and plan implementation of new technology. The central authority is needed to eliminate the duplication of services and to approve expenditures of funds in the most expeditious manner. The central authority also has the ability to keep technological applications within the dimensions of divisional goals. Obviously, the person appointed to this position must possess both formal authority and the trust of others in the division.

Third, involve the institutional community as much as possible in technologically related decisions. The sheer cost and magnitude of possible campus technology means that the use of technology may be shared by campus users, and therefore the cost may be shared by a variety of campus users. Furthermore, the general knowledge and experience of the campus community will assist in making proper decisions and avoiding unseen pitfalls.

The involvement of computer center directors and management information specialists should begin early in any decision process involving technology. The effectiveness of decisions will be enhanced by the vision, knowledge, and training provided by these professionals. No system is installed or operated without problems, and by enlisting technical support personnel early as allies, assistance will be more easily forthcoming.

Fourth, consider external societal developments. Environmental scanning will assist in determining technological advances, but it is imperative that factors influencing students, campus resources, and constituent attitudes also be carefully monitored. For example, if a new class of incoming students has an expectation of a highly technical campus, the campus administrators must make appropriate decisions to meet or modify those expectations. The important element in this example is that student expectations be predicted in a timely manner to assure timely decisions.

Finally, the fifth procedure is to seek stability of funding and financial support over time. Because the cost of technology frequently exceeds the available funds in a single fiscal year, it is important to have assurance that funds will be available over several years. Assurance means not only a commitment to fund technological advances but also the availability of methods to develop income sources (including user fees) that can offset expenses.

In short, the management of technology must be dynamic and oriented to change and future impacts. Decisions must be made in the context of the student affairs mission—while recognizing the external institutional and societal environment. The effort requires commitment to achieving goals effectively and efficiently.

Management of technology also requires a focus on utilization rather than sophistication. A focus on utilization protects users from hardware and software that may have not only immense powers but also a complexity beyond the ability of average users. Ultimately, usefulness is the final criterion for effective technology.

Cost-Benefit Analysis. Properly determining the benefits of technological advances in relation to their costs is extremely difficult. Determining specific purchase prices of computers or other technological equipment is relatively simple, but the benefits are much more elusive. Although some benefits can be determined easily, placing a value on them is more difficult. "Costs are the resources-dollars, people, machines, etc.—which, when locked to one alternative, cannot be used for other purposes. Benefits are those worthwhile elements which are derived as a result of some action.

. . . In order to determine the overall worth of an alternative, both cost and benefit (effectiveness) must be considered" (Cleland and King, 1975, p. 60).

Benefits are not always measured in dollars. What programs will not be accomplished when funds are spent on technological progress? Are students better served by having computers available for use in residence halls or by having additional journals available in the library? Is a campus environment enhanced by technology, or does it lose part of its distinctive character? These and other questions must be answered by administrators before they make final technological decisions. Costs, not always measured in dollars, may be variable, based on the level of sophistication and desired outcomes. Costs may be short-range, one-time costs, or they may be ongoing. The effective manager will recognize that virtually all technological advances have continuing costs in addition to original or purchase costs.

Most student affairs administrators are not expert in determining cost-benefit ratios. But even though both costs and benefits are often variable, the ratio of the costs to the benefits is a value that the student affairs professional must incorporate into an effective decision-making process.

In short, not only must a decision to proceed technologically be affordable, but also the outcome of the decision must lead to benefits for both students and the institution—benefits that outweigh those that would result from other possible courses of action.

Security. The availability of technology creates additional management problems for the student affairs administrator. For example, computer systems must have built-in security devices to protect against unauthorized intrusion. Certainly, the well-publicized efforts of so-called computer hackers should eliminate a false sense of security that any system is totally safe from outside interference.

Typically, cases of academic dishonesty using computers involve changes in student records, especially grades. However, other types of academic dishonesty occur through copying unauthorized files, using data obtained through access to files not open to students, changes in bursar's office charges, and copying software from copyrighted material. Because of these types of behavior, institutions must develop explicit definitions of academic dishonesty and must establish security procedures to protect against unauthorized use of data. Finally, the range of penalties to be assessed for this type of unethical behavior must be determined and widely publicized.

Staff Development. Staff development may be the most important management tool for improving staff performance, and the proper use of technology will continue to aid administrators in this important task. The self-paced programs and assessments that are useful for students are equally useful for staff. Perhaps of even greater value are teleconferences linking campuses by satellite technology. These programs, frequently interactive through phone hookup as well as video, bring together experts from across the country for developmental experiences that formerly were available only through traditional conferences requiring travel to a specific location. Computer conferences also enable persons to communicate through computers to solve problems, to discuss issues, and to collaborate on projects. The only cost is a phone call and the computer time on a host computer. This approach offers relatively inexpensive, high-tech means of staff development.

Further opportunities for staff development using technology abound. Access to data bases, development of research programs, review of research conducted on other campuses, and review of bibliographic entries related to specific topical interests are available through personal computers or from an institution's central computer. Videotapes also are excellent sources of staff development programs.

However, for technology to be effective, the user must be comfortable with it. Too frequently, new technology is introduced by technicians using a vocabulary unfamiliar to student affairs administrators. This unfamiliarity may raise considerable anxiety in staff and prevent staff from effectively using the technology, so one of the most important staff development programs may be to introduce technology in ways that reduce anxiety.

A number of methods can be used to reduce staff anxiety regarding technology. First, carefully describe to staff the outcomes and benefits associated with technology. Second, involve staff in the process of decision making by having them assess their own needs. Third, permit staff to experiment with new technology, and do not expect immediate productivity. Fourth, provide staged training programs building on acquired skills rather than programs providing training only at the time of installation. Finally, provide time and funds for self-paced training programs and off-campus training opportunities with student affairs staff from other institutions.

Decision Making. Through the use of spreadsheets and other software tools that model "what if" questions, administrators can make decisions based on data that closely resemble the likely future reality. The forecasting possibilities of a computer give administrators a tool that enhances decision making and assists in establishing priorities.

Problem solving is aided by the more effective use of information. Technology, especially computers, enables student affairs administrators to categorize information more efficiently and to manipulate data. It does not replace the analysis of data required by administrators, but it does provide empirical evidence to be used in solving problems.

Technology assists in policy development in similar ways. While some policies flow directly from an institution's mission statement, others are dependent on environmental setting, so information becomes important. For example, if an institution wishes to establish policies for parking, the gathering and organization of data about autos on campus, student ownership, student residence location, student and faculty driving patterns, and so on will help in developing a policy that is both workable and fair. Without the assistance of technology, the development of policy requiring large amounts of data is much more difficult to effect.

The management challenges are significant, but the opportunities to enhance a student affairs program are equally significant. The possibility of integrating data among divisions of the institution will assist in institutional planning. "As information becomes integrated and readily accessible, administrators will better be able to manage institutional planning. Budgets will be prepared from actual and projected resources using sophisticated budgeting applications, and administrators will know where cutbacks can be made without threatening valuable institutional initiatives and projects" (Ferrante, Hayman, Carlson, and Phillips, 1988).

Equity. Finally, managers must confront the problem of equity. There are serious decisions to be made regarding the process by which technology is to be added to a student affairs division. The allure of technology means that jealousies may occur, so criteria by which technology decisions will be made must be established. These criteria should be established in a collegial atmosphere and must be well understood by all staff. Otherwise, questions of equity will undoubtedly arise, causing personnel and productivity problems.

The addition of technology must be part of a longer-range program of staged installation. Within a division of student affairs, there are competing technological needs that must be considered within the total scope of the student affairs mission. And since available funds are likely to be insufficient to meet all technological needs in a single year, a process must be developed to allow incremental technological progress that is equitable and has the commitment of all areas of the division of student affairs. Therefore, student affairs should base planning decisions on the need to accomplish essential services, the ability to further the developmental and educational needs of students, and the determination of the technology necessary to meet the long-range goals of the division. Funding should also come from throughout a division, based on the assumption that divisional goals are being satisfied. It is appropriate that reallocation of money among departments or special incremental fund increases take place on an annual basis to meet technological purchase requirements.

The equity question clearly affects students as well. As discussed earlier, cost considerations will pose hardships for some students who need computers. Serious questions of fairness arise if an institution requires a computer or computing capability in some courses of study. Easy access to computers must be assured for all students if equity is to be maintained.

Conclusion

Higher education and student affairs professionals are becoming increasingly connected with technology. Student affairs administrators must move beyond mere connections to a planned approach to incorporating technology. There must be consistency in policy and cooperation in implementation. There must be a recognition that for all the advantages of technology, a significant danger exists that technology will be a force that separates people. Certainly a campus is a collegial community; yet as technology becomes more sophisticated, much of what is accomplished in the name of progress may actually serve to limit the achievement of those goals of student development indicated in "A Perspective on Student Affairs, 1987" (National Association of Student Personnel Administrators, [1987] 1989).

Popular culture has made the concept of the *bottom line* familiar to virtually everyone in society, and the easiest way to determine the bottom line is to quantify it. Technology, particularly computers, provides forms of quantification in almost every arena of American society. The quantification looks at the short term as a measure of success, and secondary impacts are often ignored. The danger is that, as computers are used more by students and others, quantification may seem more important than the high-touch value of ethics, tolerance, personality development, and social justice. The continued development and use of technology may force persons into isolation and separate them from other people.

Lewis Mumford (1973, p. 480) states, "The difficulty is that our machine technology and our scientific methodology have reached a high pitch of perfection at a moment when other important parts of our culture, particularly those that shape the human personality, religion, ethics, education, the arts have become inoperative or, rather, share in the general disintegration and help to widen it."

An additional challenge is the confidence that people place in technology, as if it were a form of salvation from the problems confronting society. The urge to let technology solve problems makes it imperative for student affairs administrators to consider the consequences of solutions defined by technology primarily because technology is seen as being able to reach a solution. Only if the solution has associated with it the values of society and the institution will the solution be appropriate. The campus environment must be one in which the value questions are asked before the involvement of technology. It falls to student affairs to make sure this happens.

In his book *The Tomorrow Makers,* Grant Fjermedal (1986) quotes a researcher in robotics at M.I.T.: "If you really do take the view of humans as just being machines, which I do—we just happen to be made out of this wet stuff—then there is nothing to say that it's not possible to build robots that we can make intelligent and more intelligent. And there's an advantage to building robots out of silicon and stuff like that, because we know how to control the fabrication process pretty well. We have trouble with biology, although we have learned some tricks . . . . So there is much more potential for rapid evolution of machines than there is for humans" (p. 33). This is a frightening view of a high-tech future.

The central mission of student affairs remains. Student affairs administrators must be the architects of campus social structures using technology to create opportunities for staff and faculty to interact with students, to conduct routine work with efficiency, and to be effective in our primary work. Students must be taught that technology is a tool, not an end in itself. The wonder of what it can do should not blind persons to what it should do.

Weinberg (1975, p. 2) may have summarized it best: "Science and engineering have been the catalyst of the unprecedented speed and magnitude of change. . . . But science and engineering have been unable to keep pace with the second-order effects produced by their first-order victories. . . . Of what we are doing to our progeny, we still have only ghastly hints. . . . We have learned how to transform prairies into dustbowls, lakes into cesspools, and cities into mausoleums. Can we turn around before it is too late?"

References

American Council on Education. "The Student Personnel Point of View, 1937." In *Points of View.* Washington, D.C.: National Association of Personnel Administrators, 1989a. (Originally published 1937.)

American Council on Education. "The Student Personnel Point of View, 1949." In *Points of View.* Washington, D.C.: National

Association of Student Personnel Administrators, 1989b. (Originally published 1949.)

Bennis, W. *The Unconscious Conspiracy: Why Leaders Can't Lead.* New York: AMACOM, 1976.

Cleland, D., and King, W. *Systems Analysis and Project Management.* New York: McGraw-Hill, 1975.

Cornell University Health Services. *Alcohol I.Q. Network.* Stevens Point, Wis.: National Wellness Institute, 1989.

Ditlea, S. "IBM: Practicing What They Preach." *PC World,* May 1986, pp. 192–200.

Ferrante, P., Hayman, J., Carlson, M., and Phillips, H. *Planning for Microcomputers in Higher Education: Strategies for the Next Generation.* ASHE-ERIC Higher Education Report No. 7. Washington, D.C.: Association for the Study of Higher Education, 1988.

Fjermedal, G. *The Tomorrow Makers.* New York: Macmillan, 1986.

Fried, J. "Principles of Design." In J. Fried (ed.), *Education for Student Development.* New Directions for Student Services, no. 15. San Francisco: Jossey-Bass, 1981.

Johnson, K., and Wernig, S. "Life Directions: A Comprehensive Wellness Program at a Small College." In F. Leafgren (ed.), *Developing Campus Recreation and Wellness Programs.* New Directions for Student Services, no. 34. San Francisco: Jossey-Bass, 1986.

Kane, S., and Keeton, R. "Digital Dialing." *Sky,* July 1989, pp. 12–20.

Markovich, G. *Total Involvement Educational System.* Stevens Point, Wis.: Institute for Lifestyle Improvement, 1983.

Mumford, L. *Interpretations and Forecasts: 1922–1972.* San Diego, Calif.: Harcourt Brace Jovanovich, 1973.

National Association of Student Personnel Administrators. "A Perspective on Student Affairs, 1987." In *Points of View.* Washington, D.C.: National Association of Student Personnel Administrators, 1989. (Originally published 1987.)

National Wellness Institute. *The Lifestyle Assessment Questionnaire.* Stevens Point, Wis.: National Wellness Institute, 1989.

Weinberg, G. *An Introduction to General Systems Thinking.* New York: Wiley, 1975.

Chapter 8

Growing Staff Diversity and Changing Career Paths

Margaret J. Barr

Effective student affairs programs are built on competent staff. Student affairs is a very people-intensive enterprise, and our greatest strength, as well as our greatest potential liability, lies with staff members who work with students and design programs and services for them. Other chapters in this volume outline the forces that will shape the future of student affairs; these same forces will shape the characteristics, background, and training of student affairs professionals.

As we look to the future, we will be compelled to expand our concept of professional staff in student affairs. The way we see ourselves and our colleagues will change due to two major factors. First, the functional areas associated with student affairs are bound to change as new students come to our campuses and new needs emerge. In the last two decades alone, the role and scope of student affairs on many campuses has changed dramatically. These new and different functions will require us to employ individuals whose experiences and backgrounds reflect specialty training.

Second, there is no clear set of academic experiences and training that are prerequisites for employment in student affairs. In contrast with our colleagues in law or medicine, for example, a typical student affairs staff profile exhibits a wide range of preparation and training. We do not share common educational experiences or training, nor are we licensed to practice the profession of student affairs; this is how it should be, for student affairs staff reflect a composite of skills and academic backgrounds. Our challenge, as a profession, is to identify individuals with potential, to recruit them to the profession, and to train them so they will become committed to the unique role student affairs has in higher education.

In this chapter, we will explore the factors that will promote increased diversity in student affairs staffs, we will outline the major career paths that contribute to that diversity, we will identify the barriers associated with attracting and retaining competent staff, and we will provide suggestions for surmounting these barriers. Finally, we will present an agenda for the future—an agenda we must address.

Factors Influencing Increased Staff Diversity

Staff requirements in student affairs will be influenced by all the forces of change outlined in this volume. All will have a real and direct influence on who is hired, who succeeds, who is retained, and what tasks will be accomplished. Three factors appear to be most critical: changing students, technological changes, and altered expectations for student affairs organizations within institutions.

Changing Students. Kuh's Chapter Four outlined the demographic changes that will influence who attends a college or university. As students change, professional staff in student affairs must have the skills and competencies to respond to them. For example, if institutions meet the challenge of attracting more minority students to higher education, student affairs staff members must be prepared to respond. The call and documented need for minority professionals in student affairs is not new. In addition to their specific professional responsibilities, they also serve as role models, mentors, and teachers to both minority and nonminority students. In a world that is rapidly changing, the need for qualified minority staff will become even more intense in the decades ahead.

Student affairs professionals, regardless of their own ethnicities, face a mandate to increase their knowledge base with regard to cultural and ethnic differences among students. Research is already in progress on the influences of ethnicity and gender on human development theory (Delworth, 1989). That work must be continued, and methods must be developed to translate these new theoretical perspectives (see Chapter Three) into professional practice. Further, student affairs professionals must be able to assist nonminority students to function effectively in a multicultural world.

As we look to the future, every indication is that higher education in the United States will continue to serve as a center for education of students from other lands. Such international students also bring with them unique concerns and issues, and student affairs staff members must be able to understand the cultural differences to assist both international students and the rest of the campus community in bridging cultural differences.

In addition, women have become the majority population enrolled in undergraduate education in the United States (National Association of Student Personnel Administrators, [1897] 1989). This trend is likely to continue and will require staff members in student affairs to understand gender differences and to translate that understanding into programs and services that genuinely serve women students.

Assessment of current teaching and operating practices also will need to be made. Student affairs will need to provide consultation for faculty and other administrative staff and to share information about gender differences in learning and responding. To meet these needs, student affairs must include staff members who can serve as positive role models for students, and staff members who can assist in the translation of knowledge of gender differences into programs and services.

Finally, the traditionally aged college student of eighteen to twenty-two years is now in the minority of those enrolled in higher education (National Association of Student Personnel Administrations, [1987] 1989). This trend will continue, and new skills and competencies will be needed as student affairs professionals work with older student populations. Traditional services will need to be evaluated to determine if they are meeting the needs of the older students; new services may be needed. (See Chapter Four.)

Technology. Advances in technology (see Chapter Seven) also will profoundly influence how the work of student affairs is to be accomplished and will determine some of the skills and competencies needed by student affairs staffs in the future. Professionals will not only have to increase their own effectiveness in the realm of technology, but they will also increasingly be called upon to provide the "high touch" in the high-tech (Baldridge, 1971) environment of higher education. Further, student affairs divisions must be able to manipulate and synthesize available data in order to respond to rapidly changing conditions. Experts in information management will be needed to aid student affairs in becoming active, participatory problem solvers in our institutions.

In addition, technology will bring questions of ethics and responsibility—questions that must be addressed within the campus community. For example, what constitutes academic dishonesty in group projects using the computer? Or what are the freedom-of-speech dimensions of using computer networks to exchange information? These issues will not be easy to resolve, but student affairs professionals must assume responsibility to ensure that such questions are discussed, debated, and answered in the campus community.

Changing Expectations. New areas of responsibility are inevitable for student affairs in the future—because of organizational changes, the need to respond to new priorities, or the reality that student affairs is often the only area within the academy that will confront difficult issues. And with new areas of responsibility comes the requirement for specialty-trained staff to provide the needed services.

One recent example of such new program and service imperatives rests in the growing number of substance abuse prevention programs on campus. Just a decade ago, alcohol and drug issues were referred to the counseling and health center for programming or intervention, but the growth of the substance abuse problem in the United States and the high incidence of problems among college populations demanded increased response. Thus, through institutional, state, and federal funding, new agencies have been formed to focus specifically on substance abuse education, prevention, and treatment. And with this change came a concurrent need to hire staff members with specialty training in substance abuse.

In addition, the future will reflect increased demands for accountability and management. Multiple funding sources, complex budgets, and facility management expectations combined with fiscal constraints will set new requirements for student affairs. Specific training will be needed to augment the skills of generalists in managing the human and fiscal resources of the organization.

Finally, student affairs professionals will need to continue and enhance their role as experts regarding students. "We are a profession committed to, and expert in, the integrated development of college students" (Delworth and Hanson, 1989, p. 604). As our student bodies become more diverse, this responsibility of ours will increase in importance. We must not make assumptions regarding the skills, knowledge, and competency of staff members in this domain. Instead, we must assess their knowledge and provide remediation if needed. Further, it will not be unusual in the future to see, as a central part of the student affairs organization, staff members whose primary function is research.

In order to meet the challenges of required diversity in professional staff, however, we must first understand the career paths that bring individuals to student affairs.

Major Career Paths

"Students do not grow up with aspirations to pursue student affairs careers. It is also unlikely that you are going to find many college sophomores or juniors giving serious thought to entering the student affairs profession" (Brown, 1987, p. 5). Pathways to professional positions in student affairs are many and exhibit some unique characteristics. There appear to be at least five approaches to professional positions in student affairs: intentional decision, unintentional decision, organizational realignment, specialty preparation, and remaining uncommitted. Each approach to professional employment brings a unique perspective and influences the ability of staff to meet student and institutional needs.

Intentional Decision. Some staff members intentionally choose a career in student affairs. Usually that choice is made fairly late in the collegiate experience and is related to a positive experience as an undergraduate (Brown, 1987). Often the intentional-decision professional has had a positive experience with a student affairs staff member or has had a leadership or paraprofessional experience during his or her undergraduate education.

Once a decision is made to seek a career in student affairs, intentional-decision staff enroll in one of the many graduate preparation programs available in student affairs (see Chapter Eleven). Often when we discuss the profession, intentional-decision individuals provide our model for the ideal student affairs staff member. We must recognize, however, that intentional-decision professionals may not always share common academic experiences or be equally prepared to assume leadership in the profession. As we plan for the future, we must also acknowledge that this approach to a career in student affairs is not likely to reflect the background of the majority of our professional staff.

Unintentional Decision. Many competent staff come to student affairs by other paths and other means. Some come to student affairs by accident: a position is open, they meet the minimal qualifications, they apply, and they are hired. Some come from outside the academy and did not intend to spend their professional lives working with college students. Some, most notably faculty, come from within the academy and seek employment in student affairs as a result of enrollment changes or fiscal problems.

Whatever the initial reason for employment in student affairs, the unintentional professional often discovers that the work is rewarding and that a significant contribution to education can be made. Many times, unintentional professionals find that their skills and abilities match well with the tasks that must be accomplished. In the process, unintentional professionals may also find that they share the assumptions and beliefs of intentional-decision professionals (see Chapter Two). When such a match occurs, unintentional professionals become committed and assume a vital role within the organization. They need assistance in acquiring basic knowledge about the profession and its theoretical underpinnings, but they can and do make a significant contribution to the welfare of students.

Organizational Realignment. Some individuals become student affairs staff members due to circumstances beyond their control. New leadership may come to the institution, and reporting relationships may be altered. Offices and agencies that once reported to the chief business officer or academic officer become part of student affairs. Often the identity of such organizationally realigned professionals rests not with the general profession of student affairs, but rather is focused on their specific responsibilities and direct services to students.

Sometimes, an organizationally realigned staff member assumes the leadership role in a division of student affairs. Due to the philosophical orientation of the chief executive officer, a policy might be set requiring all institutional officers to hold academic rank. Perhaps the president has developed a good working relationship with a faculty member and wants that individual to serve a central role on the administrative staff. A vacancy in the leadership position for student affairs provides such an opportunity and the appointment is made. Often these organizationally realigned faculty members bring enormous skills and competencies to the new position and may already have been actively involved in the work of student affairs. But to function effectively, despite these qualifications, they must overcome gaps in both direct experience and knowledge.

Organizationally realigned professionals, at all levels, can make substantive contributions to students, student affairs programs, and the institution. We would make a mistake, however, to think that such professionals always share a common set of assumptions and beliefs or have a common base of understanding shared by others who join student affairs by other paths.

Specialty Preparation. A large number of student affairs staff do not see themselves as student affairs professionals at all. They are deeply rooted in a primary professional identity such as physician, nurse, counselor, or psychologist. While they may understand and appreciate that they are part of an organizational structure called student affairs, their professional identities are shaped by their specialty areas, and their interests and involvements are primarily focused on these areas rather than on student affairs issues and problems.

As new areas of responsibility open for student affairs and as new challenges must be met, the number of specialty-prepared professionals in student affairs is likely to grow. This approach to student affairs certainly is not negative, for many of our current leaders in student affairs have emerged from specialty disciplines, and they certainly make strong and vital contributions to student affairs. We must recognize, nonetheless, that their backgrounds and experiences are markedly different from student affairs generalists. Further, intentional effort must be made to aid them in understanding the large organization of which they are a part.

The Uncommitted. Uncommitted individuals view employment in student affairs as a job rather than a career. They may come to student affairs by any of the paths described above, but they do not commit to the profession. Student affairs may be a temporary home while they mark time waiting for some other opportunity. Employment in student affairs is a means rather than an end. Identity with the profession always remains marginal, and length of employment may be short. Usually, uncommitted staff do not share common experiences, knowledge, assumptions, or beliefs with other staff members in student affairs.

Summary. Among our tasks for the future is to identify just who our staff members are and how they entered the profession. Our diversity as a profession will remain both our greatest strength and our greatest weakness. The challenge is not new. Nearly forty years ago, "The Student Personnel Point of View, 1949" (American Council on Education, [1949] 1989) stated that "each personnel staff should be maintained in a balanced manner with respect to desirably varied professional points of view and professional backgrounds of specialists" (p. 43). Our future success will rely on our ability to connect staff members of diverse backgrounds with the profession. Barriers do exist in that process and must be overcome.

Barriers to Full Commitment

A number of barriers exist as the student affairs profession seeks to attract and retain competent staff. Barriers must be identified and strategies developed to reduce the influence the barriers have on the recruitment and retention of qualified staff. To do less would mean that we would not be able to serve both our students and our institutions effectively in the future.

Lack of Professional Identity. The multiple approaches to a career in student affairs create a large part of this professional-identity barrier. Diverse backgrounds, skills, and competencies bring multiple perspectives on problems and issues, but they also bring diffusion. There is a lack of clarity about what the requisite skills, knowledge, and competencies are in student affairs. Minimal qualifications and required academic preparation vary widely for similar positions, and clear-cut criteria for both initial employment and promotion simply do not exist in student affairs. For example, it would be very unusual for a person with a graduate degree in student affairs to be hired as an instructor in mathematics. All too often, however, individuals without formal experience, training, or academic background are hired as entry-level staff members in student affairs. As a profession, we often do not present ourselves as a clear career alternative with criteria and standards.

Lack of a Career Path. The issue is exacerbated further by a lack of a clear career path in student affairs. For persons desiring to enter higher education as a faculty member, there is a clear career path, and criteria are established to achieve the next step along that path. Although some might not feel that the criteria for tenure and promotion are fair and equitable, they are clear. Further, processes for faculty promotion and tenure are very similar among all colleges and universities. No such clear rank and promotion system exists in student affairs. Promotional opportunities within institutions are limited, and advancement often requires professionals to leave their current places of employment. This situation creates a confusing and frustrating environment for a new staff member.

The problem is compounded by the lack of quality and content control in student affairs graduate preparation programs. Even if a decision is made to require a master's degree or a doctorate in college student personnel, there is no guarantee that candidates from various programs have been exposed to the same content areas or have had similar experiences. There is no accreditation process for graduate preparation programs in student affairs; thus, there are no standards to judge the adequacy of a specific educational experience of a potential candidate.

Working Conditions. The typical entry-level generalist position in student affairs presents less than ideal working conditions. Expectations for performance and availability to students are high, hours are erratic, and rarely does a student affairs staff member have a routine and predictable environment in which to do his or her work. While the rewards of working with bright, energetic college students are many, the nature and unpredictability of the task can produce both stress and lack of comfort.

For example, consider the typical entry position or middle management position in student activities or residence halls. We expect professional staff to be available to students at times outside of regular office hours, to attend student programs, to plan events, and to fulfill all required administrative duties. Unless supervisors monitor involvements closely, there is a high potential for stress. Supervisors must give attention to helping staff members in such positions gain a sense of perspective on their work and to develop a personal life. Such efforts require intentionality on the part of the staff members and flexibility and responsiveness on the part of the supervisors. If we fail to attend to the most difficult problems associated with staff positions in student affairs, we face the possibility of losing positively contributing staff members.

Compensation. The compensation barrier is closely related to working conditions. Expectations for performance and availability are high, hours are erratic, yet compensation for positions in student affairs remains relatively low. Compensation will remain a central issue in student affairs, and the solutions to the problem will not be easy.

There are a number of confounding issues. First, it is not easy to get accurate comparative data on compensation among positions in student affairs. The same title, for example, may mean entirely different things at different institutions, in terms of the range and scope of responsibilities expected of the professional. Second, the generalist positions in student affairs, particularly at the entry level, have the least leverage in terms of compensation. Since a universal career path and agreement of minimal qualifications do not exist, compensation often becomes what the market will bear. Specialty-area professionals in student affairs, such as psychologists or physicians, usually fare much better in a comparative analysis; their degree requirements and work expectations are similar to those within the academy. Further, these professionals have different options in terms of employment outside higher education.

Competition from Outside the Academy. Students who may have considered higher education and student affairs as a career option are often recruited for positions in business and industry. Higher initial compensation packages and more predictable career paths have made such outside employment very attractive. Minority students are in high demand in business and industry, and attractive options are especially available to them.

The competition factor has also increased in intensity due to the heavy debt burden many students assume in their undergraduate years. Immediate rewards appear to be more desirable than assuming an additional debt burden for graduate education or postponing payment of debt during a period of continuing education.

Competition from Within the Academy. Competition for qualified staff also occurs within the academy. In most institutions, there is no uniform system of compensation for professional staff, and student affairs has resisted such systems. Therefore, individuals with similar qualifications and responsibilities may not receive salaries comparable to those of their colleagues in other divisions of the institution. Thus, when a position becomes available in another area and the position offers a larger salary with a more predictable work environment, it becomes very attractive. Many times the result is the loss of qualified staff from student affairs.

The Future Agenda

The need for increased staff diversity, growing specialization, lack of uniform career paths, and barriers to commitment combine to create a formidable agenda for staffing in student affairs. We must take steps to ensure that qualified staff are available to help the students of the future. The following agenda items, if they are actively embraced, can provide strategies for success.

Agenda Item One: Define the job that must be done. Upcraft (1988) reminds us of the importance of evaluating the tasks associated with a position to determine who should be hired. Too often we assume that what was and what will be are identical conditions. Careful assessment of what a specific position requires can aid in determining needs, skills, and competencies for new hires; and the process can also identify barriers to commitment, if such factors are involved.

Agenda Item Two: Reevaluate performance expectations, particularly for entry-level positions. Woodard and Komives, in Chapter Eleven, discuss the performance expectation issue in detail. We need to examine the expectations in terms of hours, availability, and balance between personal and professional lives for entry-level staff. Unless we find ways to reduce some of the negative effects of unrealistic expectations, we will have a chronic problem with staff retention.

Agenda Item Three: Carefully review compensation packages, particularly for those in generalist positions in student affairs. Compensation review is a responsibility that rests clearly with the chief student affairs officer (CSAO), and effective review also requires cooperation between and among CSAOs sharing relevant data. The emphasis is placed on generalist entry-level positions because of two factors. First, more data are already available on managerial positions through both national associations and informal networks.

Second, specialty positions (such as psychologist, nurse, or medical doctor) all have salary referent points outside the academy.

There are no comparable positions (such as program adviser, residence hall director, activities assistant, assistant dean of students, or so forth) in either business or government. After appropriate research is completed, the CSAO has an absolute obligation to present the case forcefully as salary decisions are made.

Agenda Item Four: Become intentional about recruiting potential staff members to student affairs. Again, Woodard and Komives have a number of specific suggestions for both professional associations and graduate preparation programs—suggestions that should be given careful consideration. In addition, the development of a student paraprofessional program is one way to "grow your own." A structured student paraprofessional program, with a high-quality training component, can introduce undergraduate students to student affairs as a field. Paraprofessional programs, as recruitment tools to student affairs, will only meet that goal if they are supported by high-quality training and on-the-job experience.

One goal of such efforts should be to aid students in gaining a perspective on what it really means to be a professional student affairs staff member. With careful design and implementation, paraprofessional programs can increase the quality of services for current students and concurrently serve as a vehicle to attract potential staff to the field. An excellent resource for developing such programs can be found in *Students Helping Students* (Ender, McCaffrey, and Miller, 1985).

Agenda Item Five: Define the core knowledge, attitudes, and beliefs that need to be held by all student affairs staff regardless of position. "A Perspective on Student Affairs, 1987" (National Association of Student Personnel Administrators, [1987] 1989) outlined a set of assumptions and beliefs that are common to student affairs. Lyons's Chapter Two in this volume expands on these concepts and provides initial guidance. In addition to these attitude issues, there is a core knowledge base, which should be held in common by all professional staff in student affairs, regardless of role. At a minimum, this core includes basic knowledge about human development theory, knowledge of the history and philosophy of student affairs and higher education, knowledge of the specific institution, and the ability to translate that knowledge into practice.

Agenda Item Six: Differentiate the skills, competencies, and

requisite knowledge needed for generalist and specialist positions. This agenda item relates to agenda items one, two, and five above, but it is much more specific. We have often made an error in assuming and requiring the same skills and competencies for all staff regardless of position or specialty area. Careful examination will reveal that not all staff have to know all things. This kind of analysis should also relate to the level of the staff position required, with increased knowledge expectations directly related to the increased responsibilities of the position.

Agenda Item Seven: Design and implement staff development opportunities that will aid specialty-training staff in mastering the core knowledge base. Each student affairs staff should have an intentional program for staff development to assist individuals without formal training in student affairs to understand the core knowledge base that undergirds the work of student affairs. Such programs need not be expensive, but they must be intentional. Moore and Young (1987) provide a professional education model that is extremely useful in assessing staff needs, and Baier (1985) and Dalton (1989) both provide excellent reviews of techniques and strategies for staff development.

Agenda Item Eight: Design and implement a staff development program for all staff. Student affairs, by its nature, invites conditions of burnout and staff stress. We must pay attention to the interpersonal needs as well as the skills and competencies of all participants in staff development programs. Comprehensive staff development programs increase collaboration and cooperation between and among professional staff, and this kind of interaction increases staff morale and provides support for a high-quality working environment.

Agenda Item Nine: Assess the skills and competencies of current staff. Specific knowledge with regard to the skills and competencies of current staff will assist student affairs organizations to prepare for the challenges of the future. If, for example, staff do not have technological expertise, remediation can be provided. If they do not understand the implications of a changing student population, intentional effort can be made to close the knowledge gap. This type of assessment will assist the CSAO in determining what specific staff skills are essential as he or she makes decisions about filling vacancies.

Agenda Item Ten: Expand the concept of who really are professional staff in student affairs. Earlier in this chapter, I discussed the multiple career paths to student affairs. As a profession, we need to acknowledge this diversity and the increased specialization in staff that will be required in the future. We need to match academic backgrounds and experience with the tasks we need to do rather than to make the assumption that generalists are the only true professionals. In addition, we must be intentional about introducing these "new" staff to the profession through involvement in student affairs associations and exposure to the literature.

Agenda Item Eleven: Become affirmative in the process of attracting minority individuals to student affairs. Item eleven is closely related to all the other agenda items outlined above, but it is of critical importance if we are going to serve our future students adequately. We must give specific attention to attracting minority students to graduate education programs, identifying minority persons who may have specialty preparation, urging them to consider student affairs, and using all the networks available to us to identify qualified candidates.

Agenda Item Twelve: Pay specific attention to strengthening traditional preparation programs in student affairs. The American College Personnel Association (ACPA) and the National Association of Student Personnel Administrators (NASPA) have established a joint task force on the relationship between professional practice and preparation programs. Such efforts need to be continued and strengthened (see Chapter Eleven). Delworth and Hanson (1989) also provide specific recommendations that should be carefully considered for preparation programs. Quality control is currently an issue and must be addressed. Finally, the profession should carefully consider a national registry program, as proposed by Woodard and Komives.

Agenda Item Thirteen: Student affairs staff in all areas must enhance their role as experts on students. Staff members must remain on the cutting edge of the profession. In positions with high time demands and high stress, keeping up with developments in the field is often easier said than done. In order to remain knowledgeable, each student affairs professional must make a commitment to keep up with the field, including research and new program ideas. Finally, the student affairs professional of the future must make intentional efforts to keep up with the demographic and attitude characteristics of students on their own campuses.

Agenda Item Fourteen: Individual professionals must assert pride in their work and be able to identify the contributions made by student affairs. For far too long, professionals in student affairs have not been able to articulate clearly the specific contributions that they make to higher education and students. Articulating the importance of our work is not easy, but being diffident accomplishes nothing. A key skill for the future will be our ability to translate what we do and to communicate it to colleagues within the academy. To do less would undermine the attractiveness of the profession to those whom we wish to attract and retain as competent staff.

Summary

Student affairs staffing patterns are in the process of evolution and change. This process is likely to continue in the future, and student affairs must respond appropriately. Changing student characteristics, changes in technology, and evolving expectations for both higher education and student affairs will influence profoundly what combination of background, skill, and knowledge student affairs staff will need in the future. In addition, staff members are coming to student affairs with increasingly diverse academic backgrounds, training, and experience. Increased specialization due to changing expectations will mandate a continuation of this trend.

A number of barriers exist and interfere with the quest of attracting and keeping competent staff in the profession. In order to assure quality staff that can respond to both student and institutional needs in the future, an active agenda regarding staff issues must be embraced by the student affairs profession, institutions of higher education, and individual student affairs professionals. We must learn ways to include genuinely both generalist and specialty staff in the profession and to develop strategies to ensure that our professional staff is prepared to meet the challenges of the future.

Student affairs, higher education, and our students cannot afford to adopt the stand that Milton (1941) took when he said, "They also serve who only stand and wait." Our future depends on firm and assertive action by staff members at all levels within the profession, and the leadership for that effort must be provided by chief student affairs officers and professional associations.

References

American Council on Education. "The Student Personnel Point of View, 1949." In *Points of View.* Washington, D.C.: National Association of Student Personnel Administrators, 1989. (Originally published 1949.)

Baier, J. "Ensuring Competent Staff." In M. J. Barr, L. A. Keating, and Associates, *Developing Effective Student Services Programs: Systematic Approaches for Practitioners.* San Francisco: Jossey-Bass, 1985.

Baldridge, J. V. *Power and Conflict in the University.* New York: Wiley, 1971.

Brown, R. D. "Professional Pathways and Professional Education." In L. V. Moore and R. D. Young (eds.), *Expanding Opportunities for Professional Education.* New Directions for Student Services, no. 37. San Francisco: Jossey-Bass, 1987.

Dalton, J. C. "Enhancing Staff Knowledge and Skills." In U. Delworth, G. Hanson, and Associates, *Student Services: A Handbook for the Profession.* (2nd ed.) San Francisco: Jossey-Bass, 1989.

Delworth, U. "Identity in the College Years: Issues of Gender and Ethnicity." *NASPA Journal,* 1989, *26* (3) pp. 162–167.

Delworth, U., and Hanson, G. "Future Directions: A Vision of Student Services in the 1990s." In U. Delworth, G. Hanson, and Associates, *Student Services: A Handbook for the Profession.* (2nd ed.) San Francisco: Jossey-Bass, 1989.

Ender, S., McCaffrey, S., and Miller, T. *Students Helping Students.* Athens, Ga.: Student Development Associates, 1985.

Milton, J. "On His Blindness." In H. F. Fletcher (ed.), *The Complete Poetical Works of John Milton.* Boston: Houghton-Mifflin, 1941.

Moore, L. V., and Young, R. B. (eds.). *Expanding Opportunities for Professional Education.* New Directions for Student Services, no. 37. San Francisco: Jossey-Bass, 1987.

National Association of Student Personnel Administrators. "A Perspective on Student Affairs, 1987." In *Points of View.* Washington, D.C.: National Association of Student Personnel Administrators, 1989. (Originally published 1987.)

Upcraft, M. L. "Managing Staff." In M. L. Upcraft and M. J. Barr, *Managing Student Affairs Effectively.* New Directions for Student Services, no. 41. San Francisco: Jossey-Bass, 1988.

PART THREE

Taking Action to Shape the Future

It is not enough to know change will occur and the directions those changes are likely to take. If student affairs is going to be a vital part of higher education in the future, certain conditions must be met. In this section, our authors share their thinking about actions we must take to improve our ability to respond in the future and to ensure that student affairs will continue to contribute to the higher education enterprise.

First, we must define and articulate new organizational roles for student affairs. No one organizational structure meets the needs of all institutions, but it is clear that a certain minimum set of institutional and student affairs conditions must be met if we are to be successful. In Chapter Nine, Margaret Barr and Robert Albright discuss these necessary conditions and propose strategies to help student affairs professionals meet their unique responsibilities in higher education.

Second, changes in organizational conditions are not sufficient to ensure success. Student affairs professionals will need many skills in the future, but the most important will be our ability to manage conflict and change. The issues we will face will not easily be resolved, for we will be confronting many paradoxical questions. Competing values and ideas will demand attention and resolution. In Chapter Ten, Anne Golseth and Margaret Barr identify the paradoxical questions we must face, and they provide suggestions and strategies to help student affairs professionals increase their effectiveness in conflict management and problem resolution.

Third, preparing and training competent staff to meet the challenges of tomorrow is a primary agenda item. In Chapter Eleven, Dudley Woodard and Susan Komives present staff preparation and training challenges to graduate preparation programs, individual campuses, and professional associations. Their provocative suggestions for change should stimulate debate among professionals. Competent and well-prepared staff will continue to be the most critical variable in our ability to provide quality services and programs to our students and our institutions.

Fourth, although cooperation between academic affairs and student affairs has always been an issue of concern, we believe that it will be a pressing priority in our shared future. In Chapter Twelve, Suzanne Brown provides a number of suggestions to increase collaboration between academic and student affairs and identifies the barriers we must overcome to achieve success.

Fifth, we can no longer simply rely on anecdotal information and spotty research and evaluation processes to determine our effectiveness. In Chapter Thirteen, Gary Hanson proposes an agenda for research, evaluation, and outcome assessment for the future. This chapter will provide valuable guidance on how data can aid student affairs to meet both student and institutional needs more effectively.

Finally, we believe we are moving in a positive direction; and although the problems are enormous, the promise still shines. In the final chapter, we summarize the trends we see and provide a set of challenges for the profession of student affairs.

Chapter 9

Rethinking the Organizational Role of Student Affairs

Margaret J. Barr
Robert L. Albright

In 1972, Fredric Ness said, "Campus governance has been changing so radically in recent years that no one can really predict what it is likely to be even by the end of this decade" (p. 39). The end of the decade of the seventies has long passed, but his prediction remains true today. As we look forward to the twenty-first century, issues regarding campus governance and the roles of the individuals and internal groups involved in governance remain unclear. We do know that higher education must adapt to a number of changes in people, priorities, and programs. We are aware that fiscal resources are becoming more restricted. We know that the larger society is concerned about outcomes and accountability in the educational enterprise. We understand that the legal and regulatory environment is more demanding. We comprehend some of the influence that social changes, health issues, technology, and expanded expectations will have on the academy. What we do not know, however, is what all of this may mean for the organizational entity known as student affairs. What changes are in our future? What are the conditions we must meet for student affairs to be an effective component of a college or university?

In this chapter, we will review the current status of student affairs, we will explore issues in role definition of student affairs, and we will present a more defined role for the profession. Finally, we will lay out a set of organizational conditions that will increase the effectiveness of student affairs in the future. To understand our future, however, we must first make sure that we appreciate our past and our present.

Background

We will not present a long discourse on the history of student affairs. Instead, we will do a cursory review of the rapid development of student affairs as an organizational entity within higher education. The growth and development of student affairs as part of higher education is directly related to the changes in philosophy that have guided the enterprise. As the philosophy of higher education in the United States evolved from that of education for the aristocracy to a philosophy of egalitarianism, expectations for post-secondary education also expanded (Knock, 1985). New students entered college, new institutions were formed to meet new demands, new services were added in an effort to attract and retain students, and the complexity of each individual campus grew. Concurrently, faculty were faced with increased pressures to conduct research and to publish.

Responsibilities related to the out-of-class life of students became less of a priority for faculty, and new personnel were added to the organization to work with students. Evolving from these new positions were the roles of dean of women and dean of men as "mainstays of morality and decorum" (Dressel, 1981, p. 94). After World War II, student affairs units rapidly expanded to encompass a whole range of services and programs. Although the domain of student affairs varies from campus to campus, the range and scope of the organization often are wide.

The formal organizational role of student affairs exhibits great variability from campus to campus. "Student affairs in a college or university is influenced by the distinctive character of the institution, including its history, academic mission, traditions and location. The composition of the student body and faculty, the priorities of the chief executive officer and governing board, and the beliefs and knowledge of the student affairs staff also shape the responsibilities and the manner in which programs and services are delivered. The character of an institution largely determines the nature of student affairs programs, therefore organizational structures may vary widely from one campus to another" (National Association of Student Personnel Administrators, [1987] 1989, p. 15). This acknowledged diversity has created some of the dilemmas student affairs will face in the future as we try to define our role and function in a rapidly changing environment.

Student affairs organizations are faced with three major issues: confusion about organizational purpose both within and without the institution, lack of consistency regarding student affairs organizational structures, and ambiguous goals for student affairs that must nevertheless be appropriate to the enterprise. All must be resolved.

Confusion of Purpose

The purpose of student affairs within the organization of a college or university always has been diffuse. "Presidents are frequently confused as to the purposes of student personnel services. Many presidents have felt that the role of the unit was to devise and maintain reasonable controls on student behavior, provide safeguards on morals, and immediately get rid of homosexuals, pregnant women and any others whose behavior might reflect adversely on the institution. Student activities have also been regarded as a means to keep students busy in ways of little concern to the faculty and administration" (Dressel, 1981, p. 95). This view of the purpose of student affairs was shared, at least in part, by many during the era of in loco parentis. The validity and utility of this point of view matters less than does the widespread conviction that the chief purpose of student affairs was to control student behavior.

Expectations that student affairs should control student behavior still exist for many associated with colleges and universities, including some parents and members of local communities. In addition, we must recognize that in loco parentis remained an operating principle for many institutions even through the court challenges of the early sixties and seventies.

For most institutions, however, the constitutional challenges in the courts caused a change in the relationships of the student to the institution. While institutions continued to be concerned about student behavior, on some campuses, discipline and control were reduced in importance. A question arose for student affairs. With the role of controller of behavior and enforcer of institutional standards deemphasized, what was to be the appropriate role of student affairs organizations in higher education?

When the traditional purpose of student affairs was under assault, many professionals and student affairs organizations used student development theory as a vehicle to redefine their role and function. (See Chapter Three.) New terms came into our vocabulary to define the professional function of student affairs: *student development educator* (Brown, 1972, 1980) and *campus ecologist* (Banning, 1978; Morrill, Hurst, and Oetting, 1980). But these new concepts did not communicate clearly, either to the profession or to colleagues in academia, what the student affairs organization can and should do to contribute to the campus. In fact, for some time, an unproductive debate ensued within student affairs regarding the emerging role of student development educator and the traditional role of manager-administrator.

During the period when the concept of in loco parentis was waning and student affairs professionals were searching for a new purpose, great changes occurred in American higher education. The decades of the sixties and the seventies were ones of great growth. Expansion occurred in the number of institutions, the sizes of institutions, the types of students served by the enterprise, and the range of programs and services provided by colleges and universities. Unbridled growth brought increased demands for housing, health care, food services, admissions, placement services, and the like. New students pressed for programs and services to meet their needs, including access for the handicapped, minority student services, adult services, and child care. As more and different students entered American colleges and universities, the need to provide adequate psychological and physical health care and programs responding to the diversity of the student body grew in both number and size.

Student affairs organizations were often the places where new programs for special populations were nourished and developed. In addition, the rapid expansion of housing, recreational sports, and student unions caused a concurrent expectation for student affairs to manage complex facilities and budgets effectively (Ambler, 1980). This expanded facility and budget management responsibility for student affairs is a reality on most campuses today. Effective student affairs administrators recognize and honor this important aspect of their responsibilities.

The debate over the question of educational quality in the undergraduate experience also has and will continue to have an influence on the purpose of student affairs. Boyer's (1989) criticism of the quality of the undergraduate experience is but one of many reports focusing on what is wrong with American higher education. Although Boyer adheres to a somewhat idealistic version of collegiate life, his valid criticism of the lack of civility, poor living conditions, and cultural apathy among college students must be examined carefully.

The social issues of the day—substance abuse, AIDS, eating disorders, and chronic psychological problems—have led many to reexamine the concept of in loco parentis. There is a growing trend for institutions of higher education to take more responsibility for the behavior and welfare of students. The difference in focus, however, is notable; it emphasizes the total development of students—not just morality.

A new and yet incomplete purpose for student affairs is emerging, but it still focuses responsibility for student lives in student affairs organizations. Some would argue that this new concept of in loco parentis has always been there, even during the great social upheavals of the sixties and seventies. But whether this argument is valid or not, student affairs is faced with a dilemma of purpose. Are we controllers of behavior? Are we educators? Are we managers and administrators? Are we facilitators of student growth and development? Are we all of these things and more? The answers to these questions will define the future of student affairs.

Organizational Uncertainty

A faculty member moving from one campus to another will encounter similar organizational structures in both places. The work of the faculty is usually organized in departments as part of a school or college. Administrative titles are consistent: department chair, dean, and chief academic officer—whether called vice-president, vice-chancellor, or provost. The professional career ladder for faculty is clearly defined by faculty rank: instructor, assistant professor, associate professor, and professor. While criteria for achieving academic rank may vary from institution to institution, there is a certain pattern of familiarity across colleges and universities for faculty.

Colleges and universities are also governed in predictable ways, although the specific titles and structures will vary from campus to campus. All American colleges and universities are governed by lay boards, although appointment to the governing board may vary according to the public or private nature of the institution. A chief executive officer for the institution is appointed by the board and is called either president or chancellor. If the institution is part of a larger system, the campus chief executive reports to an overall chief executive officer. Although there have been major changes regarding the autonomy of the decision-making process on campus, and although no one would claim that governance in higher education is an easy task, there remains a certain predictability in the overall administrative structure.

For student affairs professionals, predictability is not the case. As is the case for our colleagues in business affairs and other support units on campus, student affairs professionals are often in the position of not having clearly defined rank, professional career paths, or organizational stability. At the individual level, there are no universal titles, nor are there criteria for certain levels of responsibility in student affairs.

The terms *director, dean, assistant dean, assistant director, coordinator, specialist, university staff,* and *professional staff* are used freely to describe the roles and functions of the student affairs staff. Further, there is no agreement about what these terms mean from one campus to another. Academic rank conveys a certain sense of meaning from campus to campus, but that is not true for student affairs. (See Chapters Eight and Eleven.)

Just as much variability exists on an organizational level. The chief student affairs officer may be either a vice-president, a vice-chancellor, or a dean of students. The chief student affairs officer may report directly to the campus chief executive or through a vice-president for academic affairs, business affairs, or administration.

The functions assigned to student affairs vary from campus to campus. On some campuses, for example, admissions and registration are part of the student affairs organization. On others, they report to academic affairs. "Colleges have built their student services after the fashion of the New England farmhouse. As new needs were discovered, new services were added. The result has been a rambling construction, attractive and serviceable enough after its fashion but not a very economical model and hardly a structure one would set out to build" (Jellema, 1972, pp. 71–72).

A variety of internal organizational structures also characterizes student affairs. In some institutions, the internal organization is built around funding sources—auxiliaries and general revenue. In some, the organization is built around functions, with developmental programs reporting through one chain of command and direct services through another. At some institutions, the business functions of housing and the union report to another organizational entity while the program functions within those units report to student affairs. Clearly, universal commonalities do not exist among institutions with regard to student affairs.

Ambiguous Goals

"Goals simply state where an individual, unit, or division wants to go" (Johnson and Foxley, 1980, p. 410). Unfortunately, student affairs goals are often diffuse, unmeasurable, and vague. Although all of higher education is plagued by the problem of unspecific goals (Baldridge and Tierney, 1979), the issue is particularly acute for student affairs.

A lack of specific goals can interfere with the development of both organizational and fiscal support. Many of the goals on the academic side of the house are fairly easy to measure and understand.

For example, a goal to provide English instruction to all first-semester freshmen in classes enrolling no more than twenty students is fairly clear. If enrollments exceed the number of available sections, then pressure is mounted to add additional instructional staff. When enrollments decline, debate ensues whether the upper limit should be reduced to fifteen students. At no time is the fundamental goal of providing English instruction really questioned.

In student affairs, the goals are usually less concrete and are not easily understood by others. A vague goal of helping students to "develop," for example, not only is unclear but also causes a number of other questions to arise (Barr, 1988).

Vague goals are also not easily translated into fiscal support for student affairs programs. To illustrate, it is much easier to support a request for additional instructors in mathematics than to support a vague request for a new position to help students develop. Student affairs administrators must be able to state clearly both what will and will not happen if fiscal support is not forthcoming.

Finally, vague and ambiguous goals contribute to the perception that student affairs units are not well managed. When that perception exists, access to decision making is reduced, and the student affairs unit fares less than well during the budget process.

As we face the twenty-first century, three tasks appear to be primary to the organizational role for student affairs. The first is to reach agreement on the role and purpose of student affairs within higher education. The second is to develop organizational patterns that support that agreed upon purpose. And the third task is to propose a set of institutional conditions and student affairs organizational conditions that must be in place before the positive contributions of student affairs can be realized.

Issues Involved in Role Definition for Student Affairs

A number of distinct, conflicting, and sometimes unrealistic roles have emerged for student affairs organizations over the years: controller of student behavior, manager of facilities, administrator of programs, student development educator, and campus environment expert. In their time and place, all have had legitimacy, although they have been difficult to achieve. The task for the future becomes one of defining the limits of these many and diverse expectations and blending them into a coherent whole.

A Fundamental Premise. Belief in the primacy of the academic mission of the institution provides the basis for a redefinition of the role and purpose of student affairs in the future. "The work of student affairs should not compete with and cannot substitute for that academic experience. As a partner in the educational enterprise, student affairs enhances and supports the academic mission" (National Association of Student Personnel Administrators, [1987] 1989, p. 12). Such a premise does not in any way denigrate the importance of student affairs in the college and university of today or tomorrow. "Although the entire university community must contribute to an institutional environment conducive to learning, it is undeniable that the major part of that support system resides within the student affairs division" (Monat, 1985, p. 51).

Only when institutional community supports both the concept of the primacy of the academic mission and the necessary and fundamental role that student affairs plays in achieving that mission can there be success. (See Chapter Two.)

Who Is Served. Student affairs serves both the institution and the students. A clear understanding of the dual responsibilities of student affairs is a prerequisite for redefining the role and purpose of that function. This dual responsibility inherently brings conflict to the role of student affairs. Institutional purposes, student expectations, and agendas may diverge (see Chapter Ten). Outside forces may shape institutional responses to issues in unpredictable ways (see Chapters Four, Five, Six, and Seven). New student demands or expectations may emerge, and the institution may be either unwilling or unable to respond.

Serving two clients who will sometimes come in conflict is never a comfortable situation. It is a reality that more than any other factor shapes the role of student affairs in higher education. Individuals who serve a bridging role are sometimes viewed as not being in either or any camp. Achieving a sense of balance while engaging in bridging activities is central, however, for the success of student affairs as an organizational component in higher education.

Duties and Responsibilities. "A Perspective on Student Affairs, 1987" lists a number of duties and responsibilities that student affairs has for both institutions and students (National Association of Student Personnel Administrators [1987] 1989, pp. 16–18). These list the ideal—what should be on the campus—and are replicated in Exhibits 9.1 and 9.2.

Some duties and responsibilities for student affairs are readily agreed upon by many in higher education. Of these, some have

Exhibit 9.1. Institutional Responsiblities for Student Affairs.

Student affairs staff provide programs and services directly to institutions including the following (National Association of Student Personnel Administrators, [1987] 1989, pp. 17–18):

- Support and explain the values, mission, and policies of the institution
- Participate in the governance of the institution and share responsibility for decisions
- Assess the educational and social experiences of students to improve institutional programs
- Provide and interpret information about standards during the development and modification of institutional policies, services and practice
- Establish policies and programs that contribute to a safe and secure campus
- Effectively manage the human and fiscal resources for which student affairs is responsible
- Support and advance institutional values by developing and enforcing behavioral standards for students
- Advocate student participation in institutional governance
- Provide essential services such as admissions, registration, counseling, financial aid, health care, housing and placement which contribute to the institutional mission and goals
- Serve as a resource to faculty in their work with individual students and student groups
- Encourage faculty-student interaction in programs and activities
- Advocate and help create ethnically diverse and culturally rich environments for students
- Assume leadership for the institution's responses to student crises
- Be intellectually and professionally active
- Establish and maintain effective working relationships with the local community
- Coordinate student affairs programs and services with academic affairs, business affairs, development, and other major components of the institution

Exhibit 9.2. Student Affairs Responsibilities to Students.

Student affairs staff provide programs and services directly to students, including the following (National Association of Student Personnel Administrators [1987] 1989, pp. 17–18):

- Assist students in successful transition to college
- Help students explore and clarify values
- Encourage development of friendships among students and a sense of community within the institution
- Help students acquire adequate financial resources to support their education
- Create opportunities for students to expand their aesthetic and cultural appreciation
- Teach students how to resolve individual and group conflicts
- Provide programs and services for students who have learning difficulties
- Help students understand and appreciate racial, ethnic, gender, and other differences
- Design opportunities for leadership development
- Establish programs that encourage healthy living and confront abusive behaviors
- Provide opportunities for recreation and leisure-time activities
- Help students clarify career objectives, explore options for further study, and secure employment

---

come to student affairs as a result of growth, and some as a result of a change of mission or lack of interest by other members of the academic community. But agreement is not as easy to reach on other duties and responsibilities because of issues of history, territory, and power. There are even many who will not agree with those listed in the NASPA statement. It is important, however, that a greater consensus and sense of agreement be reached on the legitimate role, function, duties, and responsibilities of student affairs. But even when that agreement is reached, other issues will invariably intervene, including the politics of decision making on the campus.

Politics. Higher education is characterized by multiple constituency groups and approaches to governance. Structures including committees, task forces, and legislative bodies abound and contribute to the political nature of the enterprise (Cohen and March, 1974; Walker, 1979; Baldridge and Tierney, 1979; and Barr, 1985). Student affairs administrators generally have not been adept at understanding and using the political processes of higher education. This skill deficit must be corrected if student affairs is to be an equal partner in the future higher education community. Walker (1979) discusses the political environment of higher education in great detail, and his book is highly recommended. Two concepts are key in managing the political environment. First, "Respect the people with whom you work" (p. 193). And second, "Understand the university for which you work" (p. 193).

Lack of political skill on the part of student affairs administrators contributes to the sense that student affairs is a marginal enterprise. Well-honed political skills can aid student affairs administrators in accessing and influencing the decision-making structures on campus—and in improving the quality of leadership of the institution and within the student affairs organizations.

Who Leads. A great deal has been written about the need for strong, effective, and transforming leadership in higher education. It should be noted, however, that "to the extent the failure of a college can be attributed to a failure of leadership, it is usually not the result of a lack of charisma but to a lack of basic organizational competence" (Bensimon, Neumann, and Birnbaum, 1989, p. 75). For student affairs to be effective, that grasp of basic organizational competence must be present in both the chief executive officer of the campus and the chief student affairs officer. The quality of relationship between these two leaders, as well as the quality of their shared understanding of the role and function of student affairs, will either enhance or detract from the ability of the student affairs organization to contribute effectively to the institution and students.

Most studies of leadership in higher education have focused on the presidential role (Cohen and March, 1974; Fisher, 1984; Kerr, 1963; Kerr and Gade, 1986; Walker, 1979). These studies have value for the chief student affairs officer, but more information is needed on the leadership role in student affairs. Some promising work has been done, or is in-process (Sandeen, 1980; Rickard, 1985, 1988). One important agenda item for the future will be an intentional focus on the skills and competencies needed for effective leadership in student affairs; regardless of the organizational alignment, leadership does make a difference.

The Role of Student Affairs: A New Definition

Notwithstanding the previous discussion, we believe there is an essential and coherent role for student affairs on any campus. That role is based on the following broad duties and responsibilities.

Student Experts. Professionals in the division of student affairs should be expected to be experts on students, their attitudes, concerns, and environments. Student affairs professionals must be able to provide information regarding the student population in a timely and useful fashion as the campus community makes decisions. For example, research on student attitudes, values, and perceptions should be conducted on a routine basis, and those findings should be made available to the academic community (see Chapter Thirteen). Data about student living patterns, involvements, and use of facilities and services must be collected and interpreted for the campus community. The role of expert on students also assumes a knowledge of student development theory and the ability to translate that theory into useful information to aid in planning, policy formation, and program development. It also assumes expertise on demographic trends, economic forecasts, and the like—and the ability to understand the implications for the institution.

Bridgers. Student affairs should be expected to provide a bridge between various constituency and interest groups, both on and off campus. A distinct part of the portfolio for student affairs is the responsibility to communicate with all sides on issues and to aid individuals and groups with the resolution of conflict. In student affairs, we see this function as a routine part of our responsibilities, yet it takes a great deal of time, energy, and expertise to help conflicting individuals and groups reach resolution on issues (see Chapter Ten). This expectation implies expertise in group and organizational dynamics as well as in conflict resolution.

Intervenors. Intervention is a well-supported role for student affairs and is a logical outcome of the first two expectations. Student affairs should have demonstrated expertise in crisis intervention with both individuals and groups and should assume primary responsibility for managing crisis situations. Such crisis situations may be as diverse as a student suicide attempt, a tragic automobile accident, the death of a student, or a demonstration on either national or campus issues. In all these cases and more, student affairs staff must assume primary responsibility for managing the crisis of the moment while seeking long-term solutions to the problem.

Program Developers. Based on student affairs expertise regarding students, their responsibility for bridging communication gaps, and their knowledge of crisis intervention, it logically flows that cocurricular program development is also a legitimate expectation for student affairs. Such programs should enhance the primary academic experience of students and aid students in applying their academic experiences to their lives. In addition, student affairs should place intentional emphasis on the development of learning opportunities for students and on leadership skills. This role is firmly rooted in the assumptions and beliefs underlying our professional practice (see Chapter Two).

Managers. Student affairs professionals hold responsibility for a large amount of human and fiscal resources. In an age of accountability, they must exercise sound management of these resources to meet institutional and student goals. Sound budget skills, supervision skills, and concern for reduction of the potential liability of the institution are inherent in the role of manager. Further, effective management requires the development of strong and positive working relationships with other parts of the institution, including business and administrative services.

Spokespersons. Often the student affairs professional is expected to be the institutional spokesperson on policy matters and in problem situations. In times of crisis, the ability of student affairs to articulate clearly the position of the institution is critical. Just as important, however, is the importance of this role in the day-to-day operation of the institution—keeping lines of communication and understanding open.

Institutional Conscience. William Monat (1985) described the need for student affairs to serve as "institutional conscience." It is an ongoing role and a primary responsibility for student affairs. During the process of decision making, budget allocation, and crisis management, student affairs must assume primary responsibility for reminding others of the importance of inclusion and managing differences as part of the process. Student affairs professionals are not the only people in the institution with consciences. We do, however, carry a special responsibility, because of our unique role as intervenors and bridgers, to be sure that questions of justice, fairness, and equity are considered when decisions are made.

Behavioral Standards Enforcers. Each institution has a unique set of student behavioral standards, which must be consistently and fairly enforced. This enforcement has been a traditional role of student affairs and one that will continue into the future. It requires understanding of the legal implications of decisions and the constant need to monitor those standards in light of changing conditions.

The foregoing duties and responsibilities describe the role of student affairs for the future. Although the emphasis may change depending on time and place, they will remain essential elements.

Necessary Organizational Conditions

For student affairs to be successful, both institutional and internal organizational conditions must be met.

Institutional Conditions. First, a clear, distinctive institutional mission enhances the ability of student affairs to improve the academic experience of students (Kuh and others, 1989). If the institution is unclear about what the role and purpose of the enterprise are, the student affairs organization will also be unfocused. A clear institutional mission focuses the energies of all involved in productive and useful ways.

Second, we must encourage and support open communication. Student affairs professionals must never be reluctant to "speak up for students but never down to them" (Monat, 1985, p. 57).

Third, we must foster freedom to innovate. "A clear, unwavering commitment to celebrating, encouraging and enabling multiple communities" (Kuh and others, 1989) must be present.

Fourth, it is affirmed that the distinctive character of a campus shapes the reporting relationship for student affairs, and whatever the reporting lines, access to and participation in decision-making structures are essential for success. Student affairs must not be relegated so far down the organization that the unique perspective this staff brings to issues and problems is never heard when decisions are being made. A direct reporting relationship to the chief executive officer would foster such communication, but not all institutions have that arrangement. The essential element is the ability of student affairs to have access to and to influence persons or groups that hold the "real" decision-making power on campus.

Fifth, resources within the institution must be allocated on the basis of educational purposes, and debate on resource allocation should be actively encouraged. If student affairs is not an equal partner during the resource allocation process, support for their programs, activities, and services is not likely.

Finally, the philosophy that guides the institution's relationship with students must be clear and unambiguous. The academic community must view students as more than revenue units or social security numbers; they must see them as whole persons.

Student Affairs Conditions. First, the student affairs organization must be able to articulate clearly what it does. Vague statements regarding contributions to the growth and development of students are not enough to ensure organizational success. Specific statements regarding services offered, numbers of students served, and outcomes of that service are essential. Research and evaluation must be conducted on an ongoing basis.

Second, if student affairs professionals are not already, they must become experts on students. More than any other part of the institution, student affairs must know students, their characteristics, their needs, and their aspirations. This kind of knowledge requires a strong foundation in student development theory and the expertise to translate that theory into action—and it requires strong commitment to continued professional education. Third, student affairs must accept the primacy of the academic mission of the institution while maintaining the commitment to student affairs as an equal partner in fulfilling that mission. This view requires understanding of the multiple roles of student affairs and a willingness to act on those expectations when needed.

Fourth, student affairs organizations must demonstrate sound and well-developed management skills. Optimal use of human and fiscal resources must be made to meet well-articulated objectives.

Fifth, using their base of knowledge and skills, members of the student affairs organization must be forecasters and anticipators of problems—roles that will become even more essential as students change and resources constrict.

Finally, the student affairs organization needs to demonstrate a sense of enthusiasm for students, for the tasks at hand, and for the institution. To do less would impair the ability of student affairs to function as an essential part of the institution.

Summary

The future will bring many changes to higher education and, as a result, to student affairs. All student affairs organizations must define clear roles and purposes consistent with the missions of their institutions, and they must resolve issues of organizational uncertainty and professional identity if student affairs is to prosper.

It is essential that the student affairs organization serve both students and the institution. This dual role will sometimes bring conflict and is not always comfortable. If, however, student affairs can effectively enhance the understanding between the students, with their needs and desires, and the institutions, with their goals and missions, the student affairs organization will become indispensable.

Student affairs must develop new and expanded roles, including those associated with knowledge about students, crisis intervention management, and bridging between conflicting constituency groups. The traditional roles of program developer and enforcer of behavioral standards must be reshaped to meet changing student needs and institutional priorities.

Finally, for student affairs to be active partners with the rest of the academy, certain institutional conditions must be present in addition to certain conditions in the student affairs organization. There is no universal structure for student affairs that is applicable to all institutions of higher education. There must be, however, a clear commitment on the part of institutions to serve all dimensions of the student if student affairs is to survive and flourish.

References

Ambler, D. "The Administrator Role." In U. Delworth, G. Hanson, and Associates, *Student Services: A Handbook for the Profession.* San Francisco: Jossey-Bass, 1980.

Baldridge, J. V., and Tierney, M. L. *New Approaches to Management: Creating Practical Systems of Management Information and Management by Objectives.* San Francisco: Jossey-Bass, 1979.

Banning, J. H. (ed.). *Campus Ecology: A Perspective on Student Affairs.* Portland, Oreg.: National Association of Student Personnel Administrators, 1978.

Barr, M. J. "Internal and External Forces Influencing Programming." In M. J. Barr, L. A. Keating, and Associates, *Developing Effective Student Services Programs.* San Francisco: Jossey-Bass, 1985.

Barr, M. J. "Managing the Enterprise." In M. L. Upcraft and M. J. Barr, *Managing Student Affairs Effectively.* New Directions for Student Services, no. 41. San Francisco: Jossey-Bass, 1988.

Bensimon, E., Neumann, A., and Birnbaum, R. *Making Sense of Administrative Leadership.* ASHE-ERIC Higher Education Report No. 1. Washington, D.C.: School of Education and Human Development, George Washington University, 1989.

Boyer, E. L *College: The Undergraduate Experience in America.* New York: Harper & Row, 1989.

Brown, R. D. *Student Development in Tomorrow's Higher Education—A Return to the Academy.* Washington, D.C.: American College Personnel Association, 1972.

Brown, R. D. "The Student Development Educator Role." In U. Delworth, G. Hanson, and Associates, *Student Services: A Handbook for the Profession.* San Francisco: Jossey-Bass, 1980.

Cohen, M. D., and March, J. G. *Leadership and Ambiguity: The American College President.* New York: McGraw-Hill, 1974.

Dressel, P. L. *Administrative Leadership.* San Francisco: Jossey-Bass, 1981.

Fisher, J. L. *The Power of the Presidency.* New York: MacMillan, 1984.

Jellema, W. W. (ed.). *Efficient College Management.* San Francisco: Jossey-Bass, 1972.

Johnson, C. S., and Foxley, C. H. "Devising Tools for Middle Managers." In U. Delworth, G. Hanson, and Associates, *Student Services: A Handbook for the Profession.* San Francisco: Jossey-Bass, 1980.

Kerr, C. *The Uses of the University.* Cambridge, Mass.: Harvard University Press, 1963.

Kerr, C., and Gade, M. *The Many Lives of Academic Presidents.* Washington, D.C.: Association of Governing Boards of Universities and Colleges, 1986.

Knock, G. H. "Development of Student Services in Higher Education." In M. J. Barr, L. A. Keating, and Associates, *Developing Effective Student Services Programs.* San Francisco: Jossey-Bass, 1985.

Kuh, G., and others "Factors and Conditions Common to Involving Colleges." Unpublished manuscript, Department of Administration and Educational Leadership, Indiana University, 1989.

Monat, W. R. "Role of Student Services: A President's Perspective." In M. J. Barr, L. A. Keating, and Associates, *Developing Effective Student Services Programs.* San Francisco: Jossey-Bass, 1985.

Morrill, W. H., Hurst, J. C., and Oetting, E. R. *Dimensions of Intervention for Student Development.* New York: Wiley, 1980.

National Association of Student Personnel Administrators. "A Perspective on Student Affairs, 1987." In *Points of View.* National Association of Student Personnel Administrators. Washington, D.C., 1989. (Originally published 1987.)

Ness, F. W. "Campus Governance and Fiscal Stability." In W. Jellema (ed.), *Efficient College Management.* San Francisco: Jossey-Bass, 1972.

Rickard, S. T. "Titles of Chief Student Affairs Officers: Institutional Autonomy or Professional Standardization?" *National As-*

sociation of Student Personnel Administrators Journal, 1985, *23* (2), 44–49.

Rickard, S. T. "Toward a Professional Paradigm." *Journal of College Student Development,* 1988, *29* (5), 388–397.

Sandeen, A. "Student Services in the '80's: A Decade of Decisions." *National Association of Student Personnel Administrators Journal,* 1980, *19* (3), 2–9.

Walker, D. E. *The Effective Administrator.* San Francisco: Jossey-Bass, 1979.

Chapter 10

Managing Change in a Paradoxical Environment

Margaret J. Barr
Anne E. Golseth

Higher education in the United States has proved to be extremely adaptable. Even a cursory review of history reveals the many and rapid changes that have been embraced by higher education as a whole. New students have been served, curriculum choices have increased, content in courses has been modified, service domains have expanded, institutions have been developed to meet specific needs, technology has become part of the teaching-learning process, and societal expectations for higher education have grown. In one sense, the future will be no different. Change is an inevitable part of any vital educational enterprise.

In some very fundamental ways, however, the future of higher education will be different. First, the pace of change in society has accelerated, and the issues that influence educational change have become increasingly complex (Monat, 1985). Second, the forces of change have increased in both number and power, partially as a result of the information age in which we live. Earlier chapters in this volume have discussed some of the forces that will shape the future tone, style, and direction of colleges and universities. Student bodies will continue to become more diverse in terms of age, gender, race, ethnicity, and socioeconomic status. The legal and regulatory environment of the country will make many more demands on higher education, and technology will continue to be a potent force in shaping human interactions. Finally, the social agendas facing society and education are enormous and will not be easily confronted. "The agenda for higher education has never been more challenging. Colleges and universities must reflect the values of a pluralistic society, provide a forum in which those values can be tested and seek solutions to persistent issues and problems" (National Association of Student Personnel Administrators, 1987, p. 18).

For student affairs, the management of change is particularly important. By history, tradition, and professional values, student affairs professionals are expected to resolve conflicts and to aid groups with competing agendas to reach constructive solutions. Although that role has never been easy, the unpredictability of the future will make it even more difficult. Higher education and student affairs will not be managing change in an atmosphere characterized by agreement on goals, mission, and philosophy. Instead, the future will be filled with choices that must be made between and among legitimate goals. Choices will be difficult because the alternatives that face us are neither inherently good nor inherently bad. Student affairs must assume leadership on campuses during an era when the process of managing change has shifted to the process of managing an environment filled with paradox.

The Question of Paradox

The word *paradox* is most often defined as a contradiction or competition of alternatives, both of which contain truth or rightness or value. Paradoxical issues are most frequently presented in the form of questions. For example, can an institution embrace both the value of equality of access and the value of excellence?

A key skill for student affairs professionals in the future will be the ability to define and recognize paradoxical issues. Paradox is not, however, new to higher education. In fact, paradoxical questions are part of the daily lives of faculty, students, administrators, and staff. In the classroom, such questions are central to the processes of intellectual challenge, creative thinking, and pedagogy.

For example, a vigorous classroom debate on the question of euthanasia will bring forth a number of paradoxical questions with which students must struggle. There are many points of view, and both the rights of an individual person and the rules and laws of society must be weighed in developing an intellectual or personal answer to the question of whether euthanasia is an acceptable solution to problems of illness.

Other examples within the classroom also illustrate the complexities in determining the best course of action. Should we conduct research using animals? How do we determine when life ends? Has our technology in medical care outpaced our ability to provide good and useful alternatives for those we save? These are not abstract questions, and they must be explored if our current and future students are to be able to meet the dilemmas of the future. In campus life, paradoxical questions often relate to the mission of the institution, to the welfare of individuals and groups, and to the relationships among the institution, the larger community, students, faculty, and staff.

For example, what is the proper and correct role for the institution when dealing with students who have substance-abuse problems? Should we intervene, or should we ignore the question as long as it does not interfere with their ability to do their academic work? Or should we hold a group responsible for the damage done by its members in the community? Are we correct in assuming that faculty and staff members should be held to a higher standard of conduct than their counterparts are in the larger society? The list of such issues could go on and on. Paradoxical questions arise and must be managed constantly in an academic community.

Some paradoxes are inherent in the higher education enterprise, and others have emerged as results of change in society. Still others are emerging today and will demand increasing attention in the future. Some paradoxes endure regardless of attempts at resolution or changes in time and circumstances, some are resolved or become obsolete because of forces outside the academy, and some arise from the dynamic interaction between the institution and the greater community. All are difficult, all are complex, and all will require time and attention.

Historical Paradoxes. The relationship between the individual and the institution has been a constant source of paradoxical questions in higher education. Some of these historical paradoxes involve issues such as the value of autonomy of the student versus the value of protection of the student, the value of protection of individual freedom of expression and the sometimes competing value of social propriety, and the need to resolve the competing values of personal agendas of campus community members and the sometimes conflicting values of institutional objectives. At times, paradoxes are based in the sensitivity of certain individuals and groups and the pride of other community members in embedded institutional traditions such as mascots. In the sixties and seventies, an overwhelming paradoxical issue for student affairs involved balancing the interests of some members of the campus community in social protest against compelling interests in maintaining an orderly environment. None of these questions has been fully resolved, and they are still present on our campuses today. Any issue of the *Chronicle of Higher Education* bears stark witness to that reality.

The relationship of the individual to the institution also causes a set of ethical questions to emerge for the student affairs professional. For example, what is the responsibility of the professional when students express intention of doing harm to themselves? If the student affairs professional adheres to Kitchener's (1985) ethical principle of respecting autonomy, then mere expression of intention to harm oneself does not warrant action or intervention. If, however, the expression of intention on the part of the student causes distress to others within the community, or if the student involved has a history of suicide attempts, then the professional must consider the ethical principle of doing no harm. The question becomes one of balancing competing values.

Although student rights have been assured through institutional policies and legal cases and statements (American Association of University Professors, 1967), student responsibility is still subject to institutional expectations and disciplinary procedures.

The joint goals of freedom and responsibility remain primary though often elusive ideals within the academic community.

An additional historical paradox for student affairs is embedded in its traditional mission of meeting student needs. Balance between providing services to all and concurrently providing attention to individual needs remains difficult to achieve.

Finally, a major paradox remains regarding how student affairs professionals can support freedom of student expression and concurrently meet an institutional objective of maintaining order. Other examples from our recent past that are not yet resolved might also be discussed. All of our historical paradoxical issues bring to student affairs administrators the constant challenge of developing fair and just policies and procedures.

Current Paradoxes. Our historical paradoxes remain with us, and many of the major paradoxes facing higher education are focused on social issues more than on individual matters. The relationship between the greater society and the institution, for example, spawns a number of paradoxes in the area of behavior of students, faculty, and staff. For example, should an individual's behavior be judged in light of campus standards or by those of the larger community? Where do the campus boundaries and limits of authority begin and end? These are not abstract questions; they are very real parts of the work of any student affairs administrator. Resolution of such issues must be made, and not everyone will agree with the decision.

Broader questions also influence the paradoxes of the day. The increased expectations for institutional performance coupled with more limited resources have caused a number of paradoxical questions to surface. Who should be served? What program should be abandoned? Anyone who has faced a budget cut or steady-state funding can testify to the difficulty of resolving such issues. Other competing values arise: academic freedom versus political reality, providing technological training versus human development, creating an autonomous learning environment or a legally bound public service entity, for example. The choice must be both. The dilemma is how.

This decade's overriding paradox, which reflects all other

issues, is the question of access versus excellence. The literature mirrors the intensity of the debate—reports, books, and research projects in abundance. Conferences and workshops on the two concepts of access and excellence have proliferated. Legislatures in many states have passed statutes regarding the issue; the number of words, programs, projects, services, and proposed reforms is overwhelming. Yet the paradox of access and excellence remains and is reflected in a number of specific questions that must be resolved if higher education is to move forward. Does affirmative action mean commitment or compliance? Are goals or quotas appropriate? Should higher education provide special admissions programs or equal opportunity? Should achievement be judged only through standardized tests or should other options be considered? The debate is alive and well and will continue as a primary issue in the future.

Emerging Paradoxes. Both the historical and current paradoxes facing higher education provide glimpses of the future. The paradoxical questions of the future will involve both our battered baggage of experience and the possibility of new solutions. Emerging paradoxes will inevitably intensify, so as we glimpse the future, we must employ tools of prediction and prepare to confront a number of new and vexing issues.

One primary tool that we can use to predict the future is the media, which both transmit and create the dilemmas of the present and the future. Careful attention to the hot topics of the day can help each of us prepare for tomorrow. In addition, study of economic forecasts, demographic analyses, historical trends, and changes in technology will provide valuable insights into potential issues that must be resolved.

Access and excellence will continue as the primary issue of higher education and will demand attention and action. The higher education community will need to confront the basic question of whether higher education is a right or an opportunity. The question will not be one of whether the concepts of access and excellence can coexist, but rather one of how these two goals can be accomplished.

The need for cultural sensitivity will intensify in the future and will be accompanied by a backlash that is just beginning to emerge on the college campuses of today. Understanding and appreciating cultural differences will continue to be required for the students and staff of the future. The world, through advances in the media, transportation, and commerce, is continuing to shrink, and the well-prepared individual must be able to function effectively in a wide variety of cultural settings. The emphasis on cultural issues currently is accompanied by reactive behavior on the part of some to the special programs and special attention for ethnic minority groups. Clashes have broken out as students struggle with the rightness and value of affirmative action programs that are much more than mere rhetoric. Finding methods to resolve these intercultural conflicts will remain among the top agendas for the future.

Issues related to personal health and well-being will be part of the future of higher education. Substance abuse, AIDS, and yet unknown diseases will affect the lives of all members of the campus community. The historical paradox of balancing the welfare of the individual and the welfare of the group will reemerge and intensify. In the future, however, there will be an added pressure to resolve these conflicts because the consequences of nonresolution are so much more severe than they have been in the past.

Technology will serve as both a predictor of paradoxical issues and a paradox itself. Nearly every human function in higher education, including teaching, advising, testing, counseling, and student services, will face a technological challenge. The question of whether higher education can provide both technological teaching and human contact is no longer rhetorical. The paradox of technology rests in its ability to open the possibility of learning to many while concurrently threatening many aspects of higher education. With computers, electronic mail, and interactive television becoming more accessible and less expensive, will the college campus really be necessary? With many learners off campus, how can student services be provided for them? Will such services continue to be needed?

Finally, each institution of higher education will have to resolve fundamental questions regarding its mission. The unbridled growth of higher education is at an end, and institutions cannot continue to try to be all things to all people. Making choices among positive alternatives will be difficult and will be the cause of new issues. Clearly, the processes of managing the complex agenda of change that faces us is the challenge of the future.

From any point of view, the future of higher education presents a formidable challenge. The question facing higher education is not one of whether change will occur, but rather one of managing the inevitable changes that will influence our shared uncertain future. The manner in which we approach managing change may be as important as the final decisions that we reach. "In a pluralistic campus community, the manner in which policies are made, decisions are reached and controversial issues are handled may be as important as the results themselves. Indeed, an institution transmits values to students by the way it approaches policies, decisions and issues" (National Association of Student Personnel Administrators, 1987, p. 15).

Essential Elements in Managing Change

We must consider two sets of essential elements in managing paradox and change. The first set revolves around understanding the environment in which we work. The second focuses on principles that guide our approaches to the task of resolving issues and problems.

Understandings. An essential first step is to understand the mission of a college or university and how that mission may translate into a position on a specific issue. Too often, institutional mission statements are viewed as abstractions and statements of intention rather than action, so we must take time to discuss the specific relationship of an institutional mission statement and the day-to-day processes of decision making and problem resolution on the campus. It is essential that leaders within the academic community understand where the institution stands on certain issues. Active discussion and debate as part of an ongoing process can help avoid crisis responses to paradoxical questions within the context of the institution.

A second step is embracing a genuine understanding of the ethical dimensions of the profession of student affairs. Although student affairs administrators may not be ethics experts, they must be ethics officers on their campuses. They must see to it that leaders actively engage in examination of the ethical dimensions of their work as they formulate the positions of the institution. Discussion of ethical issues is essential in an educational community where decisions are rarely clearly good or bad, right or wrong. Movement to understanding and a consistent approach to ethical questions permit balance between competing positive interests to be achieved.

Third, understanding the law is essential. Frequently, administrators use the law as a last resort. Sometimes they are forced by students or others to deal with issues on a legal basis. In the past, student affairs educators and faculty often sought to maintain a separation between higher education and the law, but societal changes in the last two decades have made that stance obsolete. Higher education is not an enclave of immunity from the law, and thus legal issues are fundamental to the resolution of many differences on the campus.

On many campuses, policies and procedures have been developed to meet the explosion of mandates, regulations, and compliance requirements. What is too often lost in the process of reaction is the positive value of the partnership between higher education and the law. "Protection of individual rights, ethical and human treatment and responsible actions are principles on which student affairs is founded. The emerging trend toward legalism is in part a response to a lack of adherence to these principles in the past" (Barr, 1988, p. 348). The law can be a powerful tool in conflict resolution, and the astute administrator uses knowledge of the law as a pragmatic force in developing solutions to ongoing problems.

Guiding Principles. There are many principles related to the management of paradoxical situations. Most can be related to three areas: agreement, integrity, and utility.

One of the first principles of resolving conflicts is determination of commonality, common ground, agreements, and ways to cooperate. This principle applies to people, positions, or concepts; the agreements may be goals, limits, procedures, time lines, or decisions. Essential to reaching agreement is the process of inclusion, so it is critical that all who affect, or are affected by, the paradox or issue at hand be included in discussion regarding resolution of the dilemma. All possibilities of action must be explored. In addition, agreement must include openness to further agreements, to new commonalities, and to balance of positions and outcomes.

Integrity involves principles that are too often assumed rather than affirmed. Integrity means demonstrating consistency between beliefs and actions. Implicit in this definition is adherence to behaviors demonstrating honesty, fairness, sensitivity, and a commitment to doing no harm. The simplicity of these words hides the complexity of action based upon such principles when faced with paradoxical issues. Total honesty can sometimes be harmful, fairness to all at times seems impossible, sensitivity is interpretive, and doing no harm involves evaluation. Integrity is in itself a paradox, a continuing struggle for both the institution and the individual.

A third area of principle is utility, a term rarely used with respect to a principle. What is the utility of dealing with a paradox? What can be gained or accomplished? What can be learned? What can be contributed? Is it true that some issues do not need to be addressed but simply ignored until they go away? Perhaps it is. Indeed, not every paradox of life in our society requires attention from higher education or from student affairs. However, many issues that have been ignored, either intentionally or unintentionally, are relevant to the goals of colleges and universities. Again, college administrators have too often confronted paradox as a problem rather than as a possibility. Paradox is a tool for learning, for change, and for progress, regardless of the resolution of the specific issue. Indeed, paradox is often the medium for the message of higher education.

Strategies

Managing change and paradox is a consuming responsibility for student affairs administrators. Once a paradoxical issue or problem is identified, the question becomes one of reaching resolution. Christensen (1980) identified several specific steps in managing changes and placed a strong emphasis on identifying problems, determining problem causes, seeking alternative solutions, and testing those solutions prior to implementing any change. When all factors are reasonably within control, his approach is very useful and is highly recommended. But often we are faced with situations in which not all elements are under our control, emotions run high, and reaching a consensus is difficult, if not impossible. Faced with these circumstances, the following strategies to manage change and paradox may be useful.

Identifying Common Goals. Often when a conflict arises, the first focus is on what separates or otherwise divides the individuals and groups involved. One of the most effective methods of managing change is assisting all parties to identify those issues on which there is agreement and to establish goals on which consensus can be reached. This method involves employment of effective listening and paraphrasing skills to assist all parties in finding out where they can converge instead of divide.

Identifying Patterns. Careful study of institutional history and conflicts can uncover patterns. Certain issues are bound to bring consistent reactions from specific groups or individuals, and if such patterns can be established, communication with these interested parties can be opened before the issue escalates into a crisis. Such an approach may not prevent a crisis, but it can serve as a method to start the process of managing change.

Exercising Patience. When we are faced with a paradoxical situation, patience is genuinely a virtue. Although we may feel that the issue has been resolved and that there is no need to talk about it anymore, some in the community may feel otherwise. The length of time a college student is at the institution is generally much less than that of any administrator or faculty member. Students leave and new students enter the university, so the issue we felt was settled just last year may arise again as a new agenda item for new students. Acknowledgment of this reality helps each of us to maintain perspective.

Setting Limits. Rules, regulations, and approaches to problem solving must be clearly understood by all parties involved in a paradoxical issue. If there are consequences for unscheduled protests, let people know. If there are limits on how often and where parties to the conflict can meet, be honest about those parameters.

If there are issues involved that are outside the control of the institution, make them known. To do less invites turmoil and accusations of dishonesty when limits are eventually imposed.

Trying to Work Things Out. Working things out involves bringing people together in dialogue, seeking ways to be fair to all involved, calling upon experts for assistance, spending countless hours in study, analysis, and meetings, and knowing that there is no final or enduring resolution.

Doing More Than Is Needed. Doing extra work may include forming a committee, a task force, or a commission to study the issue; setting timetables for study of the problem; making reports to appropriate legislative bodies, students, faculty, and staff; or giving attention to the problem at the highest possible level within the organization. The extra work involves more people in the final resolution of the issue—more people who then own the solution.

Experiment. The experimental approach is a corollary to the one above. If a report is issued with recommendations for actions, experiment with the proposed solutions and set a time limit for evaluating their effectiveness. Many administrators feel this is a risky approach to solving problems, but it is one that has proved to be successful at many colleges and universities.

Taking Risks. Sometimes, successful management of paradox requires taking risks. Success may mean meeting with groups or individuals who do not have recognized entitlement within the institution. Often it involves taking risks with other administrators and faculty by telling them what they do not want to hear or deal with. It requires being a visible resource, a listener, and a target for those disenchanted with processes or solutions.

Involvement. More than ever before, campuses can and must become places of opportunity for genuine involvement by all community members in resolving the issues of the day. Many studies (Astin, 1977; National Commission on Excellence in Education, 1983) have focused on the concept of involvement as a key ingredient in learning, persistence, and completion of higher education. Student involvement is also crucial to the effective management of paradox and related issues on the campus. It is not enough merely to include students on campus committees and discipline boards. Students must become directly involved in the management of paradox in the residence hall, the classroom, the athletic team room, the newspaper office, and in any context of activity or study on the campus. The campus must be the real world in which real people are dealing with real learning, real dilemmas, and real decisions.

Compromise. One of the most effective tools for dealing with the dilemmas of paradox is compromise. Too often, compromise has been viewed as capitulation rather than as empowerment. Compromise can be a powerful tool for management of paradox because it offers the options of choosing from competing solutions and bringing forth a collaboration of many sides of an issue. Compromise can become the action of first resort—the most viable course for moving on and getting things done for the benefit of all.

Anticipatory Management. Crisis management has become the status quo in higher education and rarely brings permanent resolution to persisting problems. Although crisis management may be inevitable, anticipatory management as a tool is more available than ever before. Issues, dilemmas, and paradoxical challenges that will become parts of the campus milieu are increasingly predictable with continuing advancements in media and technology. College officials can choose to deal with the paradoxical questions of the future, either as crises for reaction or as ongoing challenges for teaching and learning.

Reaching Out. Student affairs efforts include numerous programs of outreach on and beyond the campus. Programs, workshops, and activities are prime methods for reaching students and helping them successfully complete their collegiate experiences. The effective management of paradox requires the expansion of such efforts to the entire campus community and beyond. Sharing data, presenting issues, examining alternatives, and looking to the future must become parts of the domain of student affairs.

But not only students must be involved. Board members, other administrators, faculty, and staff also must become aware of current and emerging issues and begin the process of discussion regarding those issues before they become crises that must be managed. It is time that student affairs professionals "take the lid off" problematic issues and involve others in the challenge of working with the dilemmas of the campus and society.

Doing Nothing. Time will solve the problem. The issue will go away and another will take its place. Certain students will leave, and they may take with them the challenge of contradiction. But choosing this option requires careful thought and understanding of the conditions that surround the issues. It may become the option of either the first or last resort in managing change.

The choice of strategy will depend on the issue at hand, the parties involved, and the potential influence that resolution (or failure to resolve) can have on the academic community. Solutions will not be simple or easy to reach, because the questions we will face do not fall into the category of right or wrong answers. There is usually merit in all of the many sides of the issue. The challenge is to develop solutions that make a positive difference for our institutions.

Summary

The management of change is not an easy task. The problems and dilemmas facing higher education are becoming increasingly complex and reflect the changing values in society. Issues that were once viewed in a rather straightforward manner in the past are now fraught with nuances. As higher education moves into the future, the degree of complexity facing the organization will increase, and the number of paradoxical situations that will need to be managed will grow geometrically. Effective management of change will require student affairs professionals to provide leadership as colleges and universities confront paradoxical and difficult questions and seek to turn difficult situations into opportunities for growth and development for students and institutions.

Within higher education, academic freedom ensures a climate for coexistence of conflicting points of view, of equal but differing values and priorities, of multiple perspectives and infinite possibilities. The campus, however, is more than the academy. Coexistence of paradoxical positions and goals is essential to, but not sufficient for, the management of paradox; a sense of resolution must be achieved.

The chosen strategy for managing change will depend on circumstances, skills, attitudes, and the issues at hand. Successful management of change requires the student affairs professional to be aware of the political realities of the situation while entering the process with a goal of resolving the question. Attention and skill must be brought to the emerging issues of the time, and careful consideration must be given to methods and possible outcomes. To manage change and to make it useful in an environment where many equally important issues and positions are vying for support is a challenge for student affairs now, and it will continue to be so in the future.

References

American Association of University Professors. "Joint Statement on Rights and Freedom of Students." *AAUP Bulletin,* 1967, *52,* pp. 365–369.

Astin, A. *Four Critical Years: Effects of College on Beliefs, Attitudes, and Knowledge.* San Francisco: Jossey-Bass, 1977.

Barr, M. J., and Associates. *Student Services and the Law.* San Francisco: Jossey-Bass, 1988.

Christensen, V. R. "Bringing About Change." In U. Delworth, G. Hanson, and Associates, *Student Services: A Handbook for the Profession.* San Francisco: Jossey-Bass, 1980.

Kitchener, K. S. "Ethical Principles and Ethical Decisions in Student Affairs." In H. J. Canon and R. D. Brown (eds.), *Applied Ethics in Student Services.* New Directions for Student Services, no. 30. San Francisco: Jossey-Bass, 1985.

Monat, W. R. "Role of Student Services: A President's Perspective." In M. J. Barr, L. A. Keating, and Associates, *Developing Effective Student Services Programs.* San Francisco: Jossey-Bass, 1985.

National Association of Personnel Administrators. "A Perspective on Student Affairs: A Statement Issued on the Fiftieth Anniversary of *The Student Personnel Point of View.*" Washington, D.C.: National Association of Student Personnel Administrators, 1987.

National Commission on Excellence in Education. *A Nation at Risk: The Imperative for Educational Reform.* Washington, D.C.: U.S. Government Printing Office, 1983.

Chapter 11

Ensuring Staff Competence

Dudley B. Woodard, Jr.
Susan R. Komives

Justice Oliver Wendell Holmes has been credited with the observation that "one's mind, once stretched by a new idea, never regains its original dimension." This axiom is true for any profession. Once a profession has been stretched by its talent and mission, it never regains its original status.

We have written this chapter to stimulate debate and discussion regarding the changes that have occurred in the profession and the future of professional practice in student affairs. We place specific emphasis on the need to change and strengthen college student personnel graduate programs in order to prepare professionals to educate and serve students of the future. We will also give attention to the issues involved in recruiting and retaining professionals in student affairs. Finally, we will address the continuing education and certification of professionals in the practice of student affairs, regardless of their academic preparation.

Voyager II will not reach the star Sirius for another 276,000 years, but the profession of student affairs will celebrate its one hundredth anniversary at the turn of the twenty-first century. So what can be said about the status of the profession of student affairs? It has been characterized from being on the brink of bankruptcy to being a healthy profession in its halcyon days. But before describing the condition of the profession, it is useful to examine some of the myths about student affairs and attempt to debunk them, or at least realign them.

Myths

The first myth that troubles some professionals is that student affairs may not be a profession. Emmet "indicated that student personnel workers need to find new reasons for their existence or prepare to see their time run out" (cited in Newton and Hellenga, 1974, p. 492). In revisiting Wrenn and Darley's work of nearly forty years ago on the status of the student affairs profession, Stamtakos (1981b, p. 204) concluded "that college student affairs is still en route to professional status." On the other hand, Carpenter, Miller, and Winston (1980, p. 16) claim "that the field of student affairs is, more than ever before, an emergent profession with its own distinct theory base and preparation criteria." Sandeen (1982, p. 16) commenting on the doomsday predictions states that "the facts of our present condition and history of our profession clearly contradict such pessimism . . . . Student affairs, especially in the past two years, has expanded dramatically and become a vital part of the educational program of many institutions." The issue may not be so much whether student affairs is a profession, but rather how the profession of student affairs tackles the issues of training, recruitment, and retention of professionals.

A second myth is that the field of student affairs is in disarray and that its influence has significantly diminished as a result of retrenchment and downgrading of student affairs departments—often by subsuming them under academic or business affairs organizations. But there is no evidence that this is a trend, except circumstances occasioned by local conditions such as a downturn in a state's economy, a falloff in institutional enrollment, or weak program leadership (Rickard, 1985). The evidence is clear that student affairs budgets, as percentages of institutional expenditures, have increased at approximately the same general growth rate experienced by higher education during the last decade (National Center for Educational Statistics, 1988). Moreover, a 1985 study of chief student affairs officers (Rickard, 1985) identified a trend toward establishing student affairs as autonomous units rather than subsuming its functions under other instructional organizations like academic affairs.

The most troubling myth is that the profession has been weakened by a decline in the quality and influence of graduate preparation programs. Despite significant demographic changes in graduate programs, which will be discussed later, the actual number of graduate preparation programs has increased during the last two decades (Keim, 1987). But a major problem confronting graduate programs is maintaining early-1970s staffing levels in the face of the significant faculty retrenchments of the late seventies and early eighties in colleges of education. Education colleges and departments, faced with financial exigency, protected what they perceived to be the core of the college—teacher preparation programs; other programs were considered peripheral and were targets for reduction (Stamatakos and Creamer, 1989).

Attendant to this perception of weak graduate programs in student affairs are the changing characteristics of students enrolled in college student personnel (CSP) preparation programs. Although the number of students enrolled in and graduated from CSP preparation programs has declined, the quality of students has remained comparable to the quality of students in other graduate education programs (Kuh and Komives, 1988). A factor in the declining number of students entering the field relates to the changing values of students in the seventies and eighties. The annual Cooperative Institutional Research Program (CIRP) data show a marked shift from the idealism and altruism of the sixties and seventies to valuing money and pleasurable life-styles (Astin, Green, and Korn, 1987; Stamatakos and Creamer, 1989). This shift away from the values that undergird student affairs has led potential new professionals to areas of business and other disciplines with higher financial payoff.

Finally, another myth about the profession is that it is made up of paraprofessionals, implying someone who has been trained as an aide to support a professional—gatekeepers, disciplinarians, residence hall assistants, activities advisers, but not educators. It is true that there has been a significant shift in the number of individuals who have crossed into the practice of student affairs from other disciplines. These individuals have not received, in most cases, prior or subsequent formal training in college student personnel work (Stamatakos, 1981a). It is not true, however, that the corps of the profession is populated by paraprofessionals. The issue is not whether the field is populated by paraprofessionals; rather, the issue is the increasing number of individuals entering the field who have not received any formal academic training in student affairs (Stamatakos and Creamer, 1989).

Current Status of Professional Preparation

During the last two decades, a number of changes have occurred in professional preparation programs. Full-time faculty have declined from 2.4 FTE in 1973 to 0.9 FTE in 1987, while part-time faculty increased during the same period from 4.7 FTE to 5.1 FTE (Keim, 1987). There has also been a corresponding decrease in both the number of students entering the programs and the number of students graduating. The enrollment peak reached during the early seventies was 3,800, but the number dropped to 3,100 by the mid 1980s. Graduates declined during the same period from 1,400 to 1,100 (Keim, 1987). Interestingly, the number of graduate programs actually increased slightly during this period; and the decrease in the number of professionals entering the field seems to have occurred at the same time as the emphasis on recruitment of minority students and job crossover.

With over 3,500 two-year and four-year institutions in operation and a current annual graduation rate of approximately 1,100 students from existing student affairs preparation programs (Keim, 1987), Stamatakos and Creamer (1989) conclude that it is unlikely the demand for new professionals can be met. They estimate that only half of the professionals employed in entry-level positions have been trained in student affairs preparation programs and that the other half either hold advanced degrees in other disciplines or have been hired with baccalaureate degrees. This situation represents one of the most serious challenges facing the profession today. How do we recruit and retain professionals in student affairs while training those who come into the profession without a background in student affairs?

Two other significant issues are gender and race related. More women than men are graduating from master's and specialist programs, compared with the early seventies when men and women graduated at about the same rate (Keim, 1987). The "qualitative as well as quantitative issue" (McEwen, Engstrom, and Williams, 1990) represented by this shifting gender balance among entry-level professionals toward a preponderance of women—and a resulting gender imbalance between male deans and directors and women lower-level staff positions—is the target of increasing inquiry (Evans, 1988; Hamrick and Carlisle, 1990). Moreover, the profession has not been successful in recruiting sufficient numbers of minority students into graduate preparation programs. Stamatakos and Creamer (1989, pp. 10–11) estimate that perhaps only 4 to 5 percent of graduate programs include Asian, Hispanic, African American, and Native American students, whereas a recent study by Schuh (1989) showed a more encouraging participation rate.

One of the most significant challenges we face as we move into the twenty-first century is the role modeling for students who increasingly will be from minority backgrounds. (See Chapter Four.) A field that is significantly dominated by white professionals and charged with the responsibility of educating and serving an increasingly multicultural student body portends, at best, a continuation of existing conflict and unrest.

A number of other factors regarding the condition of the profession should be mentioned. The survey done by Keim (1987) on the condition of graduate preparation programs shows there has not been much change in content and requirements of graduate preparation programs, although some requirements have been relaxed. The number of credit hours and courses required for graduation has increased at the master's level, but the number of courses needed to complete degree requirements has decreased in doctoral and specialist programs. The number of thesis hours required in doctoral and master's programs has also dropped.

What is the impact of these changes? A recent major national study of chief student affairs officers, directors of housing, and graduate preparation program faculty showed agreement on competencies needed for new professionals. Yet faculty thought graduates had developed these competencies to a greater extent than practitioners thought they had (Hyman, 1988). Several explanations are possible, including such factors as quality of students, content of programs, and the higher expectations of today's practitioners for new graduates. Chief student affairs officers included in the survey are supportive of graduate preparation programs and see direct benefits in working with faculty to improve programs (Sandeen, 1982).

The changes in student enrollment and graduation rates, the decrease in full-time faculty in graduate preparation programs, the static nature of requirements in graduate preparation programs, the turnover rates of practitioners, and other demographic changes such as gender and race all suggest that the field of student affairs faces serious challenges. The principal challenges are to consolidate the gains made by the profession during the past two decades, to meet the demand for qualified professionals, and to accommodate requirements of training and retention of those professionals for the future.

A Look to the Future

The current trends that will form the issues and opportunities in the twenty-first century are all around us: increasing cultural diversity, technological literacy, facility disrepair, and rapidly changing career fields, to name a few. These issues require new attitudes, enhanced skills, and the ability to turn massive information sources into knowledge and wisdom. During the past decade, demographers have told us who the students of the future will be. We need to use this information to focus also on who the staff will be in the twenty-first century.

Ensuring competent staff requires an examination of the futurists' projections regarding the changing expectations of future workers. The basic requirements of careful selection and training of professionals are not expected to change, but the work styles of the profession will have to be adjusted to meet the social conditions of the future.

Deutsch (1985) has predicted that the new workers of the 1990s, raised as "computer babies," will value more autonomy and the ability to direct their own work—in contrast to their bosses, the "TV babies," who prefer participatory management and work teams. Raised in a society that played to new workers as consumers, the new employees of the 1990s will look for choices in all activities just as they have in soda pop, computer programs, and cable television shows. Unlike the unified cultural message the television era brought to the youth of the fifties and sixties, new workers will likely handle diversity and ambiguity by becoming "segmented into a single-issues orientation" (p. 8).

New student affairs staff already are expressing less interest in the diverse and general functions of student affairs and are seeking specialized training in graduate school. Instead of seeing the diversity of student affairs positions as a broader system, some see it as an array of choices. And instead of seeking the past cultural career pattern of generalizable skills, master's students tend to seek specialization reinforced by employers who hire those with demonstrated specialty skills and experiences for particular jobs. The pressure toward specialization makes it difficult for students to value and manage the choices required to be competent generalists. The future requires both talented specialists and flexible generalists.

Recruiting and Enrolling Graduate Students. Established professionals and professional associations can no longer play a passive role in recruiting new students. If student affairs is an "invisible" profession (Stamatakos and Creamer, 1989), then there is a need to recruit new professionals vigorously and to market the career field. Some professionals intentionally seek out college seniors and talk with them about careers in college student personnel, but many do not. Some graduate programs have brochures or send occasional letters to the alumni and friends of their programs requesting referrals of talented students, yet most graduate programs do no recruiting and merely act on applications that come their way. Neither approach is sufficient to meet the dramatic need for acquainting more undergraduates and returning adults with this career field and the need for encouraging more master's degree staff to pursue a doctoral degree.

Dramatic steps must be taken to attract a strong, talented pool of men and women, minorities, disabled students, and other special populations to graduate study in student affairs. It is time to think of new interventions.

Development of recruitment efforts is essential. A vigorous, ongoing national recruiting program led by the national professional associations is needed. Such a program should be intentionally designed to raise awareness of student affairs as a career field in secondary, collegiate, and community agency settings; to increase the pool of applicants to graduate preparation programs; and to provide focused recruiting efforts to underrepresented populations, including ethnic minorities, men, and the disabled. We should note that a new book, *Working with People: Careers in Counseling and Human Development,* will have a chapter devoted to careers in college and university student affairs (Collison and Garfield, forthcoming).

As mentioned, national associations must take the leadership role in marketing the profession. Specifically, the American College Personnel Association (ACPA), the National Association of Student Personnel Administrators (NASPA), and the National Association of Women Deans, Administrators and Counselors (NAWDAC) must act affirmatively. Our suggestions include (1) the development and funding of new national recruitment materials that can be used by all professionals to recruit students systematically, (2) the development of distinct materials targeted at special populations, and (3) expansion of associational functions to reach beyond recruitment of members to recruitment of students to the profession.

Development of new employment strategies is a second possible intervention. Campuses that find it hard to attract new professionals, particularly minority applicants, must try new strategies such as awarding graduate scholarships, fellowships, or assistantships to key talented undergraduate students, particularly minority students—with the agreement that the students would work for that sponsoring school for three or four years following graduation. The talented black resident assistant who feels a bond to the campus might be the very person to sponsor for a graduate degree, with an understanding of two to three years of committed service. Institutions might also retrain other employees through paid leave or sabbaticals.

Another possible intervention is the development of a feeder system. There is no single undergraduate degree that feeds solely into college student personnel graduate study (Stamatakos and Creamer, 1989), but there are tremendous underdeveloped opportunity points of student contact that need attention. We definitely should consider establishing a feeder system for our profession. Professionals and professional associations working with large groups of involved students—such as student peer advisers, resident assistants, commuter and off-campus advisers, minority mentors, orientation assistants, and behavioral science graduates—should design parts of their training to explore professional careers in their functional areas and in college student personnel work in general. Collaborative work with specialty associations such as the Association of College Unions-International (ACU-I), the Association of College and University Housing Officers-International (ACUHO-I), and the National Association of Campus Activities (NACA) could provide pilot-project opportunities. Special recruitment materials to these target populations and ways to involve undergraduates in local, regional, or national conferences would be helpful.

Enhancing Graduate Preparation in College Student Personnel. The preparation of new professionals through college student personnel graduate education programs has two primary components—the classroom experience and the fieldwork requirements. The symbiosis between practitioners and faculty must be addressed as we look to the future. Essential components of that future include design, redesign, and renewal of the content of formal class work to stay relevant to practice; ensuring quality assistantships and fieldwork experiences; and envisioning new in-service professional development strategies that bring new thinking and research to experienced practitioners. We must not think that graduate education is the domain only of teaching faculty or that professional education is accomplished only in graduate study. A dynamic reciprocity must exist between practitioners and faculty for a high-quality graduate program; indeed, "Collaborative involvement between these two campus entities is an essential characteristic of quality preparation in the field of student affairs" (Miller, 1988, p. 108).

Just as undergraduate education was refocused in the wave of the many national reform reports of the early 1980s, graduate education was refocused in the late 1980s. Clarification of the profession and the definition of its mission continue to be important ingredients in the design of graduate programs. Two recent efforts in that direction include the 1989 Joint NASPA/ACPA Task Force on Professional Practice/Preparation Programs and *The State of the Art of Professional Education and Practice, Generativity Project No. 1* (Young and Moore, 1988).

Several prominent issues will need to be addressed as we improve graduate education for the future. First, we must consider the composition of the faculty. Professional standards regarding the desirable number and balance of full-time faculty and part-time practitioner faculty teaching in college student personnel programs must be established. The Council for the Advancement of Standards for Student Services/Development Programs (CAS) (1986) provides the vehicle and opportunity to develop standards and guidelines in this area in conjunction with their work in master's curriculum standards.

It appears essential that all graduate preparation programs should have at least one full-time faculty member and several practitioners teaching courses, but are there conditions under which it might be acceptable for there to be no full-time faculty? This question raises issues regarding the quality of preparation. It seems unacceptable for any major university to reduce full-time faculty and still offer a major program. How can the dilemma of isolated campuses that creatively "educate" their own staff in a small master's program taught by volunteer-practitioners be resolved without such programs becoming so-called credential mills? What standards should be developed for attaching such part-time college student personnel faculty to appropriate sponsoring academic departments—with their cadres of full-time faculty teaching core courses (for example, organizational behavior, counseling, higher education administration, family studies, or curriculum and instruction)—while maintaining the integrity and thrust of the college student personnel program?

It is clear that we must examine the focus of preparation programs. The three curriculum routes at the master's level endorsed in the standards set by the CAS serve the profession well: higher education administration, student development, and counseling. A number of curriculum models have been advanced (Allen,

Julian, Stern, and Walborn, 1987; Brown, 1985; Carpenter and Miller, 1981; Saddlemire, 1988), all with an underlying value of responding to changing needs of students and campus environments. For example, Delworth, Hanson, and Associates (1989) suggest that master's programs should include one course in the history, organization, and philosophy of higher education and student services, two courses in student development and human development theory, one course in models of practice and role expectations, four courses in a core competency such as assessment, consultation, instruction, counseling, or advising, one course in a specialized competency, one course in administration and management, and one year of practice in at least two student services agencies.

Many college student personnel programs are parts of counseling graduate programs. Prior to the implementation of the CAS preparation standards, Rodgers (1977, p. 13) found that 55 percent of the fifty-five graduate preparation programs surveyed required a core of counseling course work. Although a counseling program is valuable for many student affairs positions, Keim's 1987 study found an encouraging shift toward student development and administration programs. As existing programs engage in self-study and as new programs begin, we suggest that consideration be given to expanding programs focusing on higher educational administration or student development.

Doctoral students clearly need college student personnel administration programs to stress generalist roles and to encourage broad systems thinking with an emphasis on leadership, research futures awareness, and vision. This need seems paradoxical; the traditional push at the doctoral level has been toward specialization and singular expertise. Recent writing on graduate study devotes little attention to suggestions for doctoral preparation. While master's programs are guided by the CAS standards, doctoral programs seem to be idiosyncratic and depend on local factors like the professional interests of graduate faculty. As of this writing, CAS member institutions are considering doctoral standards that should be of tremendous benefit in moving toward more consistent quality in doctoral study. For example, Delworth, Hanson, and Associates (1989) recommend that all doctoral students should complete the equivalent of their master's curriculum and should demonstrate (1) competence in both the understanding and production of relevant research and (2) mastery of core and specialized competencies essential for leadership in at least one of the role orientations or models of practice.

Increasing Retention in the Profession. The delicate nature of the early work experience for new professionals needs attention. Just as we want to enroll new freshmen who will be successful graduates and alumni of our colleges and universities, we should want to hire new professionals who will be promotable within or outside our own campuses and who will mitigate any unnecessary attrition factors. Despite high job satisfaction among professionals in the field (Bender, 1980), the turnover rate of professionals who practice student affairs has accelerated. It is estimated that one out of three professionals has been in the field less than three years, and one out of four directors and chief student affairs officers positions turn over each year (Blum, 1989; Stamatakos and Creamer, 1989). Nonetheless, Sandeen (1980, p. 4) notes that the profession has never been as "strong" as it is now and proposes that the lack of a "monolithic structure," "diversity," and the presence of "a large number of highly competent people" in the field all support that affirmation.

Traditional new master's professionals enter the field at approximately twenty-five and twenty-six years of age. Most thirty-year-olds in any career field engage in an examination process of their life plan and career choice, but new professionals in college student personnel engage in that difficult process from the base of entry work, which (1) is usually underpaid, (2) is designed to require total life commitment with little balance of personal and professional life, (3) often lacks the intentional professional development and mentorship so expected from their graduate student experiences, and (4) requires at least regional mobility for career advancement. Some job designs and pay systems appear to be the worst of initiation stereotypes, with messages such as "If you are really dedicated, you will work sixty-hour weeks and enjoy it," or "I came up through this system and made it; it's good for you." Much has been written about the interests of new professionals (Moore and Burns, 1983; Kirby, 1984; Richmond, 1986), yet it is no longer sufficient to study the new professional. We must address some of these critical issues in the retention of new professionals.

Job Redesign. Several entry-level jobs need close examination and redesign. With declining budgets or staff reductions, existing jobs have frequently had more functions added to continue the worthy goal of maintaining a level of needed education and service to students—but at the expense of the possibility of accomplishing that job with quality, professionalism, and personal balance.

Old ways of thinking about traditional entry-level work need the most examination: live-in residence life positions, high-travel admissions officer roles, and those positions requiring intensive day and evening work like athletics, student union programming, and campus activities work, to name a few. We must examine ways to build flextime into the work week, ways to provide paraprofessional and support staff for handling more routine functions to allow maximum use of professional energy, and ways to build career ladders that include branching into related functions—not only upward in the same function. Although participation in outside organizations may require an additional burden of duties, professional associations provide opportunities for professional development and role modeling that do not exist on many campuses. Specialty professionals especially should be encouraged to examine these outside development opportunities.

Remuneration. There is broad diversity among types of institutions in any remuneration comparison, but within the same institution, there must be remuneration equity among student affairs departments and between student affairs and other professional positions, including teaching faculty. Equity in compensation demonstrates a caring and a commitment from the campus. Campuses must engage in remuneration studies for entry-level professional college student personnel positions as well as for other campus professional entry-level positions (for example, hall directors, instructors, assistant professors, and assistant directors in business affairs and finance), and institutions must correct inequities. Instead of perpetuating substandard pay, student affairs decision makers may need to manage their issues and resources creatively by combining some positions to raise pay appropriately, even if the combination means less service or a change in program; opportunities to combine positions are less available on small campuses.

Professional Development and Professional Renewal. Ensuring competent staff requires a work environment that establishes and nurtures continuous learning—not one that perpetuates a status set of hiring criteria including knowledge bases or skills already inadequate at the time they were established. Barr has made recommendations for effective professional development activities in Chapter Eight. And Young (1988, p. 77) correctly observes that "the totality of post-master's degree education requires further conceptualization, involving the career stages of practitioners, their types of work, the roles of providers, methods of instruction and the content of instruction." Intentional professional development programs are essential.

Work environments must support professional renewal in all positions in order to avoid unmanageable stress cycles, situational burnout on specific tasks or at specific times, and isolation. Effective environments foster and fulfill expectations that staff will acquire new knowledge and skills for future issues and opportunities. Professional renewal must come in the day-to-day function and must not be reserved only for spring conventions nor be possible only through job changes (Komives, 1986). Kantor (1977) reminds us that feelings of success must come from something other than upward mobility. Any campus would treasure the English professor who truly enjoys teaching freshmen composition and prefers that assignment; so why is it that the hall director who enjoys freshmen halls is expected to seek promotion and transfer in student affairs? Instead, institutions should acknowledge that motivated student affairs professionals with reasonable work loads and appropriate remuneration will excel in their functional areas and enhance the community.

Recognizing the New Work Coalitions. Student affairs divisions comprise several professions, many professionals, and different specialties; they are characterized by diversity. There will always be student affairs staff who do not have formal experience or graduate degrees in college student personnel, and, in many cases, there should be. We need to validate the many related fields (for example, recreation, social work, health education, medicine, and business management) that prepare professionals to work in their specialties in a student affairs division. Perhaps the two questions on our agenda for the future need to be (1) which positions or functions most need a formal college student personnel education? and (2) what competencies will we require of those from related professions who are engaged in the education and development of students within a student affairs division? We also need to ask what knowledge, attitudes, and skills must all in student affairs have regardless of their roles, and what common base must those who engage in direct education and development of students have?

Clearly, we would not hire unprepared staff for specialty professional roles. For example, a history professor could not become the campus nurse, and an English professor would not become a psychologist-counselor. We must identify the central roles that must be staffed with college student personnel professionals who bring expertise in student development theory and grounding in higher educational systems and intervention strategies. Further, we need to identify alternative educational preparation routes for some positions; for example, we would like the flexibility to hire sociologists in the campus activities office.

For those with other graduate degrees who are working in student education and development programs without benefit of formal college student personnel education, we need to consider a national expectation or standard for certification that would include in-service programs and creative continuing education units (CEUs). Graduate programs must be accessible to those professionals who need to take selected courses without pursuing a degree (Kuh and Komives, 1988). And those in the direct student affairs professions need to establish and define the credentialing or certificate standards for those who apply their related educations to the student personnel field. Without apology, any campus, at minimum, should require those in related fields to complete specific CEUs or certification programs in the college student, their environment, and their development—as a condition of employment.

Perhaps at the extreme, it is time to consider the benefits and drawbacks of a national registry. Unlike licensing that is regulated by state legislation, a registry would implement standards or examinations (or both) that attest to a professional's competence and skill. Various certification methods have been discussed for years. Knock (1977, p. 175) encouraged a careful review of the "professional benefits and liabilities of certification for the field of student affairs." This suggestion presents many problems yet merits serious review.

The Supervisor of the Future. The workers of the future, particularly those in human development fields, will have high expectations for a caring, nurturing supervisor. Workers are concerned about their quality of life, their personal and professional well-being, and their holistic development, including career and work. "The manager's ability to recognize individual lifestyle and preference will become even more crucial as the next new wave of workers, weaned on choice, sweeps into the workplace" (Deutsch, 1985, p. 10). Workers will increasingly expect supervisors to be transformational leaders—intellectually stimulating new solutions to old problems, motivating to extra effort, continuously embracing a shared vision, valuing work, and encouraging each worker to maintain a balanced life as a prerequisite for effective work performance (Bass, 1985).

Supervisory Talents. Supervisors of new professionals are frequently only a few years removed from being new professionals themselves. Supervisors are often frontline professionals as well, counseling students, advising organizations, and carrying their heavy management loads with planning and budgets. Supervisory tasks fade to the background and management by exception becomes the norm. For example, "You're doing fine; I'll let you know if anything needs to be different; just do it." Those who supervise the supervisors of new professionals need to develop expectations and reward systems that recognize the supervisor who develops staff talent and who effectively enhances the transition into this new field of work for their staffs. Professional associations need to provide ongoing workshops and literature targeted at developing effective supervisory skills for new professionals. CAS should explore standards for effective supervision as guidance for this essential relationship. The support of a good, caring supervisor probably contributes most to a new staff member's persistence and motivation. The impact of developmental supervision and mentorship cannot be overstated (Rentz and Saddlemire, 1988).

Formative Staff Evaluation. Supervisors should ensure staff evaluation that requires employees to assess their own knowledge, skills, and attitudes as a way of helping them to meet demands of their current and anticipated work challenges. Supervisory responsibility requires the supervisor and the professional to design and implement regular professional growth plans that ensure responsiveness. The formative nature of this type of evaluation encourages professional development.

Bob Brown's monograph (1988) on performance appraisal provides a wealth of practical suggestions to increase supervisor and professional effectiveness. Carefully designed performance appraisal systems are essential for continued staff development.

Thought Questions to Ensure Competent Staff on Individual Campuses

Embedded in this chapter have been agenda items for individual professionals, for campuses, and for professional associations. Each of us needs to ask, what are we doing locally and nationally to manage the issues? These thought questions can help individual campuses strategically examine future needs to ensure competent staff.

Recruiting New Staff. The following questions should be answered on each campus.

- What shifts in the professional labor pool will affect your future hiring practices?
- Which underrepresented populations do you continuously find it hard to attract or retain in your work setting?
- What can be done to alleviate this problem?
- What fieldwork experiences should you offer graduate students from nearby college student personnel preparation programs?
- If there is not a nearby program, could you develop a summer internship program for such students?

- What regular recruiting system can you establish to acquaint good students with college student personnel career fields?
- What feeder programs in your institution might you target?

Retaining Competent Staff. The retention of competent staff is equally critical for the profession. Answers to the following questions may provide insight into ways that an institution can attack this issue.

- What special issues, including campus and regional needs, shifting needs of students, and changes in curriculum, will require job redesign for staff members?
- What will be the effect of these special issues, and what retraining may be required for current staff to address these issues?
- How should you modify your staff evaluation system to meet developmental goals, to encourage a balance between personal and professional lives, to include staff short- and long-term goals, and to provide needed renewal?
- What work teams could be established to include a range of professionals to address common student issues?
- What leadership development program could you provide for new staff?
- Can you identify departments where there is a "glass ceiling effect" restricting upward mobility?
- Can opportunities for parallel moves be created within the division?
- Can the entry-level positions most in need of job redesign be identified?
- What is the best process for job redesign?
- Are there remuneration inequities that the chief student affairs officer (CSAO) and the institution must address?

Final Words

Student affairs will always attract competent, bright, energetic people who want to help students and work in an environment that is intellectually stimulating and diverse. The challenges for our future as a profession are many, but they can be addressed. First, we must attract enough of these talented people to the profession, and we must become intentional about that process. Second, we must determine the specific and general preparation required for each of the many and diverse positions that constitute student affairs. Third, we must create meaningful, renewing, and well-paid work opportunities; this will require assessment of the current position descriptions, particularly for entry-level positions. Fourth, we are obligated to provide systematic professional development programs focused on the knowledge, skills, and attitudes needed by staff members in the future. Fifth, we must actively supervise and evaluate staff in a manner that promotes growth and retention. Finally, we must actively encourage professional associations to provide leadership in support of these changes.

References

Allen, K. E., Julian, F. H., Stern, C. M., and Walborn, N. C. *Future Perfect: A Guide for Professional Development and Competence.* Columbia, S. C.: National Association of Campus Activities Educational Foundation, 1987.

Astin, A. W., Green, K. C., and Korn, W. S. *The American Freshman: Twenty Year Trends, 1966–1985.* Los Angeles: Higher Education Research Institute, University of California, Los Angeles, 1987.

Bass, B. M. *Leadership and Performance Beyond Expectations.* New York: Free Press, 1985.

Bender, B. E. "Job Satisfaction in Student Affairs." *National Association of Student Personnel Administrators Journal,* 1980, *18* (2), 2–9.

Blum, D. E. "24-Pct. Turnover Rate Found for Administrators; Some Officials Are Surprised by Survey Results." *Chronicle of Higher Education,* March 29, 1989, pp. A13-A14.

Brown, R. D. "Graduate Education for the Student Development Profession: A Content and Process Model." *National Association of Student Personnel Administrators Journal,* 1985, *22,* 38–43.

Brown, R. D. *Performance Appraisal as a Tool for Staff Development.* New Directions for Student Services, no. 43. San Francisco: Jossey-Bass, 1988.

Carpenter, D. S., and Miller, T. K. "An Analysis of Professional Development in Student Affairs Work." *National Association of Student Personnel Administrators Journal,* 1981, *19* (1), 2–11.

Carpenter, D. S., Miller, T. K., and Winston, R. B., Jr. "Toward the

Professionalization of Student Affairs." *National Association of Student Personnel Administrators Journal,* 1980, *18* (2), 16-22.

Collison, B., and Garfield, N. (eds.). *Careers in Counseling and Human Development.* Alexandria, Va.: American Association of Counseling and Development, forthcoming.

Council for the Advancement of Standards. *CAS Standards for Student Services/Development Programs.* Iowa City: American College Testing Service, 1986.

Delworth, U., Hanson, G. R., and Associates. *Student Services: A Handbook for the Profession.* (2nd ed.) San Francisco: Jossey-Bass, 1989.

Deutsch, R. E. "Tomorrow's Work Force: New Values in the Workplace." In E. Cornish (ed.), *Careers Tomorrow: The Outlook for Work in a Changing World—Selections from The Futurist.* Bethesda, Md.: World Future Society, 1985.

Evans, N. J. "Attrition of Student Affairs Professionals: A Review of the Literature." *Journal of College Student Development,* 1988, *29* (1), 19-24.

Hamrick, F. A., and Carlisle, L. W. "Gender Diversity in Student Affairs: Administrative Perception and Recommendations," *NASPA Journal,* 1990, *27.*

Hyman, R. E. "Graduate Preparation for Professional Practice: A Difference of Perceptions." *National Association of Student Personnel Administrators Journal,* 1988, *26* (2), 143-150.

Kantor, R. M. *Men and Women of the Corporation.* New York: Basic Books, 1977.

Keim, M. R. "Data from the Directory of Graduate Preparation Programs in College Student Personnel (1973, 1977, 1980, 1984, 1987)." Paper presented at the annual Midwest meeting of Faculty in Student Affairs, Michigan State University, Lansing, Oct. 1987.

Kirby, A. F. "The New Professional." In A. F. Kirby and D. Woodard (eds.), *Career Perspectives in Student Affairs.* Washington, D.C.: National Association of Student Personnel Administrators, 1984.

Knock, G. H. "Future Developments in Professional Preparation." In G. H. Knock (ed.), *Perspectives on the Preparation of Student Affairs Professionals.* Alexandria, Va.: American Association of Counseling and Development, 1977.

Komives, S. R. "Facing Crises: Counselors' Personal and Professional Responses." In M. Rose and S. Alexander (eds.), *Power Keys in America: Counseling Interventions.* Alexandria, Va.: American Association of Counseling and Development, 1986.

Kuh, G. D., and Komives, S. R. " 'The Right Stuff': Some Thoughts on Attracting Good People to Student Affairs Work." In R. B. Young and L. V. Moore (eds.), *The State of the Art of Professional Education and Practice, Generativity Project No. 1.* Alexandria, Va.: American College Personnel Association, 1988.

McEwen, M. K., Engstrom, C. M., and Williams, T. E. "Gender Diversity Within the Student Affairs Profession." *Journal of College Student Development,* 1990, *31,* 47–53.

Miller, T. K. "Challenge, Support and Response: An Epilogue." In R. B. Young and L. V. Moore (eds.), *The State of the Art of Professional Education and Practice, Generativity Project No. 1.* Alexandria, Va.: American College Personnel Association, 1988.

Moore, L., and Burns, M. "Recruiting the Entry Level Professional and the Middle Manger in Student Affairs." *Journal of College and University Student Housing,* 1983, *13* (1), 19–23.

National Center for Educational Statistics. *Digest of Educational Statistics.* U.S. Department of Education, OERI publication #CS 88-600. Washington, D.C.: U.S. Government Printing Office, 1988.

Newton, F. D., and Hellenga, G. "Assessment of Learning and Process Objectives in a Student Personnel Training Program." *Journal of College Student Personnel,* 1974, *15* (6), 492–497.

Rentz, A. L., and Saddlemire, G. L. "Career Paths in Student Affairs." In A. L. Rentz and G. L. Saddlemire (eds.), *Student Affairs Functions in Higher Education.* Springfield, Ill.: Thomas, 1988.

Richmond, D. R. "The Young Professional at the Small College; Tips for Professional Success and Personal Survival." *National Association of Student Personnel Administrators Journal,* 1986, *23* (2), 44–49.

Rickard, S. T. "Titles of Chief Student Affairs Officers: Institutional Autonomy or Professional Standardization?" *National Association of Student Personnel Administrators Journal,* 1985, *23* (2), 44–49.

Rodgers, R. F. "Student Personnel Work as Social Intervention." In G. H. Knock (ed.), *Perspectives on the Preparation of Student*

Affairs Professionals. Alexandria, Va.: American Association of Counseling and Development, 1977.

Saddlemire, G. "Designing a Curriculum for Student Services/Development Professionals." In R. B. Young and L. V. Moore (eds.), *The State of the Art of Professional Education and Practice, Generativity Project No. 1.* Alexandria, Va.: American College Personnel Association, 1988.

Sandeen, A. "Student Services in the '80's: A Decade of Decisions." *National Association of Student Personnel Administrators Journal,* 1980, *19* (3), 2-9.

Sandeen, A. "Professional Preparation Programs in Student Personnel Services in Higher Education: A National Assessment by Chief Student Affairs Officers." *National Association of Student Personnel Administrators Journal,* 1982, *20* (2), 51-58.

Schuh, J. H. "Selected Characteristics of Students Enrolled in Doctoral Programs in Student Affairs, 1988-89." Unpublished paper, Wichita, Kansas, 1989.

Stamatakos, L. C. "Student Affairs Progress Toward Professionalism Recommendations for Action—Part 1." *Journal of College Student Personnel,* 1981a, *22,* 105-113.

Stamatakos, L. C. "Student Affairs Progress Toward Professionalism: Recommendations for Action—Part 2." *Journal of College Student Personnel,* 1981b, *22,* 197-207.

Stamatakos, L. C., and Creamer, D. G. "The Current Condition of College Student Affairs Preparation Programs: Demographics, Analysis, and Recommendations." Unpublished manuscript, Joint ACPA/NASPA Task Force on Professional Practice/Preparation Programs, Washington, D.C., 1989.

Young, R. B., and Moore, L. V. (eds.). *The State of the Art of Professional Education and Practice, Generativity Project No. 1.* Alexandria, Va.: American College Personnel Association, 1988.

Chapter 12

Strengthening Ties to Academic Affairs

Suzanne S. Brown

Collaboration, a term long associated with intellectual and artistic endeavors, has gained new currency in higher education circles, along with a closely related term, *partnerships.* Collaborative research is a time-honored approach to academic work, but collaborative teaching, collaborative learning, partnerships between colleges and schools, and partnerships between higher education and business and industry are newer applications of the concept.

Collaboration and partnership connote relationships of somewhat greater intensity than does the word *cooperation,* and they generally imply a relationship among equals pursuing a goal of mutual interest. A group of educators promoting collaboration in undergraduate education carries the concept even further: "Rooted in the belief that learning is inherently social in nature, [collaboration] stresses common inquiry as the basic learning process. Although academically and culturally challenging, it benefits participants by making them more active as learners, more interactive as teachers, more balanced as researchers, more effective as leaders, and more humane as individuals" (Whipple, 1987, p. 3).

It may seem inappropriate for professionals in academic affairs and in student affairs to discuss moving from relations to collaborations and from cooperation to partnerships. Many feel that relations between these two groups are tenuous and that existing cooperation often derives from organizational necessity or ad hoc arrangements rather than from genuine interest in working together toward mutual goals. For years, student affairs professionals have been lamenting the lack of relationships with their academic colleagues and have been devising new ways or revamping old ways of bridging the gap. Academicians, on the other hand, have given little attention to this problem. Many faculty, especially on large campuses, are hardly aware of the existence of student affairs professionals, much less of their goals. Academic administrators are more likely to be aware of their student affairs counterparts, but they tend to view their functions as separate and unequal. Nonetheless, at most colleges and universities, relationships between academic and student affairs abound.

This chapter illustrates the range of relationships between academic and student affairs. We will consider barriers to collaboration and will define conditions for moving toward collaboration. Finally, we will focus on several major issues in our shared future that call for collaboration.

Commonplace Relations

The chart of Commonplace Relations Between Academic and Student Affairs (Exhibit 12.1) illustrates the broad range of relations that do occur with some frequency. Although a few of the examples are of fairly recent vintage (retention task forces, wellness programs, AIDS education), others date back to the days of deans of men and deans of women. A few represent bright ideas that were quickly picked up elsewhere; others are so common and obvious that they are often taken for granted. The chart also illustrates different approaches to, as well as varying intensities of, relationships between academic and student affairs.

At the lowest end of the intensity scale are practices such as providing monitored study areas, computer or typing rooms, study lounges or browsing libraries in the student center, and faculty office space or classrooms in the residence halls. Such practices demonstrate student affairs staff support for the academic mission of the institution, but they probably involve no direct relationship

Exhibit 12.1. Commonplace Relations Between Academic and Student Affairs.

Standing Committees or Councils (involving faculty, student affairs staff, and often students)

Academic standards committee
University judiciary
Cultural programming
Lecture series committee
Commission for women
Minority roundtable
Retention committee or task force
Long-range planning committee
Career planning advisory council
Student center advisory board
Health services advisory board
Advising committee
Freshman-year committee
Council on undergraduate life
Bookstore advisory board
Fee allocation committee

University Programs or Functions (often involving both academic and student affairs staff)

Admissions
Freshman seminars (focusing on topics such as goal-setting, time management, university resources, academic requirements, and academic integrity—often team taught by faculty and student affairs professionals)
Mentorship programs for minority students
Advising for undeclared students
University day-care centers
Academic support programs (development courses, early warning systems, supplemental instruction, study skills training, tutoring)
Student internship and volunteer programs
New faculty orientation
Honors program (student affairs professionals working with honors coordinator or committee to provide appropriate cocurricular experiences for students in an honors program)
Student newspaper or radio station
Assessment of student satisfaction or institutional environment

Residence Halls

Special discipline-oriented halls or academic floors
Faculty offices or classrooms in the residence halls
Regular faculty presentations or discussions in the halls and Greek houses (fireside chats after dinner or afternoon high tea sessions)
Faculty participation in the training of resident assistants
Faculty involvement in floor programs for workshops in the halls
Computer rooms, typing rooms, browsing rooms (with good newspapers and magazines), music rooms in the halls
Organization of study groups or reading and discussion groups in the halls

Exhibit 12.1. Commonplace Relations Between Academic and Student Affairs, Cont'd.

Provision of monitored study areas
Tutoring programs in the residence halls
Academic recognition dinners in the halls (recognizing special groups of students and individual faculty members identified by students)

Health and Counseling Services

Cooperative campuswide wellness programs (cosponsored, for example, by the health center and the physical education department)
Faculty involvement in noncredit educational programs (on AIDS, sexuality, interpersonal relationships, alcohol and drug abuse, dieting, for example) or student affairs involvement in classroom presentations on these or other health-related topics
Coordination between academic advising and personal counseling
Appointment of a counseling center liaison to each major academic unit
Counseling center staff providing workshops for faculty advisers
Faculty and staff working together to train and supervise students in health-related majors to serve as health aides in living units
Cooperative programming and resource sharing between the women's studies program and the women's resource center

Career Planning and Placement

Staff visits to classrooms and academic department meetings to discuss career opportunities in a given field
Faculty involvement in identifying and hosting on-campus interviewers and in identifying alumni who can advise students about careers
Career center staff offering workshops for faculty advisers on helping students with career planning
Workshops for students on business or health-related careers (for example) presented by faculty or by a team of faculty and career center staff

Student Activities and Cultural Programming

Faculty advising of student organizations (student affairs professionals may provide training, support, and recognition for faculty advisers)
Involving faculty in the student program board planning of interdisciplinary symposia on significant themes (may include speakers, debates, panels, artistic presentations)
Working with particular academic departments to mount special programs (for example, a Model United Nations, madrigal dinner, jazz festival, Latin American Week, Black History Month, dinner theater series, and so forth)
Faculty and student affairs staff involvement with students in planning an annual academic festival or university showcase

Exhibit 12.1. Commonplace Relations Between Academic and Student Affairs, Cont'd.

A committee of faculty, student affairs staff, and students to promote student participation in campus cultural and performing arts programs
Faculty requiring or encouraging students to attend programs sponsored by the student center or by the student programming board (foreign films or speakers, for example) related to specific courses
Art exhibits or sales in residence halls and the student center
Workshops, "teaser" performances, and master classes or discussion sessions by visiting artists or speakers in the residence halls, the student center, or classrooms
Informal brown-bag-lunch discussion series with faculty members on preannounced topics in the student center
Special programs to bring faculty and nontraditional or commuter students together
Involvement of faculty in student-affairs-sponsored leadership training programs for students
International programs involving faculty and students (including trips as well as on-campus programs)
Recreation programs (for example, sports competitions, camping trips, ski clubs) designed for faculty, staff, and students

Miscellaneous

Faculty serving as consultants to student affairs units or on review teams evaluating student affairs agencies or programs
Student affairs representation on academic program review teams
Working with faculty to develop student projects that assist student affairs operations, for example, having students in a marketing class do a marketing plan for the student center, students in an advertising or public relations course design a campaign for the health center or academic assistance center, students in a sociology course do a study of interracial relations in the residence halls
Faculty and student affairs professionals who hold joint appointments in an academic department and student affairs unit
Cooperation between faculty and student affairs professionals in arranging and supervising internships or practicums for graduate students (especially those enrolled in graduate training programs for student affairs professionals)

---

with academic personnel. Other instances, including most of those listed in the career planning and student activities sections of Exhibit 12.1, involve ad hoc, generally short-term relations between faculty members and student affairs professionals. Such relationships, usually initiated by a student affairs staff member, may entail a faculty member's doing a favor for a student affairs department or for students, or student affairs professionals' providing a service to faculty members. At best, each party benefits from the interaction. These relationships are of greatest value when they serve to foster or enhance out-of-class interaction between faculty and students, as they often do.

Cooperative Relationships. Cooperation between academic and student affairs personnel is most common within the borderline or boundary-spanning functions of the institution—offices or programs that report to academic officers at some institutions and to student affairs officers at others. Admissions, registration, advising, academic support and tutorial programs, new student orientation, career planning and placement, and counseling all fall into this category. Given the increased emphasis during the past decade on enrollment management, retention, and freshman-year programs, these functions have received much greater attention than they once did and, in some cases, have provided the foundation for genuine partnerships between academic and student affairs (Stodt and Klepper, 1987). Too often, however, academic and student affairs staff merely fulfill the particular tasks assigned to them in carrying out such functions rather than work collaboratively to design, implement, and evaluate a program in terms of its broader institutional goals.

Organized Groups. Standing committees or councils that meet with some regularity provide the best opportunities for many student affairs professionals to get to know a few academic colleagues. Occasionally, such groups are formed for the express purpose of bringing academic and student affairs people together to discuss matters of mutual concern (Nutter and Hurst, 1988). If an institutional committee is well managed, and if the charge is of interest to members and of significance to the institution, then relations may progress to cooperation or even collaboration. But standing university committees are rarely catalysts for dynamic interaction among the various constituencies represented on them. At best, they serve to establish acquaintances that may lead to subsequent, more substantive relationships in other contexts.

Many of the commonplace relations listed in Exhibit 12.1 offer the potential for collaborative efforts between academic personnel and student affairs professionals. In most cases, the focus is, as it should be, on students, and the purpose is to enhance some dimension of students' educational experience or quality of life on the college campus. Why, then, do such relations rarely move from simple interaction or cooperation to the more intensive, ongoing type of relationship referred to here as collaboration?

Barriers to Collaboration

Some of the barriers to collaboration between academic and student affairs are no different from those that impede collaboration among groups at most institutions. Because of the high degree of autonomy afforded faculty and the fragmented organizational structure characteristic of colleges and universities, collaboration does not emerge naturally.

Competitive Climate. Some attribute the lack of collaborative relationships in the so-called academic community to the dominance of a competitive modus operandi (Astin, 1988). Administrators and faculty may lend lip service to the value of cooperation and teamwork, but traditional approaches to teaching, testing, promotion, tenure, curriculum development, allocation of resources, and relations with other institutions involve and promote competition. Palmer (1987) traces the emphasis on individualism and competition, as opposed to collaboration and community, in academe to a deeper root—the way of knowing (characterized by objectivity, analysis, experimentation, separation of subject and object) that dominates academic disciplines, including the humanities. Kuh, Shedd, and Whitt (1987) suggest that the pervasiveness of this epistemology and the differential valuing of the objective and the subjective, of the cognitive and the affective, are at the heart of the gap between academic and student affairs.

Resource Limitations. A less complicated but equally formidable barrier is limitation of resources. If collaborative efforts represent a real or perceived addition to people's normal work assignments or appear to represent a more time-consuming approach to completing those assignments, reluctance is inevitable. Few jobs in higher education afford much spare time. And if additional funding or new uses of existing funds are required to support a collaborative effort, the resource barrier is even more difficult to surmount. Collaboration may, of course, result in more efficient use of time and money, but few are likely to make that assumption in advance.

Differences in Orientation. Barriers arise from both real and perceived differences between academicians and student affairs professionals. There are differences in the organizational structures and reward systems, in background and training, in norms and cultures, and in goals and priorities. (See Chapter Eight.) Faculty are trained to be scholars in their academic disciplines. They are biologists, physicists, anthropologists, philosophers, sociologists, historians, and art or literary critics. Ironically, only those who teach in colleges of education are trained to be educators, and since education is not an academic discipline per se, its practitioners are often regarded as second-class citizens in the academy. These practitioners include many student affairs professionals whose degrees in student personnel may not be perceived as demanding the same kind of intellectual rigor as graduate degrees in the arts and sciences. (See Chapter Eleven.)

Faculty are provided little if any background about the nature and structure of the organizations in which they are likely to spend their careers. In addition, faculty receive little training in performing the task to which they will devote much of their professional time—teaching. Until recently at least, few faculty had any conception of how students learn or of the impact of the outside-the-classroom environment on student performance and retention. Traditionally, faculty have considered the primary functions of the university to be creating, preserving, and transmitting knowledge while promoting and safeguarding the so-called life of the mind. Their professional rewards have followed from these values. Moreover, recognition, promotion, and tenure at most institutions are based more on scholarly contributions to an academic discipline than on professional contributions to the education of students or to the welfare of the institution.

The orientation of student affairs professionals is quite different. For them, the institutional emphasis is on the student and the process of growth and development that students, regardless of age, undergo during their time in college. The theoretical underpinnings of the student affairs profession derive from human development theory, translated by Chickering (1969), Brown (1972), Miller and Prince (1976), and others into student development theories. (See Chapter Three.) Student affairs professionals often have regarded human development theories as providing intellectual legitimacy for their work, thus assuring their equal status within the academic community. Student development theory indeed has provided fertile ground for both program development and research, but too often it has blinded its practitioners to the fundamental mission of most colleges and universities. Brown (1972) and Miller and Prince (1976) clearly called for collaboration between student affairs professionals and faculty in development of students as whole persons, including the physical, social, and emotional dimensions generally neglected in the college classroom. But neither faculty nor student personnel staff at most institutions ever heard or understood the call. Then, as now, too many student affairs professionals failed to understand and participate in intellectual pursuits, which are, in fact, at the heart of higher education.

Nearly a decade ago, Daryl Smith (1982, p. 55) summed up the unintended, but by that time all too evident, negative consequences of the student development model: "The isolation of [student affairs from the rest of the institution] emerges because the model does not address widely held understandings about the purpose of higher education or unique institutional goals. In particular, the model has failed to address the institution's mission and the centrality of the role of academic and intellectual development. This causes student development to appear anti-intellectual. Furthermore, because in most institutions, the designated turf of student affairs is explicitly non-academic, the problem is exacerbated. As a consequence, student affairs professionals become isolated, not trusted, and restricted in their ability to participate fully in the changes and improvements in the educational environment."

Given these fundamental differences in orientation, culture, and goals, coupled with the organizational barriers to collaboration endemic to colleges and universities, it may seem surprising that any level of cooperation and interaction exists between faculty and student affairs professionals. It may seem foolish to talk about expanding and intensifying these relationships, but the conditions for collaboration are within reach today, and the issues calling for collaboration are critical to the future of higher education.

Conditions for Collaboration

The primary condition for collaboration, from the standpoint of student affairs staff, is recognition that "the academic mission of the institution is preeminent" (National Association of Student Personnel Administrators, 1987, p. 8). From this assumption, it follows that the essential role of student affairs is supporting the academic mission of the institution. (See Chapter Two.) Judging by the current literature (Brown, 1988; Mitchell and Roof, 1989; O'Brien, 1989; Webb, 1987; Smith, 1988; Smith and Weith, 1985) and by the number of program sessions on academic-student affairs partnerships at both the National Association of Student Personnel Administrators and American College Personnel Association conferences in recent years, it appears that this assumption is widely subscribed to in the profession today.

A related condition for collaboration is improved understanding among student affairs professionals of the nature of faculty preparation, priorities, and day-to-day activities. Those in student affairs must appreciate the difficulties faculty face in meeting their obligations while trying to keep current in their academic disciplines or professional fields. Such appreciation is essential for those developing student personnel preparation programs in order that the programs contribute to young professionals' understanding of the academic culture.

A return to a common practice of welcoming into the student affairs profession people with advanced degrees in history or English or biology (people who, at the same time, have an interest in and aptitude for learning the student affairs profession on the job) could contribute to enlarged understanding as well as to the enhanced academic stature of student affairs professionals. Inclusion of persons trained in the arts and sciences would also provide a richer mix of people to become involved in collaborative efforts.

In academic affairs, on the other hand, several conditions favorable to collaboration have recently emerged. Faculty development programs, with a strong emphasis on instructional development, have expanded in the past decade. There is growing recognition among faculty that the term *professional development* invokes more than disciplinary association meetings, sabbatical leaves, or release time to pursue individual research or scholarly activity. On-campus workshops, departmental retreats, peer mentoring, instructional consultation, curriculum development projects, seminars, and programs involving interdisciplinary groups have become common features in faculty development programs. Such programs tend to broaden faculty conceptions of their role as professionals and of their obligations to students. Grants are often available, both at the institutional level and from external sources, for collaborative ventures of various kinds. Indeed, there is probably no surer way of stimulating collaboration between faculty and student affairs professionals than establishing a local small-grants program to fund worthwhile projects involving such collaboration.

On another front, the narrow "publish or perish" faculty career path is being called into question (Boyer, 1987; Schuster and Bowen, 1985; National Institute of Education, 1984). Referring to academic research as "a sacred animal much in need of attention," Joseph Katz (1988, p. 14) asked, "How productive is it really? How many faculty really do it? Does it require all the time that is being spent on it? What is the relative value to the society of research versus the benefit of helping a new generation define itself in intellectually more productive ways?"

New and broader definitions of scholarship are emerging (Rice and Sheridan, 1989). These definitions recognize that effective integration, application, and communication of knowledge, as well as the discovery or creation of knowledge through research, are viable forms of scholarly activity. Cross (1988) has called upon college faculty to engage in "classroom research," which, in effect, makes teaching the focus of scholarship. The new emphasis on assessment of student outcomes is yet another force moving some faculty to shift their focus, at least a bit, from the knowledge they teach to the students they teach.

Finally, for the first time in some years, there are significant numbers of new faculty members on many college campuses, and new faculty will be hired in ever-increasing numbers during the next fifteen years. Many of these new faculty will be socialized to the traditional standards, norms, and expectations of an academic career through their graduate school experience, but recommendations to broaden that experience are in the wind (Lapidus, 1987; Sheridan, 1988). To the extent that institutions shift their emphases and their reward systems, younger faculty may be more open to working collaboratively on projects intended to improve the quality of undergraduate education.

Improving the quality of undergraduate education is the phrase that best sums up many of the challenges with which higher education was confronted, both from within and from without, during the 1980s. These challenges provide the most significant conditions, as well as the major focal points, for genuine collaboration between academic and student affairs in the nineties.

Contemporary Issues That Call for Collaboration

The major issues in higher education, as discussed below, all have significant implications for student affairs. Only occasionally, however, are these implications spelled out by the public pundits, university presidents, academic officers, and higher education researchers who publish and pontificate on the issues. With regard to several of these issues, student affairs professionals probably have greater knowledge and experience than do most of their academic colleagues—a fact not widely recognized by either group. It is true that collaborative efforts are already underway to address some of these issues; and a few success stories can be told. However, for the most part, the organizational structures and strategies for dealing with these institutional questions in a collaborative fashion remain to be developed.

Ernest Boyer and his associates (1987) forcefully pointed out that, due to a number of conflicts, discontinuities, and tensions that characterize most undergraduate institutions, the undergraduate experience in America is much less vital and enriching than it could or should be. To restore vitality, "connections" must be made. "All parts of campus life—recruitment, orientation, curriculum, teaching, residence hall living and the rest—must relate to one another and contribute to a sense of wholeness" (Boyer, 1987, p. 8). Surely, this is a call for collaboration between academic and student affairs. And the goal of such collaboration, whatever the means, should be to improve the quality of undergraduate education.

Improvement of Teaching and Learning. As the segments of society from which college students come and the proportions of high school graduates who pursue postsecondary education have expanded, the traditional modes of college teaching have become less and less effective. Research has documented the differences in learning styles, academic values, and personal characteristics between the so-called new students and the more affluent and academically oriented college students of the fifties and sixties (Cross, 1976; Davis and Schroeder, 1983). In spite of the dramatic increase in remedial course work, the tremendous growth in research on teaching and learning in the college classroom (Claxton and Murrell, 1987; McKeachie and others, 1986), and the recent blossoming of instructional development centers, the Carnegie Foundation for the Advancement of Teaching still found widespread evidence of "a mismatch between faculty and student expectations, a gap that left both parties unfulfilled" (Boyer, 1987, p. 140).

If teaching is to be effective, three domains of knowledge must be brought into play: (1) knowledge of the subject matter, (2) knowledge of the students—who they are, "where they are at," and how they learn—and (3) knowledge of a variety of pedagogical techniques that can help bridge the gap between the subject matter and the student (Edgerton, 1988). Student affairs professionals, presumably, are the experts on students and should know something about pedagogy as well. College faculty, as a whole, have shown remarkable resistance to moving beyond the knowledge of the subject matter. Schroeder, DiTiberio, and Kalsbeek (1988) propose the role of information broker for student affairs staff and describe the program they have developed at Saint Louis University for collecting and analyzing data on students' learning styles in relation to their academic progress. They provide the information to faculty colleagues and help them translate it into changes in curriculum and classroom activities. Sherhofer (1989) recommends that student affairs staff become familiar with learning-style theory in order to help students gain a better understanding of their learning preferences and strengths and to help faculty design teaching strategies that are congruous with a greater diversity of learning styles. Such information can help in planning cocurricular programs that emphasize particular learning styles—especially more affective, concrete, and experiential modes that are less commonly brought into play in the classroom.

Involvement in Learning, the title of the 1984 final report of the National Institute of Education, rapidly became a catchphrase for the calls for improvement in teaching. Patricia Cross (1987, p. 4) summarizes this research in what she confesses are "embarrassingly obvious" conclusions: "1. When students are actively involved in the learning task, they learn more than when they are passive recipients of instruction. . . . 2. Students generally learn what they practice."

Depending on the nature and quality of the lecture and on the interest and learning styles of the students, the traditional and still most common approach to college teaching, the lecture, can be effective. On the whole, however, the lecture approach is less likely to engage students with the subject matter than are a number of other teaching strategies: discussion, collaborative learning, the case method, guided independent study, joint student-faculty research, or interactive computer programs.

The value of engaging teaching strategies comes as no surprise to student affairs professionals who understood the value of student involvement in campus life long before the countless studies of retention demonstrated the difference it makes. In addition to working to get students involved in campus life, what can student affairs professionals do to get students involved in their academic work? Working with the campus instructional development center staff or with individual faculty who have indicated an interest in experimenting with new forms of instruction, student affairs professionals have the potential to do the following:

- Serve as consultants to faculty in organizing cooperative learning projects or introducing small group discussions into their classroom activity
- Serve as so-called master learners, helping students and instructors bridge gaps through constructive feedback
- Organize discussion groups for freshmen enrolled in common courses, modeling how to use out-of-class discussion or study groups as an effective approach to learning
- Identify those courses with particularly high rates of withdrawals and low grades, and offer to work collaboratively with the instructors to improve students' success rates
- Propose collaborative classroom research projects or studies of the relationship between achievement of specific course objectives and carefully designed out-of-class activities
- Design cocurricular experiences to reinforce or extend the subject matter of specific courses, especially courses that are part of the general education curriculum

If some of the calls for change in graduate education are implemented, one of the new futures of student affairs professionals could be to participate in the preparation of the future professoriate. In order to learn more about the students they will be teaching and the organizations in which they will be working as faculty, doctoral students might be encouraged to take one-semester assistantships in student affairs departments. Higher education today is well aware of the need to attract and support a larger number of doctoral students to fill the rapidly depleting ranks of faculty nationwide. Hence, the time may be ripe for student affairs professionals to propose this kind of collaboration.

Curriculum Reform. Calls for reform in the curriculum, especially the general education curriculum, have been every bit as loud and urgent as the calls for improvement in teaching and learning. Employers, legislators, and the media have all complained that college graduates too often lack solid writing and communication skills, are inept at interpersonal relations, do not know how to think critically, and fail to transfer knowledge and skills from one realm to another. Critics from within higher education bemoan the vocationalism of contemporary students, their lack of knowledge of their cultural heritage, the overspecialization of the faculty, and the fragmentation of the curriculum. Although few may agree on the precise components of a liberal education, most have agreed in recent years that the link between a liberal education and a baccalaureate degree is in grave need of repair (Project on Redefining the Meaning and Purpose of Baccalaureate Degrees, 1985; Boyer, 1987; Gaff, 1983).

Committees to review and revise general (or liberal) education requirements have been appointed on campus after campus. Some have succeeded admirably; others have succumbed under the difficulties of gaining both intellectual and political consensus and overcoming the inevitable resistance to change (Gaff, 1983).

Generally, the first step for such committees is defining the desired outcomes of general education. The lists of objectives or outcomes that have emerged from the many efforts to overhaul general education bear remarkable resemblances. Competence in reasoning and critical thinking, effective communication skills, tolerance of ambiguity, understanding different cultures, esthetic appreciation, ability to make value-based distinctions and decisions, and understanding of social institutions and of the relationship between the individual and society are some of the commonalities among the goals that have been identified. Indeed, these goals have long been the desired outcomes of a liberal education, although they have often been implicit rather than explicit.

The striking commonalities between the goals of liberal education and those of student development have been recognized in the student affairs literature far less frequently than one might expect. Berg (1983, p. 14) illustrates the similarities, stressing that "student development, in theory and in practice, clearly supports and complements the liberal arts mission." Based on this premise, he recommends first, that student affairs professionals work harder to educate the faculty in student development theory and how it promotes the goals of the liberal arts curriculum and second, that they work to ensure their own operations are grounded in student development principles.

Kuh, Shedd, and Whitt (1987) also spell out the parallels between the goals of liberal education and those of student development, but they are less sanguine about the possibility of persuading faculty that their counterparts in student affairs should be recognized as equal partners in the educational process. They advise student affairs professionals to "build on the similarities between student affairs work and liberal education by continuing to collaborate with like-minded faculty members to create environments conducive to learning both inside and outside the classroom" (p. 257).

What is less often recognized or articulated by the student affairs profession is that the liberal education curriculum promotes student development and did so long before the student development model was created. The active learning of literature, philosophy, anthropology, psychology, history, the natural sciences—or any of the arts and sciences disciplines—contributes to the development of identity, competence, and autonomy, to the development of tolerance and appreciation of diversity, to the understanding and acceptance of interdependence, to the clarification of and commitment to values, and to the development of the whole person.

Contrary to the assumptions of some student development enthusiasts, the study of the arts and sciences offers more than just cognitive development. Human experience, complete with values, feelings, and passion, is at the heart of the humanities and most of the social sciences. Math and computer science are essential for practical competence in the contemporary world. And the natural sciences help us understand our place in a much larger universe and engender in many appreciation of the interdependence among all living things, new values, and strong commitments.

Faculty have often failed to recognize and articulate the links between their disciplinary knowledge and the lives of their students. Their teaching strategies often put the premium not just on cognitive learning but also on passive learning. Perhaps only the best among them convey to undergraduates the passion they feel for their subject matter, and more often than not, they fail to help students understand why the general education portion of the curriculum is required, why it is important, and what students should expect to gain from it. Indeed, because academic status is associated with teaching upper division and graduate courses rather than general education, many faculty devalue general education. This is an attitude quickly picked up by students ("I just have one more general education course to get out of the way") and often thoughtlessly echoed by student affairs professionals.

The recent general education reform movement—coupled with the emphasis on more active, involving teaching strategies and with ongoing efforts to improve academic advising—has tried to address these issues. The extent to which student affairs professionals can assist in this process by serving as advocates, explicators, facilitators, and reinforcers of the liberal education curriculum is the extent to which we can help students understand the developmental significance of the core academic disciplines. When that occurs, student affairs professionals will be not only contributing to the mission of the institution but also addressing the goals of student development.

Improving the Academic Climate. In a September 1988 address, Ernest Boyer lavished praise upon the "creative," "coherent," "well-crafted," "thought provoking" University Studies program recently instituted at Southeast Missouri State University. It is one of very few general education programs that has deliberately designed a parallel cocurricular component. In the course of his address, Boyer referred to the Carnegie Foundation's recent study of undergraduate education (Boyer, 1987) saying, "I was enormously struck by the fact that there are two cultures in the academy today. There's the culture of the classroom and there's the culture of life outside the classroom, and these are enormously divided. The classroom culture has a clear academic goal and on many campuses the out-of-classroom experience has no guidance, little purpose, and often the climate can only be described as 'low-grade decadence' " ("Boyer Address . . . ," 1988, p. 4).

Student affairs professionals on many campuses may justifiably take exception to his harsh characterization of the out-of-class climate. Others might simply wish to remind him that many forces beyond the control of the institution influence students' activities and behavior when they leave the classroom, laboratory, or library. Nonetheless, the student affairs profession cannot ignore this kind of criticism. Even more than their academic colleagues do, student affairs professionals recognize the influence of campus climate on student persistence, student satisfaction, and student development.

Often, however, in their effort to promote student development along those dimensions not addressed in the classroom, student affairs professionals have directed their attention primarily to ensuring that ample social, recreational, and leadership opportunities are available to students. Few would question the need for such opportunities, but today's students, many of whom do not come by intellectual pursuits naturally, need reinforcement of their academic interests, skills, and struggles outside the classroom. Those who are motivated and excited about their course work need to know that they are not alone and that they can share that excitement with their peers. Those who get their kicks from getting high grades need to learn that they are missing the heart of the matter, and those who have not yet discovered that learning can be exciting, even fun, need somehow to be led to that discovery.

Gaff (1983), a prime mover in the general education reform movement, is now calling for a "second wave" of reform, which takes as its conceptual focus "the idea of the college culture." All aspects of the college including recruitment practices, publications, approaches to faculty hiring and evaluation, and the budgeting process—as well as the extracurricular life—should further the values and goals of the college's liberal education curriculum. Recognizing that student affairs professionals and other administrative staff have been conspicuously absent from the debates about general education, Gaff notes that "they are important numerically and have much to contribute to the overall education of the students. They can help set high expectations, establish an intellectual tone in the student culture, and carry forward learning goals for students beyond formal coursework" (p. 14).

The student affairs profession claims to understand so-called milieu management and environmental intervention. That understanding should be brought to new collaborations with faculty and academic administrators aimed at creating a campus climate or, better yet, a culture that stimulates and reinforces liberal learning.

Values Education. Just as all aspects of an institution contribute, for better or worse, to the college culture, so do all aspects of the institution contribute to the values that students develop consciously or unconsciously—values that are reinforced or reevaluated during the college years. In calling for "more self-conscious attention to the values we believe our students should acquire," Edgerton (1986, p. 11) suggests that we must first understand "how values are taught—and caught—in the ordinary course of campus life" (p. 12). Values are conveyed through all facets of institutional life, including the ways classes are taught and students are encouraged to or discouraged from participating, the type and caliber of guest speakers and artists brought to campus, the topics about which student affairs professionals and faculty converse with students and the kinds of things they say, the manner in which the college goes about its business and makes decisions, the nature of the accomplishments for which faculty are recognized and rewarded, the relations between faculty and student affairs professionals, and the relations between the college and the community. Astin (1988, p. 10) argues that this "implicit curriculum" may be adversely affecting "students' ability to work cooperatively with peers and to develop a sense of trust within organizational settings." It may, in fact, be reinforcing today's student competitiveness, individualism, and single-minded self-interest that educators so often bemoan.

Calls for greater attention to the teaching of values, coming from many quarters, grow out of several concerns. Hardly a week goes by without a new story of corruption, greed, and disregard for the law (not to mention other people) on the part of college-educated professionals in business, government, medicine, law, and even religion. Closer to home, the Cooperative Institutional Research Program surveys of college freshmen, conducted annually for over twenty years now, have shown a steady increase in values associated with status, power, and money (CIRP, 1988). Among the ways that such self-interest manifests itself on campus is academic dishonesty, which has assumed staggering proportions in recent years (Gehring, Nuss, and Pavela, 1986). These concerns underscore the need for more coherent and effective liberal education, but they also raise the question of whether new approaches and emphases are needed within both liberal and professional education. Morrill (1984, p. 14) urges educators to make "a conscious effort to make students aware of the values they hold, of the values implicit in the subjects they are studying, and of the values at work in the larger society," and then to lead them in questioning whether the values so identified "are consistent, coherent, adequate to the situation, comprehensive, authentic." Welty (1988, p. 24) calls for "values education across the curriculum."

Student affairs professionals have the tools today to tackle this challenge, and many are doing so. Referring to the works of Perry (1970), Kohlberg (1971), and Gilligan (1982), Dalton (1985, p. 22) claims that "student personnel professionals now have a much better empirical base from which to approach values development in college students than perhaps at any time in their history." He indicates that there are ample models for practice within the profession, as well as issues to be addressed. These issues include the responsibilities students incur as members of a resident community, the obligations they owe to themselves and others in interpersonal and sexual relations, the sources and consequences of vandalism and violence, the ethical dimensions of drug and alcohol abuse, the values implicit in various approaches to leadership, and the moral implications of racism, sexism, and homophobia. Given this array of issues that arise in the everyday work of student affairs professionals, can we ask that they go still further? Should they seek to collaborate with faculty in dealing more effectively with academic dishonesty, for example, and in helping students understand and prepare for the ethical issues that will confront them as professionals and as citizens? Through such collaboration, both parties may come to recognize, and may be able to help students recognize, the intermingled problems rooted in our society: date rape, hazing, vandalism, cheating on exams, persistent racism and sexism in the world of work, using inside information to make a killing on Wall Street, playing on people's worst impulses to sell products, and trading multi-million-dollar favors with friends in Washington at the expense of taxpayers.

Higher education can hardly be expected to unearth these buried roots or fully cleanse the current generation of their contamination. But at the same time, higher education cannot ignore either the ideals of truth and the reason for which it stands or the critical issues and problems of the society it serves. Helping students develop both the ability to examine values and the capacity to commit themselves to principles that transcend self-interest and the pleasures of the moment must be a goal of higher education, however great the barriers to its fullest realization.

Most of us, including student affairs professionals, still know far less than we would like to know about how to pursue teaching values effectively. By sharing what we do know across the boundaries of disciplines and departments, and by bringing faculty and student affairs professionals together to develop new approaches, we can collaborate to respond to this critical need. In the process of doing so, we may model as well as teach values.

Dealing with Diversity. Among the values that higher education has become a good deal more self-conscious about in recent years are those of equity and diversity (see Chapter Four). But too often, the strategies suggested today for enhancing access and strengthening performance of minority students in predominantly white institutions generally sound very much like those proposed and acted on fifteen years ago (Hawkins, 1989). Without question, we need more financial aid for minority students—from the federal government and other sources. We must have more effective academic support for underprepared students. We need to continue to provide the orientation programs, cultural activities, mentorship arrangements, and social opportunities that student affairs professionals, working closely with minority students themselves, have tried to provide for many years. We need to continue and expand our outreach to minority students in junior high to bring these young students to campus for special programs and to work with their teachers, counselors, and parents to prepare them for college.

All of this effort has not been enough in the past and probably will not be enough in the decades ahead. In order to prepare America's disadvantaged groups for the year 2000, when a majority of all new jobs will require postsecondary education (Johnson and Packer, 1987), and to prepare the rest of us for life in a truly pluralistic society, more must be done.

Higher education has failed dismally in recognizing and dealing with the discomfort that probably a majority of our faculty and students still feel in working with and relating to members of minority groups. Some would call it racism, latent if not blatant. It is this discomfort that creates a chilly climate for minority students and staff. It is this discomfort that has led to the "ghettoization, marginalization, and isolation" of minorities on college campuses (Smaw, 1989, p. 16) and, at least partially, to the reluctance of so many of their brothers and sisters even to consider a college education.

In dealing with diversity, as with the broader challenge of values education, student affairs professionals probably have more experience and expertise than do their academic colleagues. In fact, it is fair to say that student affairs professionals as a group have done more than any other group of college personnel (with the possible exception of affirmative action officers) to develop sensitivity to the experience of minority students and staff on predominantly white campuses and to learn how to work effectively with them. The time has come to share that expertise, sensitivity, and commitment through collaboration with faculty.

Out of such collaboration might come the kind of courses that Smaw recommended in an address at the 1989 national conference of the National Association of Student Personnel Administrators. He proposed a required six-week module for incoming freshmen in which attitudes, assumptions, and behaviors related to racism, sexism, and homophobia would be openly and intensively discussed—to be followed up with a six-week module the senior year to explore the issues of living in a pluralistic society. Out of such collaboration might come greater understanding of the need to incorporate multicultural perspectives across the curriculum, which is already being addressed at a few institutions. Greater faculty recognition that the learning styles of many minority students may be at odds with the traditional teaching styles of college classrooms might develop, and student affairs professionals might assist in the initiation of attempts to adapt to the needs of these students.

Most important, however, is the cross-fertilization of thinking that such collaboration could produce and the new ideas that it might yield. New ideas, fresh strategies, and broader, more open dialogue among different groups on campus are desperately needed if racism is to be eliminated and diversity genuinely valued as we move toward a new century.

Community and Commitment. A major theme in *College: The Undergraduate Experience in America* (Boyer, 1987) is the collapse of the community. Although the term *academic community* is still part of the higher education lexicon, the reality at all but the smallest schools is lack of communication and lack of shared experience among the many subcultures that constitute an institution of higher education. The size of contemporary colleges and universities, their fragmented organizational structures and confusion over goals, and the adversarial relationships between faculty and administration on all too many campuses contribute to the problem. In addition, the demands on students' time (with many working half-time or more to help pay the cost of higher education today), the increasing proportions of commuting and adult students, the competitiveness promoted by the college policies and practices, and the very diversity that we claim to value are all barriers to creating and sustaining a sense of community. Still, Boyer argues that the ideal of a "community of learners" is too important to relinquish. "At a time when social bonds are tenuous," he writes, "students, during their collegiate years, should discover the reality of their dependence on each other. They must understand what it means to share and sustain traditions. Community must be built" (p. 195).

Social Responsibility. Closely related themes that emerged during the 1980s are those of commitment and social responsibility. The concept of *community,* when the term is used to refer to something more than a group of people who live in the same geographical area, suggests shared concerns, mutual support, and some level of individual commitment to welfare of the group. The book *Habits of the Heart* (Bellah and Associates, 1985) documented the cyclical history of individualism and commitment in American life and underscored the critical role of social responsibility in a democratic society. Social responsibility and commitment to a larger community are just what seemed to be lacking in the students and young college graduates of the 1980s.

Although the undergraduate experience traditionally has been associated with idealism and dedication to social causes, a Carnegie Foundation follow-up study of high school seniors, originally interviewed in 1980, found that of those who attended four-year colleges or universities, 15 percent felt that "working to correct social and economic inequalities" was "very important" when they graduated from high school. Six years later, however, only 13 percent expressed that opinion. The decline was even more pronounced among those who attended two-year colleges (Carnegie Foundation . . . , 1988). Colleges evidently did little during those years to foster a sense of social responsibility in their students.

In 1985, the presidents of Stanford, Brown, and Georgetown universities set out to turn this situation around. They quickly assembled a group of 100 universities, mostly other elite private institutions, to form the Campus Compact, a national organization that aims "to reestablish students' commitment to service for others, to help develop policies that academic leaders and educational administrators and legislators can employ to make the climate more hospitable to such service, and to develop networks that will match students seeking opportunities to local and regional needs" (Kennedy, 1986, p. 7).

Since that time, the compact has grown and thrived; many similar organizations have emerged at the state level and on individual campuses. A number of compact schools have received substantial public and private grants to support student volunteerism and have initiated efforts to link community service and the curriculum (Stanton and Wallace, 1989). Some nine pieces of legislation to create a national service program were under debate in Congress in 1989 (Newman, 1989). But recent surveys to determine the impact of this barrage of rhetoric and burgeoning activity on the numbers of students actually involved in volunteer service seem inconclusive. One can still ask whether the movement is new populism or "smoke and mirrors" (Theus, 1988), but many are hopeful that it signals the beginning of a pendulum swing back from an era of individualism, self-interest, and isolation to one of social responsibility, commitment, and community.

Nowhere is the failure to refer to the role of student affairs professionals more startling than in the spate of speeches and articles on college students and community service. Perhaps, the following somewhat cynical analysis explains this absence: "Historically, volunteer activity has been unsung and unrewarded on college campuses. When it did exist, campus voluntarism was the stepchild of student activities offices and campus social organizations. Fraternities and sororities often encouraged their members to 'do good,' though mostly to elevate their house's image in the community. Student organizations often garnered participation with promises of social contact (dance-a-thons or fun runs, sold as dating bonanzas) or, more practically, with promises of credentials for employment. Little of this activity had as its object the nurture of civic spirit or reflection on the meaning of service" (Theus, 1988, p. 30).

Certainly, student affairs professionals have been associated with these sorts of quasi service. And, no doubt, they have responded to the dominant student ethos in recent years by "selling" leadership and organizational involvement, even volunteer work, as avenues for building skills and resumes rather than as opportunities for service to the campus community. Nonetheless, student affairs professionals understand the nature of and need for community and have had years of experience teaching the value of social responsibility. Undoubtedly, many colleges and universities have turned to student affairs professionals as they have sought to respond to the national call for student voluntarism and social responsibility. This call offers a clear opportunity for collaboration between student affairs professionals and faculty or academic administrators.

Summing Up: Some Tough Questions

All of these contemporary challenges calling for collaboration between academic and student affairs also inevitably call for reflection on the student affairs profession, how it fits into the broader institutional mission, how people are best prepared for the profession, and what its most meaningful futures might be. For the most part, these challenges transcend the traditional commonplace relations between academic and student affairs and demand that the traditional barriers between the two groups of professionals be transcended as well. To some extent, conditions seem ripe for doing so. But important questions remain.

In order to tackle these new challenges, should current functions be left undone or done differently or by somebody else? Given the constraints of time, money, tradition, and turf, can we really expect student affairs professionals to launch new initiatives in the unfamiliar terrains of classroom teaching, curricular reform, or academic climate? And given the increasing demands on faculty, can we really expect them to enter wholeheartedly into efforts to teach values, develop greater sensitivity to diversity, foster community, and promote social responsibility? Would it not be more reasonable, as well as much easier, to regard collaboration as an extra and partnerships as something to be pursued when the occasion arises and time permits? Or are the potential benefits of collaborations between academic affairs and student affairs so great that we should seek and develop them as vigorously as possible? Should such collaboration be a major strategy for transforming the campus community and enriching the quality of the undergraduate experience in American higher education? It is our students, after all, who have the most to gain.

References

Astin, A. W. "The Implicit Curriculum: What Are We Really Teaching Our Undergraduates?" *Liberal Education,* 1988, *74* (1), 6-10.

Bellah, R. N., and Associates. *Habits of the Heart: Individualism and Commitment in American Life.* New York: Harper & Row, 1985.

Berg, T. G. "Student Development and Liberal Arts Education." *NASPA Journal,* 1983, *21* (1), 9-16.

"Boyer Address, September 30, 1988." *The University Record,* Southeast Missouri State University, Oct. 1, 1988, p.1.

Boyer, E. L. *College: The Undergraduate Experience In America.* New York: Harper & Row, 1987.

Brown, R. D. *Student Development in Tomorrow's Higher Education: A Return to the Academy.* Washington, D.C.: American College Personnel Association, 1972.

Brown, S. S. "Approaches to Collaboration Between Academic and Student Affairs: An Overview." *NASPA Journal,* 1988, *26* (1), 2-7.

Carnegie Foundation for the Advancement of Teaching. "College and Changing Values: Two-Year and Four-Year Institutions." *Change,* 1988, *20,* 21- 25.

Chickering, A. W. *Education and Identity.* San Francisco: Jossey-Bass, 1969.

Claxton, C., and Murrell, P. H. *Learning Styles: Implications for Improving Educational Practice.* ASHE-ERIC Higher Education Report No. 4. Washington, D.C.: Association for the Study of Higher Education, 1987.

Cooperative Institutional Research Program (CIRP). *1988 Freshman Survey Results.* Los Angeles: American Council on Education and University of California, 1988.

Cross, K. P. *Accent on Learning.* San Francisco: Jossey-Bass, 1976.

Cross, K. P. "Teaching for Learning." *AAHE Bulletin,* 1987, *39,* 3–7.

Cross, K. P. "In Search of Zippers." *AAHE Bulletin,* 1988, *40,* 3–7.

Dalton, J. C. (ed.). *Promoting Values Development in College Students.* NASPA Monograph Series, no. 4. Columbus, Ohio: National Association of Student Personnel Administrators, 1985.

Davis, M. T., and Schroeder, C. C. " 'New Students' in Liberal Arts Colleges: Threat or Challenge?" In J. Watson and R. Stevens (eds.), *Pioneers and Pallbearers: Perspectives on Liberal Education.* Macon, Ga.: Mercer University Press, 1983.

Edgerton, R. "Six Core Convictions." *AAHE Bulletin,* 1986, *38,* 7–12.

Edgerton, R. "All Roads Lead to Teaching." *AAHE Bulletin,* 1988, *40,* 3–9.

Gaff, J. G. *General Education Today: A Critical Analysis of Controversies, Practices, and Reforms.* San Francisco: Jossey-Bass, 1983.

Gehring, D., Nuss, E. M., and Pavela, G. "Issues and Perspectives on Academic Integrity." Columbus, Ohio: National Association of Student Personnel Administrators, 1986.

Gilligan, C. *In A Different Voice.* Cambridge, Mass.: Harvard University Press, 1982.

Hawkins, B. C. "Minority Students on Predominantly White Campuses: The Need for Renewed Commitment." *NASPA Journal,* 1989, *26* (3), 175–179.

Johnson, W. B., and Packer, A. H. *Workforce 2000: Work and Workers for the 21st Century.* Indianapolis, Ind.: Hudson Institute, 1987.

Katz, J. "Turning Professors into Teachers." *AAHE Bulletin,* 1988, *41,* 12–14.

Kennedy, D. "Can We Help? Public Service and the Young." *AAHE Bulletin,* 1986, *39* (4), 3–7.

Kohlberg, L. "Stages of Moral Development." In C. M. Beck, B. S. Crittenden, and E. V. Sullivan (eds.), *Moral Education.* Toronto: University of Toronto Press, 1971.

Kuh, G. D., Shedd, J. D., and Whitt, E. J. "Student Affairs and Liberal Education: Unrecognized (and Unappreciated) Common Law Partners." *Journal of College Student Personnel,* 1987, *28,* 252–259.

Lapidus, J. B. "Preparing Faculty: Graduate Education's Role." *AAHE Bulletin,* 1987, *39,* 3–6.

McKeachie, W. J., and others. *Teaching and Learning in the College Classroom: A Review of the Research Literature.* Ann Arbor: National Center for Research to Improve Postsecondary Teaching and Learning, University of Michigan, 1986.

Miller, T., and Prince, J. S. *The Future of Student Affairs.* San Francisco: Jossey-Bass, 1976.

Mitchell, A. A., and Roof, M. "Student Affairs and Faculty Partnerships: Dismantling Barriers." *NASPA Journal,* 1989, *26* (4), 278–282.

Morrill, R. L. "Standards for Choice: A Roundtable on the Role of College in Developing Character and Values." *AAHE Bulletin,* 1984, *36,* 3–6, 14.

National Association of Student Personnel Administrators. "A Perspective on Student Affairs: A Statement Issued on the Fiftieth Anniversary of *The Student Personnel Point of View.*" Washington, D.C.: National Association of Student Personnel Administrators, 1987.

National Institute of Education. *Involvement in Learning: Realizing the Potential of American Higher Education.* Washington, D.C.: U.S. Department of Education, 1984.

Newman, F. "National Policies to Encourage Service: Where Do We Stand?" *Change,* 1989, *21,* 8–17.

Nutter, J. F., and Hurst, J. C. "A Structural Partnership: The Academic Deans/Student Affairs Advisory Council." *NASPA Journal,* 1988, *26* (1), 33–39.

O'Brien, C. R. "Student Affairs and Academic Affairs: Partners in Higher Education." *NASPA Journal,* 1989, *26* (4), 284–287.

Palmer, P. J. "Community, Conflict, and Ways of Knowing: Ways to Deepen Our Educational Agenda." *Change,* 1987, *19,* 20–25.

Perry, W. G., Jr. *Forms of Intellectual and Ethical Development in College.* New York: Holt, Rinehart & Winston, 1970.

Project on Redefining the Meaning and Purpose of Baccalaureate Degrees. *Integrity in the College Curriculum: A Report to the Academic Community.* Washington, D.C.: Association of American Colleges, 1985.

Rice, R. E., and Sheridan, H. W. "Tomorrow's Professoriate: The Search for a New Vision." Paper presented at the 1989 American Association of Higher Education National Conference on Higher Education, Chicago, Apr. 1989.

Schroeder, C. C., DiTiberio, J. K., and Kalsbeek, D. H. "Bridging the Gap Between Faculty and Students: Opportunities and Obligations for Student Affairs." *NASPA Journal,* 1988, *26* (1), 14–20.

Schuster, J. H., and Bowen, H. R. "The Faculty at Risk." *Change,* 1985, *17,* 12–21.

Sherhofer, R. "Teaching and Learning Outside the Traditional Classroom: What do Academic and Student Affairs Administrators Have to Offer?" Paper presented at the 1989 National Association of Student Personnel Administrators National Conference, Denver, Colo., Mar. 1989.

Sheridan, H. W. "The Compleat Professor, Jr." *AAHE Bulletin,* 1988, *41,* 3–7.

Smaw, D. "Diversity: Discovering Similarities, Celebrating Differences." Paper presented at the 1989 National Association of Student Personnel Administrators National Conference, Denver, Colo., Mar. 1989.

Smith, D. G. "The Next Step Beyond Student Development—Becoming Partners Within Our Institutions." *NASPA Journal,* 1982, *19* (4), 53–62.

Smith, D. G. "A Window of Opportunity for Intra-Institutional Collaboration." *NASPA Journal,* 1988, *26* (1), 8–13.

Smith, T. B., and Weith, R. A. "Value-Added: The Student Affairs

Professional as Promoter of Intellectual Development." *NASPA Journal,* 1985, *23* (2), 19–24.

Stanton, T., and Wallace, J. "Linking Community Service and the Curriculum." Paper presented at the 1989 American Association of Higher Education National Conference on Higher Education, Chicago, Apr. 1989.

Stodt, M. S., and Klepper, W. M. (eds.). *Increasing Retention: Academic and Student Affairs Administrators in Partnership.* New Directions for Higher Education, no. 50. San Francisco: Jossey-Bass, 1987.

Theus, K. T. "Campus-Based Community Service: New Populism or 'Smoke and Mirrors'?" *Change,* 1988, *20,* 27–38.

Webb, E. M. "Retention and Excellence Through Student Involvement: A Leadership Role for Student Affairs." *NASPA Journal,* 1987, *24* (4), 6–11.

Welty, J. D. "Values Education as an Opportunity for Collaboration: A President's Perspective." *NASPA Journal,* 1988, *26* (1), 21–26.

Whipple, W. R. "Collaborative Learning: Recognizing It When We See It." *AAHE Bulletin,* 1987, *40* (2), 3–7.

Chapter 13

Improving Practice Through Research, Evaluation, and Outcomes Assessment

Gary R. Hanson

The future of the student affairs profession depends on researchers and practitioners working in a symbiotic relationship to help students. The strength of the profession will be judged by how well practitioners use information about student growth and development to guide and shape their educational interventions. In the future, that judgment will not only be made by knowledgeable professionals within higher education, but increasingly will also be made by those outside our colleges and universities. The importance of showing that we know when, how, and under what conditions students learn will be superseded only by the importance of showing that we can use that information to improve what we do for them. Helping students know themselves, improving our practice, and being accountable to an external public together constitute the new research agenda.

The purpose of this chapter is to establish a new research agenda for the next generation of student affairs practitioners. This agenda must anticipate the trends that will shape higher education and the student affairs profession, because these trends will determine the context in which we work. Within that context, I will outline the reasons why we need information, the kinds of information that will be most useful, and the ways that we should acquire and use our information. In the last section of this chapter, I will present a new agenda for understanding the college students of tomorrow.

The Context: Four Trends in Higher Education That Will Shape the Research Agenda

The winds of change in higher education will blow from four directions in the 1990s and beyond. First, monumental changes in the nature of who goes to college will occur over the next twenty years. Not only will the demographics of college-bound students change, but also the value students place on education and their preferred styles of learning will be different. Second, the sparks that kindled a new fire in the reform of the elementary and secondary educational system in the United States during 1980s will sputter and die. Students will continue to finish high school poorly prepared for the academic rigor of college. Third, external pressures to shape and govern higher education from outside the ivy-covered walls of academe will intensify. New partnerships with vested interests in the quality of higher education will demand that colleges be accountable for the educational product they produce. Fourth, a significant paradigm shift in the ways we learn about students will occur. This paradigm shift toward naturalistic inquiry began in other disciplines and has led to new ways of asking questions. The new mode of inquiry, the naturalistic or post-positivistic paradigm, will lead us to new knowledge about students and the ways they grow and develop. These four trends, more than any others, will shape the research agenda for student affairs over the next decade.

A More Diverse Campus. The most significant change in higher education over the next twenty-five years will be the nature of the student body. Traditionally, white middle-class students have constituted the majority on campus. During the 1990s, the demography of who goes to college will change dramatically. Levine and Associates (1989) suggest four reasons why college students of the future will come from more diverse backgrounds. First, the total population available for higher education will decline, especially the number of traditionally college-age individuals. In addition, the adult population most likely to attend college (the baby-boom generation) peaked in 1988 and will likely decline for the rest of the century.

Second, the college-age population of the future will be people of color. In the four states with the largest projected increases in population—California, Florida, New York, and Texas—the current minority populations will become the majority. Similar demographic changes will occur in other states, though not to the same degree. Will these students pursue college? Traditionally, these ethnic groups have had the lowest rates of educational attainment, and their participation in higher education has been declining, not increasing, over the past decade. Astin (1982) noted that secondary school attrition is largest among these very ethnic populations for which the population growth is projected to be the largest. Our campuses of tomorrow may be more multicultural than they are today, but not unless preventive action is taken immediately.

Third, demographic shifts in our population will vary geographically, and each state will face a unique situation. Although nearly all areas of the country will experience losses of population, encouraging selected minorities to enroll in college will greatly influence the impact of this demographic shift.

The fourth factor concerns the pattern of enrollment across various types of institutions. Levine and Associates (1989) suggest that nonselective public institutions, colleges from the Midwest and Northeast, and private institutions in general will be at greatest risk for a substantial enrollment loss. All these trends will lead to a more demographically diverse campus and to changes in the curriculum and student services. How we educate students will evolve to deal with a changed demography of higher education. (See Chapter Four.)

At the same time that the demography of higher education is changing, the values students bring with them to campus will change. Astin, Green, and Korn (1987) found large increases in the number of students who valued money, power, and status. If these trends continue, we can expect an oversupply of students pursuing business and technical degrees and an undersupply of those who are interested in an education.

Levine (1980) also suggested how student values may change in the future. He charted the cyclical changes in student attitudes toward individual and community ascendency. The interest in social issues and in the community versus a focused interest on the self or the individual changed in an interesting symmetry with the country's involvement in major wars and international conflict. As the United States became more involved in armed conflict with other countries, the interest of the college student population shifted to community ascendency and social issues. After the conflicts were over, a resurgent interest in the individual was evident. Following this analysis, one would predict a continued focus on money, power, and status, unless our country becomes involved in a major conflict of some sort.

The Failure of Secondary School Reform. During the last twenty years, there has been a well-documented decrease in the quality of students graduating from high schools (National Commission on Excellence in Education, 1984; Astin, Green, and Korn, 1987). Students graduating from today's high schools cannot read, compute, write, or think as well as students twenty years ago. Nor are today's high school graduates as well prepared as students from other countries (Center for Education Statistics, 1986). To make matters worse, grade inflation within our high schools has created a false sense of academic well-being among the graduates. Astin, Green, and Korn show that in spite of the documented decrease in ACT and SAT admission test scores, larger percentages of today's students rate their writing and mathematics abilities higher than students did in 1966. Further evidence that high school graduates are not well prepared was documented by Ravitch and Finn (1987). Less than 45 percent of a national sample of high school seniors knew in which time period Columbus discovered America, and less than 30 percent knew who wrote *The Republic.*

Recognizing that the solution to this generalized decline in the quality of high school graduates required long-term changes in the fundamental nature of secondary education in the United States, colleges and universities developed short-term solutions to the immediate problem of underprepared students entering higher education. The response was the development of mandated basic skills assessment for all freshmen entering public institutions (New Jersey Basic Skills Council, 1986; Texas Academic Skills Program, 1988). Consequently, colleges and universities, especially two-year community colleges and vocational technical institutes, are in the business of remedial education. Most states expect this to be a relatively short-term problem that will dissolve as secondary schools improve, but the experience of one state suggests educational reform is likely to be a twenty- to twenty-five-year problem rather than a five- to ten-year problem. As evidence, note that during the last twelve years of basic skills testing in New Jersey, the percentage of freshman students who failed one or more portions of that exam increased (New Jersey Basic Skills Council, 1986).

The conclusion from these data is that the problem of underpreparation of students who leave our high schools will not be solved in the near future, if at all. Colleges and universities will continue to admit large numbers of students ill prepared to perform college-level work. Consequently, institutions of higher education will be involved in developmental and remedial education in the classroom and in our learning skills centers. To help these students, we will need well-defined diagnostic assessments of their learning skills.

External Pressure Points. The days of institutional autonomy for higher education are gone forever. The nature of how and when and under what conditions students learn will be monitored by various individuals and organizations external to our individual campuses. For example, the call for institutional accountability was voiced in the National Institute of Education's report called *Involvement in Learning: Realizing the Potential of American Higher Education* (1984). Over the next several years, additional reports echoed the same theme from the perspective of several different constituent groups (Association of American Colleges, 1985; Bennett, 1984; Education Commission of the States, 1986; National Governors' Association, 1988; Newman, 1985). Each group has a vested interest in how well the educational job is accomplished.

External public interest in the educational process has focused on higher education in two ways. First, the definition of educational quality has changed from placing emphasis on the input characteristics of the students and the resource and asset allocation of the institution to placing emphasis on quality in terms of what students have learned (Astin, 1987). What do they know when they leave your campus? Documentation of what students have learned and documentation showing that the educational institution has contributed to that learning will be the basis for determining institutions of quality.

Second, the external constituencies interested in higher education will force a difficult choice between accountability and institutional self-improvement (Ewell, 1986). With this new definition of quality, external accrediting boards, state higher education coordinating councils, and boards of regents will want evidence of what students have learned. When institutions find that their students have not learned and have not achieved the expected educational outcomes, they must look to the process of learning. To improve the teaching and learning process, different kinds of assessment data will be needed. Information about the process of learning will be of critical importance, but most institutions that respond to the call for accountability data will only know what students have learned—not how they learned it. The research agenda for the future must include a way to respond to these very different demands for information about students.

A Paradigm Shift in Our Mode of Inquiry. At the very core of the research agenda for student affairs is the notion of how we come to know our students. That too will be very different in the future. Traditionally, we have adopted a scientific, positivistic mode of inquiry—a way of asking questions heavily influenced by scientific thought from the time of Galileo to the middle of the twentieth century. This mode of inquiry placed a heavy emphasis on an objective, controlled examination of the evidence (Cziko, 1989). Consequently, the analysis of human behavior was reduced to bits and pieces that could be manipulated and controlled by so-called experimental methodology. But beginning about the middle of the current century, scientists from many different disciplines recognized that the scientific paradigm was not helping them find answers to important questions. Slowly at first, researchers in physics, chemistry, meteorology, geology, genetics, and mathematics abandoned the traditional scientific paradigm and looked to a more naturalistic mode of inquiry—one that would allow them involvement in the process of observing phenomena more directly. Control, prediction, and the reduction of observed phenomena to a controlled laboratory setting were replaced by the search for patterns of order among seemingly chaotic behavior that occurred in natural settings. A fascinating history of this change in our mode of inquiry can be found in Gleick (1987).

Only in the last fifteen years have we begun to study students from this new perspective. Banning (1980, 1989) described the earlier history of the ecological approach to working with students. This perspective was developed by the Western Interstate Commission on Higher Education (1973) and extended by Huebner (1979). The interested reader may refer to Huebner (1989) for an update and overview of recent research, new revisions to the conceptual model, and practical implications.

Another new dimension of the paradigm shift toward naturalistic inquiry is the extension of student development theory, particularly as it applies to women and other subgroups of students. Griener and Delworth (1988) urge student affairs professionals to consider the naturalistic mode of inquiry and to use qualitative research methods in the study of women's issues. Allen (1989) also recommends that the naturalistic mode of inquiry will allow us to reconceptualize student development as a dynamic, nonlinear process. The implications of this move to a new mode of inquiry will be discussed in a later section of this chapter.

Why Is Context Important?

What we do as researchers in student affairs for the next twenty-five years will be driven by four trends: (1) Our students will become more diverse, (2) they will continue to enter college poorly prepared to perform well, and (3) higher education institutions will be joined by an external public with an intense interest in how well we do our work. (The focus may begin with how well faculty teach in the classroom and what students learn as a consequence, but not far behind will be a focus on the other important types of learning that occur outside the classroom.) Finally, (4) the research questions we must pursue will be guided by a new mode of inquiry—one that tries to understand students in their naturalistic setting, the campus community. All of these trends point to our need to learn more about students and the educational context in which we work. Given this context, what are the critical research questions the student affairs profession should pursue?

Questions That Drive the Research Agenda. There are just four very broad questions that drive the research agenda for student affairs: (1) How can we describe students in meaningful ways when they first enter college? (2) How can we describe what students learn by the time they leave our institutions? (3) How can we describe the process of how students learn and develop? (4) How can we show that what they learn is a result of what we do? In a very general sense, these are the only questions that are important for student affairs professionals to answer. Yet over the last fifty years, we have barely begun to find answers.

The sections that follow provide more details for finding answers to these four basic questions. It is important to understand why we need information to answer these questions. Each question begs certain kinds of data for its answer, and assuming we find answers, each question suggests ways of using data to help students learn, grow, and develop.

Why Do We Need Information About Students? The research agenda for student affairs will be dictated by the purposes behind the assessment of students. Before we can know how to assess students, we must understand why we assess students. The reasons why we gather data about students in our research efforts are related to three major purposes, all closely tied to the educational context cited in an earlier section of this chapter.

The first purpose is accountability. The trend to greater interest and involvement in higher education by external constituents is with us today and will intensify in the future. Taxpayers, governing boards, parents, and accrediting agencies will want to know what students know and what they can do when they exit our institutions. The assessment of student educational outcomes will be a key to establishing our accountability to these external interest groups (Banta, 1988; Erwin, 1989; Ewell, 1987). There is a growing demand on the part of these external groups that these educational outcomes include noncognitive factors such as leadership, moral character, social competence, and communications skills (Lenning, 1988; College Outcomes Evaluation Program, 1987; Texas Higher Education Coordinating Board, 1989). Because much of our educational effort in student affairs is directed toward the attainment of these goals, we will be asked to account for our success in achieving these important educational outcomes.

A second purpose that will drive our research agenda is to understand the process of student learning and development, with the goal of improving our educational practice. We hope that all of our educational efforts contribute to the growth and learning of students and that all students attain their educational goals. However, we know many students leave school before they achieve their dreams and aspirations, and we know students leave school before they achieve our standards of achievement. When that happens, we have to ask how the process of educating students could be improved. What could we do differently? What new educational interventions must we develop? What old practices must we discard? Answers to these questions are of interest to program developers and directors, and for the most part, data related to this purpose will be used internally for improving our daily practice. In the long term, more students should achieve the educational goals they and the institution deem important, and ultimately, our institutional accountability will improve.

The third purpose that drives the student affairs research agenda is the use of data to help students better understand themselves—data for self-assessment. Much remains to be learned about the kinds of information students find useful in charting their educational experiences. For decades, information about students has been collected, stored, analyzed, and used for a wide variety of purposes without the student learning directly from the information. If learning and development are never-ending processes, then we are obligated to teach students how to gather, analyze, and interpret information about themselves. Students must learn how to use information in the decisions that shape their lives. What could be more important than helping students choose a college, a career, a friend, or a life-style?

These three purposes—accountability, improvement, and self-assessment—directly shape the research agenda for the student affairs profession; the purpose of the research will determine what information will be collected and how it will be used. The next section will relate these purposes to the four major research questions in determining the kinds of information we should seek about and for students.

What Kinds of Information Do We Need? When the four primary research questions that define the research agenda for student affairs are embedded in the educational context for the future, clear implications emerge for what we need to assess. The kinds of information we will need for the future can be categorized under three headings. We will need *diagnostic information* about students that describes developmental status, level of academic preparation, and preferred learning strategies. Second, we will need to assess the extent to which students achieve the desired *outcomes of higher education.* These outcomes represent both the student's and the institution's goals, and they include the cognitive and affective dimensions of the student. Third, we must assess the manner in which *the process of education* influences students to learn and grow. We need information that links how and what students learn to the programs and services we offer.

These three categories of information are interrelated in that some of the diagnostic information regarding the developmental status of each student at the time he or she enters college forms a foundation for assessing the degree and nature of learning and growth. Subsequent measures of the same dimensions at a later point in time may serve as the outcomes we wish to monitor. Likewise, relating the amount and nature of student learning to specific program interventions will help us understand the process of learning. The next step in defining the research agenda for student affairs is to expand on these general categories of information and to provide enough detail to establish some direction for our future efforts.

Diagnostic Information. The need for diagnostic information is based on the premise that we will use that information to help students learn and take advantage of their educational experiences. Important underlying assumptions are that not all students either need or will benefit from the same educational experience and that our role as educators is to help students gain the best fit between the institutional demands and their individual needs.

Diagnostic information helps the student affairs practitioner describe and understand the student in developmental terms. In the future, three kinds of diagnostic data will be useful—the student's level of academic preparation, the student's preferred learning strategies, and the student's developmental status at the time of entry.

If the educational reform movement within the secondary educational system is not successful in preparing students for college, colleges and universities must be willing and able to assess student mastery of basic academic skills. A growing number of states have mandated the assessment of basic skills of all students entering public higher education—New Jersey, Florida, Texas, and Tennessee, to mention a few. These basic skills assessments focus on a student's ability to read, compute, and write at a level that will lead to successful completion of a college degree. To the extent that student affairs professionals are involved in counseling and advising with students, they will need to help each student understand his or her level of preparation. In addition, as Fenske (1980) pointed out nearly ten years ago, the underpreparation of students offers a new opportunity for student affairs professionals to take an active role in the teaching of basic, developmental skills. To the extent that faculty do not have the time, interest, or expertise to teach remedial and developmental educational courses, student affairs professionals may be asked to assume a central role in preparing students for college-level academic work.

Diagnostic information about students' learning styles and strategies is also necessary if we are to help students become academically successful. Student affairs professionals in learning skills centers have been assessing student study skills for years, but recent research in cognitive psychology has shown that students have distinctive methods they use to learn and that students can be taught how to learn (Pintrich and Associates, 1988; Weinstein, Schulte, and Palmer, 1987). Learning strategy assessments that measure how well students select the main idea from reading passages, how well they use visual imagery to memorize classroom material, and how well they persevere at studying are now available in such instruments as the Learning and Study Strategies Inventory (Weinstein, Schulte, and Palmer, 1987). In addition, the assessment of student learning style and the sharing of that information with faculty to improve instruction have been tried with great success (Kalsbeek, 1989b).

The third area in which diagnostic information will be useful is the assessment of the developmental status of students at the time they enter college. A growing list of assessment instruments is available to assess a variety of dimensions of student growth and development. Instruments to assess Chickering's vectors of psychosocial development (Hood, 1986; Winston, Miller, and Prince, 1987) and Perry's stages of cognitive development (Kitchener and King, 1985; Moore, 1987) are readily available. In addition, some colleges have begun to use behavioral events interviews during the first few weeks of school or during freshman orientations to assess the developmental status of students and to provide them with personalized learning plans (Younce, personal communication, 1989).

Assessment of Educational Outcomes. The assessment of educational outcomes is not new (Erwin, 1989; Pace, 1979), but the focused interest of our external public has placed greater emphasis on the need to assess what students have learned. At least one accrediting agency now requires that institutions systematically collect and use outcomes assessment data in their strategic planning and in the evaluation of their programs and services (Southern Association of Colleges and Schools, 1984), and most other accrediting agencies are moving toward similar requirements. As indicated in an earlier section of this chapter, numerous states have mandated the assessment of educational outcomes, and several of these states have demanded documented evidence of the effective learning that takes place outside the classroom (Marantes, 1987). Although the mandate for the assessment of educational outcomes requires information about students, few states or accrediting agencies have defined what outcomes should be assessed in a systematic fashion. The uniqueness and variety of educational institutions would make a generalized taxonomy of student educational outcomes nearly impossible. Nevertheless, institutions will be asked to define the important outcomes they expect to produce and to collect information about their success in achieving those goals. Assessing and documenting that these educational outcomes are achieved will be an important component of our accountability.

An important part of the research agenda for student affairs in the next generation will be the definition of those affective outcomes of higher education that are influenced by the college experience. The interested reader is referred to Lenning (1977) for a systematic review of more than seventy-five models of affective student outcomes; other models also have been developed (College Outcomes Evaluation Program, 1987; Texas Higher Education Coordinating Board, 1989). While these generalized conceptual models are useful as a foundation, broad-based campus discussion and consensus should be used to determine the ultimate criteria for what affective educational outcomes are important to assess.

Assessment of the Educational Process. Hutchings (1989) has called for educational researchers to look behind the assessment of outcomes to explore the process of how students learn. She points out that the promise of assessment is improved student learning, and improvement requires attention not only to the final results but also to how the results occurred. Hence, a major challenge for the student affairs research agenda is to link the important outcomes that students achieve to our educational efforts. This is no small task, because the conceptual, methodological, and statistical problems associated with linking outcomes with practice are particularly complex (Baird, 1988; Hanson, 1988; Pascarella, 1987).

To conduct this type of needed research, it is necessary to monitor student involvement in many different educational programs over time. New data collection and analysis strategies will be required to monitor or track the amount of time and the quality of the effort students expend in the various facets of their educational experiences. Tracking and monitoring student academic progress in the curriculum has been accepted practice in higher education for years. The result has been a transcript of grades that represent the faculties' evaluations of that progress.

Systematic ways to monitor how students participate in the out-of-class experiences of college have not been widely developed. Though Brown and Citrin (1977) suggested that student affairs professionals establish a so-called developmental transcript that would document a student's involvement in developmental activities, few colleges have implemented that suggestion. For the most part, student participation and any measure of the quality of that participation are not recorded by student affairs professionals who deliver educational programs. Consequently, little is known about the contribution of any given program to the developmental status of a particular individual.

Looking at the combined influence of a combination of programs over the educational history of an individual or a group of students is nearly impossible. Yet, in the future, just such studies will be required to show that the programs we offer do, in fact, contribute to a change. These studies will require that we know the developmental status of students at the time they enter the institution and at what level they have achieved prior to participating in a program or combination of programs. We must collect data to document when and how often students participate in the services and programs we offer, and we must assess the quality of the experiences and the developmental status at the end of program participation. If the program or service occurs over an extended period of time, we may need to make several assessments. Change in the developmental status can then be monitored and linked to the kind of participation.

When students participate in multiple programs, we can assess the combined effect in much the same way. This process is little different from the one colleges and universities have been using for years to set the curricular requirements and monitor student progress toward meeting degree requirements. There is one primary difference, however. Recently, researchers have tried to link student learning with participation in multiple programs. One interesting model is the work of Ratliff and Associates (1989). Measured gains in student learning (using item gain scores on the GRE) were related to specific patterns of college course work across several different college campuses. Ratliff found that gains in standardized measures were related to particular combinations of academic course work. McGinty (1989), in a recent dissertation, showed that students who participated in various combinations of programs involving freshman orientation, living in a residence hall, tutoring, and supplemental instruction obtained significantly higher grades than did students at the same ability level who did not participate in any of the programs.

A New Research Agenda

The research agenda for the future will be shaped by the context of higher education. Our students will be more diverse, and they will continue to come to college poorly prepared for the rigor of their academic course work. We will need information about students to improve our practice and to be accountable to an external public who cares greatly about how well we do our job, and we will need information to help students understand themselves so they may take more direct control over the quality of their educational experiences.

The research agenda is also shaped by our pursuit of three relatively broad but highly important questions: (1) What do we need to know about students at the time they enter college in order to make their experiences educationally rewarding? (2) What do we need to know about students at the time they leave our institutions so we can assure ourselves and our external public that their educational experiences are of high quality? (3) How will we know our programs and services contributed to student learning and growth?

Finally, the research agenda is shaped by the purposes that drive our need to study students. We must develop the skill to diagnose the status of students at various points along their unique pathways through our institutions. More important, we can no longer ignore how students experience our institutions; rather, we must monitor and document that students involve themselves in our programs and services and that they benefit from that participation. And we must have the information to make judgments of worth about the quality of the experience relative to the cost of its delivery. Simply stated, we must evaluate the effect of our programs on students. Given these factors that will shape the research agenda, where do we start and what should we research for the next twenty-five years?

A Research Agenda for the Student Affairs Profession

The following recommendations are offered as guidelines for a long-term research agenda for the profession. Because of the scope and breadth of these recommendations, it is unlikely that any given individual or institution could pursue all of them. However, over the next twenty-five years, these are the research issues that should consume our energies as a profession.

Recommendation #1: Student affairs researchers should be involved in the definition and development of diagnostic assessment techniques and strategies of student learning and developmental status. The emphasis in this recommendation is on the diagnostic nature of the assessment strategy. Note that we are assuming a very broad definition of assessment and that the strategies and techniques may include interviews, behavioral event checklists, computer-assisted self-reports, and more formal paper-and-pencil assessment instruments.

This work should focus on three areas. First, student affairs researchers must work hand in hand with faculty members to define the basic academic competencies that lead to success in the classroom. These diagnostic measures should provide a descriptive picture of how well a student can perform the basic reading, writing, mathematical, analytical, and reasoning skills that are prerequisites to successful performance in college-level course work. By defining and building diagnostic assessment instruments, student affairs researchers and other professionals will be in a much better position to help students understand their academic strengths and weaknesses and to help students begin their educational careers at a level that will maximize the chances for successful achievement of their goals.

The second type of diagnostic assessment needs to be defined and developed to measure learning strategies. Again, the emphasis is on developing diagnostic measures of important student characteristics. To teach students how to learn, we must be able to assess the kinds of skills and techniques they have developed for learning. A few instruments such as the Learning and Study Strategies Inventory (LASSI) and the Michigan Motivated Strategies for Learning Questionnaire (Pintrich, 1988) are now available, but additional research into the methods students use to learn college material is needed.

The third type of diagnostic instrument that student affairs researchers should help develop is an assessment of the developmental status of important affective educational outcomes. This kind of assessment would differ from current personality measures and assessments of student development in that the results of these assessments would be directly related to educational experiences. For example, such an assessment might try to measure several dimensions of leadership behavior. The diagnostic results may show that a student has well-developed skills in running a well-organized business meeting and may be able to recruit members to a group or organization but that he or she has weak skills in managing a budget, acquiring new resources, and providing a sense of direction or vision for the organization. The student affairs professional could then direct the student to selected kinds of educational programs designed to build those skills.

Recommendation #2: Student affairs researchers should actively participate in the definition of educational outcomes. External pressure and the demand for accountability will not disappear in the next twenty-five years. Within our institutions, it will be important that we show our effectiveness in helping students achieve their educational goals, especially when we are asked to justify the funds we spend. To be accountable, it will be absolutely imperative that we have well-defined outcomes. Achievement of these educational outcomes will be used as a standard for judging our effectiveness in helping students.

It is not important that we have a universal taxonomy of educational outcomes. But in the future, it will be important that a continuing dialogue about these outcomes be initiated among campus constituents—students, faculty, and student affairs administrative staff. This dialogue should define those goals that are most important to each campus. Different missions, students, faculty, and generations will require uniquely defined statements of student educational outcomes, so knowing how to go about defining educational outcomes is more important than having a standard statement of outcomes.

Recommendation #3: Student affairs researchers should expand their working knowledge of assessment techniques. As outcomes are defined, assessment techniques can be identified to document whether these outcomes occur. However, to measure effectively some of the important educational outcomes, student affairs researchers will have to expand their repertoire of assessment strategies. In reviewing a wide variety of student development assessment instruments and techniques, Hanson (1989) found that the majority involve paper-and-pencil assessment techniques. Student affairs researchers simply must move beyond the paper-and-pencil mode of measurement. As Lenning (1988) suggested, there are many new and interesting methods available for the assessment of educational outcomes, particularly those methods that assess the affective or noncognitive domain.

Another reason why student affairs researchers must expand their working knowledge of assessment techniques is connected to the paradigm shift toward naturalistic inquiry. The naturalistic mode of inquiry begins with a different set of assumptions and demands that different questions be asked. As a consequence, different assessment information will be necessary, and new methods of assessment will be needed. The naturalistic mode of inquiry demands a greater level of involvement in the problem being studied.

Recommendation #4: Student affairs researchers should study the process of educational learning and development in order to link student growth to specific educational interventions. In the past, student affairs researchers have studied the process of student development by focusing on how students change over time. Our profession now has numerous student development theories that describe the progress of stages or sequences of growth that students experience. Almost without exception, these models and theories describe, from an internal, psychological perspective, the learning and growth that occur over time; but they provide very little insight into the external conditions and factors that contribute to individual learning and development. Consequently, very little information exists about how to structure educational experiences that will facilitate student growth and development. Do we have the kind of research that would help a student affairs practitioner design an educational program to facilitate the development of Chickering's (1969) vector of emotional autonomy? Do we know what kinds of educational programs will move a student toward more complex thinking stages suggested by Perry (1970)? The answer is that we do not know early enough.

Hutchings (1989) has argued that we need to spend more time studying the process behind the educational outcomes we want to accomplish. As stated earlier in this chapter, we must become more sophisticated about tracking and monitoring student involvement in the educational experience, and we must be more sophisticated in the assessment techniques we use to measure student growth and development. Linking student growth and development to our educational programs and services will require that we document how and when they participate. Kalsbeek (1989a) and Madsen, Benedict, and Weitzer (1989) recommend that student affairs professionals develop a working familiarity with management information systems, decision support systems, and the development of educational research longitudinal data bases in order to use information about students effectively in making our programmatic decisions.

Recommendation #5: Student affairs researchers should actively participate in testing and validating student development theory. Our assessment and research practice is closely tied to our current theory and models of student development behavior. Adding the naturalistic paradigm to our toolbox of assessment strategies and techniques provides a way to question our theory as well. Allen (1989) pointed out that our assessment practice has followed current student development theory by supplying instruments that assume student development and learning are sequential, orderly, and cumulative processes. As a result, our assessment instruments have given us quantifiable ways of measuring student growth. However, recent studies, using a naturalistic mode of inquiry, have begun to question those assumptions (Baruch, Barnett, and Rivers, 1983; Belenky, Clinchy, Goldberger, and Tarule, 1986; Gilligan, 1982; Josselson, 1987). These new studies suggest that development may be much more idiosyncratic, fluid, nonlinear, multioptioned, and interconnected. If development follows these naturalistic assumptions, assessment will be more complex, because we will need to measure multiple pathways to development, to look for patterns and themes for development instead of linear stages, and to examine both external and internal conditions that trigger development (Allen, 1989).

Summary

As we look to the future, higher education and the role student affairs plays will change. Skillful use of research about our students and about our delivery of student affair programs and services can and will strengthen the profession, because we will have the information to describe the diversity of our students. In the future, we will learn more about the link between the practice of our profession and the impact it has on the lives of students, both within and outside the classroom setting. We will be partners in educating students. As we learn more about students when they arrive on our campus, and as we provide learning opportunities that enhance their development, we will become more accountable to our external public. But more important, we will become increasingly accountable to our students and to ourselves.

References

Allen, K. E. "A Non Linear Model of Student Development: Implications for Assessment." Paper presented at the 1989 American Association of Higher Education Assessment Forum, Atlanta, Ga., March 1989.

Association of American Colleges. *Integrity in the College Curriculum: A Report to the Academic Community*. Washington, D.C.: Association of American Colleges, 1985.

Astin, A. W. *Minorities in American Higher Education*. San Francisco: Jossey-Bass, 1982.

Astin, A. W., Green, K. C., and Korn, W. S. *The American Freshman: Twenty Year Trends, 1966–1985*. Los Angeles: Cooperative Institutional Research Program, 1987.

Baird, L. L. "Value Added: Using Student Gains as Yardsticks of

Learning." In C. Adelman (ed.), *Performance and Judgment.* Washington, D.C.: U.S. Department of Education, 1988.

Banning, J. H. "The Campus Ecology Manager Role." In U. Delworth, G. Hanson, and Associates, *Student Services: A Handbook for the Profession.* San Francisco: Jossey-Bass, 1980.

Banning, J. H. "The Campus Ecology Manager Role." In U. Delworth, G. Hanson, and Associates, *Student Services: A Handbook for the Profession.* (2nd ed.) San Francisco: Jossey-Bass, 1989.

Banta, T. (ed.). *Implementing Outcomes Assessment: Promise and Perils.* New Directions for Institutional Research, no. 59. San Francisco: Jossey-Bass, 1988.

Baruch, G., Barnett, R., and Rivers, C. *Life Prints: New Patterns of Love and Work for Today's Women.* New York: New American Library, 1983.

Belenky, M. F., Clinchy, B. M., Goldberger, N. R., and Tarule, J. M. *Women's Ways of Knowing: The Development of Self, Voice and Mind.* New York: Basic Books, 1986.

Bennett, W. *To Reclaim a Legacy.* Washington, D.C.: National Endowment for the Humanities, 1984.

Brown, R. D., and Citrin, R. S. "A Student Development Transcript: Assumptions, Uses, and Formats." *Journal of College Student Personnel,* 1977, *18* (3), 163–168.

Center for Education Statistics. *The Condition of Education: A Statistical Report.* Washington, D.C.: U.S. Department of Education, 1986.

Chickering, A. W. *Education and Identity.* San Francisco: Jossey-Bass, 1969.

College Outcomes Evaluation Program (COEP). *Report to the New Jersey Board of Higher Education from the Advisory Committee to The College Outcomes Evaluation Program.* Trenton: New Jersey Board of Higher Education, 1987.

Cziko, G. "Unpredictability and Indeterminism in Human Behavior: Arguments and Implications for Educational Research." *Educational Researcher,* 1989, *18* (4), 17–25.

Education Commission of the States. *Transforming the State Role in Undergraduate Education: Time for a Different View.* Denver, Colo.: Education Commission of the States, 1986.

Erwin, D. T. *Outcomes Assessment.* In U. Delworth, G. Hanson, and Associates, *Student Services: A Handbook for the Profession.* San Francisco: Jossey-Bass, 1989.

Ewell, P. T. "Implementing Assessment: Some Organizational Issues." In T. W. Banta (ed.), *Implementing Outcomes Assessment: Promise and Perils.* New Directions for Institutional Research, no. 59. San Francisco: Jossey-Bass, 1986.

Ewell, P. T. *Assessment, Accountability and Improvement: Managing the Contradiction.* Boulder, Colo.: National Center for Higher Education Management Systems, 1987.

Fenske, R. "Current Issues in Student Services." In U. Delworth, G. Hanson, and Associates. *Student Services: A Handbook for the Profession.* San Francisco: Jossey-Bass, 1980.

Gilligan, C. *In a Different Voice: Psychological Theory and Women's Development.* Cambridge, Mass.: Harvard University Press, 1982.

Gleick, J. *Chaos: Making a New Science.* New York: Viking Penguin, 1987.

Griener, M., and Delworth, U. "The New Scholarship on Women: An Innovative Perspective for Student Affairs." *Journal of College Student Development,* 1988, *29,* 485–491.

Hanson, G. R. "Critical Issues in the Assessment of Value Added in Education." In T. W. Banta (ed.), *Implementing Outcomes Assessment: Promises and Perils.* New Directions for Institutional Research, no. 59. San Francisco: Jossey-Bass, 1988.

Hanson, G. R. *The Assessment of Student Development: A Review of Assessment Instruments.* Trenton: New Jersey Board of Higher Education, 1989.

Hood, A. B. *The Iowa Student Development Inventories.* Iowa City: Hi Tech Press, 1986.

Huebner, L. A. (ed.). *Redesigning Campus Environments.* New Directions for Student Services, no. 8. San Francisco: Jossey-Bass, 1979.

Huebner, L. A. "Interaction of Student and Campus." In U. Delworth, G. Hanson, and Associates, *Student Services: A Handbook for the Profession.* (2nd ed.) San Francisco: Jossey-Bass, 1989.

Hutchings, P. *Behind Outcomes: Contexts and Questions for As-*

sessment. Washington, D.C. American Association for Higher Education, 1989.

Josselson, R. *Finding Herself: Pathways to Identity Development in Women.* San Francisco: Jossey-Bass, 1987.

Kalsbeek, D. "Linking Learning Style Theory with Retention Research: The Trails Project." *AIR Professional File.* Tallahassee, Fla.: Association for Institutional Research, 1989a.

Kalsbeek, D. "Managing Data and Resource Information." In U. Delworth, G. Hanson, and Associates, *Student Services: A Handbook for the Profession.* (2nd ed.) San Francisco: Jossey-Bass, 1989b.

Lenning, O. T. *Previous Attempts to Structure Educational Outcomes and Outcome-Related Concepts: A Compilation and Review of the Literature.* Boulder, Colo.: National Center for Higher Education Management Systems, 1977.

Lenning, O. T. "Use of Noncognitive Measures in Assessment." In T. W. Banta (ed.), *Implementing Outcomes Assessment: Promise and Perils.* New Directions for Institutional Research, no. 59. San Francisco: Jossey-Bass, 1988.

Levine, A. *When Dreams and Heroes Died.* San Francisco: Jossey-Bass, 1980.

Levine, A., and Associates. *Shaping Higher Education's Future: Demographic Realities and Opportunities, 1990–2000.* San Francisco: Jossey-Bass, 1989.

McGinty, D. "A Path Analysis of the Effects of Multiple Programs on Student Persistence." Unpublished doctoral dissertation, College of Education, University of Texas, Austin, 1989.

Madsen, D. L., Benedict, L. G., and Weitzer, W. H. "Using Information Systems for Decision Making in Planning." In U. Delworth, G. Hanson, and Associates, *Student Services: A Handbook for the Profession.* (2nd ed.) San Francisco: Jossey-Bass, 1989.

Marantes, E. "A Statewide Comprehensive Outcomes Assessment Program." Paper presented at the 5th annual Regents' Conference of the State University and Community Colleges of Tennessee, Nashville, Oct. 1987.

Moore, W. S. "The Learning Environment Preferences: Establishing Preliminary Reliability for an Objective Measure of the Perry Scheme of Intellectual and Ethical Development." Unpublished doctoral dissertation, Department of Counseling Personnel Services, University of Maryland, 1987.

National Commission on Excellence in Education. *A Nation at Risk: Imperative for Educational Reform.* Washington, D.C.: National Commission on Excellence in Education, 1984.

National Governors' Association. "Developing State Policy on College Student Assessment." *Capital Ideas,* Jan. 5, 1988, pp. 1–8.

National Institute of Education. *Involvement in Learning: Realizing the Potential of American Higher Education.* Washington, D.C.: National Institute of Education, 1984.

New Jersey Basic Skills Council. *Results of the New Jersey Basic Skills Placement Testing, Fall 1985.* Trenton: Basic Skills Assessment Program, New Jersey Department of Higher Education, 1986.

Newman, F. *Higher Education and the American Resurgence.* Princeton, N.J.: Carnegie Foundation for the Advancement of Teaching, 1985.

Pace, R. *Measuring Outcomes of College.* San Francisco: Jossey-Bass, 1979.

Pascarella, E. T. *Some Methodological and Analytic Issues in Assessing the Influence of College.* Paper presented at a joint meeting of the American College Personnel Association and the National Association of Student Personnel Administrators, Chicago, April 1987.

Perry, W. G., Jr. *Forms of Intellectual and Ethical Development in the College Years.* New York: Holt, Rinehart & Winston, 1970.

Pintrich, P. R., and Associates. *Motivated Strategies for Learning Questionnaire (MSLQ).* Ann Arbor: National Center for Research to Improve Postsecondary Teaching and Learning, College of Education, University of Michigan, 1988.

Ratliff, J. L., and Associates. *Determining the Effect of Different Coursework Patterns on General Student Learned Abilities: A Working Paper.* University Park, Pa.: Center for the Study of Higher Education, 1989.

Ravitch, D., and Finn, C. E., Jr. *What Do Our 17 Year-Olds Know?* New York: Harper & Row, 1987.

Southern Association of Colleges and Schools. *Criteria for Accred-*

itation. Atlanta, Ga.: Southern Association of Colleges and Schools, 1984.

Texas Academic Skills Program (TASP). *Program Summary.* Austin: Texas Higher Education Coordinating Board, 1988.

Texas Higher Education Coordinating Board. *Improvement for Undergraduate Education in Texas: College Level Competencies.* Austin: Texas Higher Education Coordinating Board, 1989.

Weinstein, C. E., Schulte, A., and Palmer, D. *Learning and Study Strategies Inventory Manual.* Clearwater, Fla.: H & H Publishing, 1987.

Western Interstate Commission for Higher Education. *The Ecosystem Model: Designing Campus Environments.* Boulder, Colo.: Western Interstate Commission for Higher Education, 1973.

Winston, R. B., Jr., Miller, T. K., and Prince, J. S. *The Student Development Task and Life Styles Inventory Manual.* Athens, Ga.: Student Development Associates, 1987.

Chapter 14

New Futures for Student Affairs: A Summary Agenda

M. Lee Upcraft
Margaret J. Barr

As we stated in Chapter One, predicting the future is an educated guess, at best. Perhaps we should have followed the advice of that great twentieth-century philosopher Yogi Berra, who said, "I don't predict nothin', especially the future." But the authors of our chapters, happily, did not take his advice but instead took the risk of attempting to identify the challenges facing the student affairs profession into the nineties and the twenty-first century.

The Agenda for Student Affairs in the Nineties and Beyond

What are the new futures for student affairs? What might we expect? What are our agendas, and what must we do to enhance and strengthen our profession? Our authors focused on many different issues, using many different approaches. We believe the agenda for student affairs in the nineties and beyond will include the following mandates:

1. We must continue to maintain basic student services, programs, and facilities.
   - Maintain basic services such as counseling, placement, financial aid, admissions, and other essential student services in an efficient and effective manner.
   - Continue to develop programs that enhance students' academic and personal development, including health services, student activities, multicultural and gender awareness, leadership development, student government, residence halls, and other vital programs.
   - Continue to manage our facilities, such as residence halls, student unions, and recreational facilities, in ways that meet the needs of our students.
2. We must develop campus environments, as well as student services, programs, and facilities while recognizing the increasing diversity of our students, promoting equality, and eliminating prejudice, bigotry, and discrimination.
   - Be advocates for, and be responsive to students who are older or who have different racial and ethnic backgrounds, disabilities, different sexual orientations, or other differences that distinguish them from traditional students.
   - Work with students who have difficulty dealing with racial, cultural, ethnic, age, disability, and sexual differences to help them overcome prejudiced attitudes, values, and behaviors.
   - Develop policies that assert our unwillingness to tolerate intolerance and that also reflect our respect for the constitutional liberties of all persons.
3. We must continue to adapt our services, programs, and facilities to the changing needs of all students.
   - Be more responsive to students whose psychological and health problems may interfere with their academic and personal development.
   - Be responsive to students' changing career patterns and interests.
   - Be more responsive to students who do not live on campus, who study part-time, or who take more than four years to graduate.

- Be more responsive to at-risk students who have skill deficiencies that may reduce their opportunities to succeed in college.

4. We must adapt our services, programs, and facilities to be more responsive to the changing needs of female students.
    - Work to overcome the negative impact of the so-called chilly classroom and out-of-classroom climates that negatively affect women.
    - Educate both men and women about the negative consequences of sexism and about the value for both men and women of the elimination of sexism from our campuses.
    - Create campus environments free of sexism, sexual harassment, sexual violence, and other practices that discriminate against women.
5. We must reaffirm the academic preeminence of higher education and the central role of student affairs in supporting that mission.
    - Forge collaborations and partnerships with the academic side of our institutions to increase our involvement in teaching and learning, curriculum reform, improving the academic climate, and developing a sense of community.
    - Make faculty more aware of the powerful influence of the out-of-class environment on the academic achievement and retention of students, and increase their involvement in the out-of-classroom life of students.
    - Establish ourselves as experts on students and campus environments, based not only on our experiences, but also on our theories and research.
    - Expand our efforts to help at-risk students succeed in the classroom by providing services, programs, and facilities to enhance their academic and personal development.
    - Make better use of academic courses, such as freshman seminars and health education courses, to support the academic and personal development of students.
6. We must respond to the changing organizational climate of student affairs.
    - Be able to articulate clearly the mission and goals of stu-

dent affairs in ways that acknowledge the primacy of the academic mission of our institutions.

- Be more assertive in creating an organizational presence that ensures our participation in the overall governance of our institutions.
- Acknowledge our role as manager, and develop more precise managerial skills to fulfill this role.
- Improve our political skills as part of our management responsibilities.
- Improve our ability to manage paradoxes such as freedom and responsibility, individual and general welfare, students and the institution, students and our society, and the institution and our society.
- Enhance our skills related to defining, clarifying, and implementing our emerging organizational roles as student experts, student advocates, bridgers, intervenors, program developers, managers, spokespersons, and behavioral standards enforcers.

7. We must develop research and assessment programs that support the mission of student affairs.
   - Conduct more research that expands our theories and knowledge about students and their environments.
   - Do a better job of describing our students upon entering, explaining what they learn while enrolled, and demonstrating that what they learn is a result of what we do.
   - Conduct assessment studies that demonstrate the effectiveness of our efforts—including improved systems to account for those who use our services, programs, facilities, and assessments—and studies that relate our efforts to student academic and personal development.
   - Improve use of research and assessment in policy development, problem solving, decision making, and allocation of resources.
   - Get better at conducting research and assessment, and expand our knowledge of assessment techniques.
   - Expand the use of information in helping students to understand themselves better.

- Improve the articulation between student affairs practitioners and student affairs researchers.

8. We must continue to expand the theory base of our profession.
    - Continue to develop, revise, and expand theories that reflect the diversity, cultural backgrounds, enrollment patterns, and needs of our students.
    - Continue to develop, revise, and expand theories that explain the environments in which students grow, develop, and learn, including both campus and community environments.
    - Conduct more research to test the validity of our theories regarding personal development.
    - Get better at translating theory into practice.
9. We must be responsive to, and anticipate, the changing federal, state, and legal regulatory mandates.
    - Continue our commitment to affirmative action.
    - Continue to stress both quality and access, even though regulatory mandates may focus on quality to the detriment of access.
    - Anticipate the likelihood of a decline in the federal role in education, with a corresponding increase in state and local regulation, accountability, and assessment.
    - Anticipate that the federal government is likely to increase its requirements for institutions to respond to such issues as substance abuse by tying those requirements to financial aid regulations.
    - Deal with continuing legal constraints, such as the tension between freedom of speech and creation of a climate of tolerance.
10. We must join the computer and information system revolution.
    - Develop computer-assisted ways of managing information about students, services, programs, and facilities—and our institution in general.
    - Make better use of computer technology for planning, facilities management, resource allocation, record keeping, and other management functions.
    - Ensure that student affairs staff are computer literate, and

update professional staff development to include technological advances.
- Serve as the guardian against the dehumanization of students and staff that can occur with the increased use of computer technology.
- Assist in the development of policies regarding both academic freedom and academic dishonesty when using computers.

11. We must develop our professional staff in ways that reflect the changing conditions of higher education, our students, and our profession.
    - Increase the representation of racial and ethnic minorities and men in our profession.
    - Ensure that women and minorities are better represented in upper management positions in student affairs.
    - Develop staff in ways that help them meet the needs of our increasingly diverse student population, particularly those whose professional preparation took place before the decade of the eighties.
    - Develop staff in ways that take into account the ethical standards, principles, and practices of our profession.
    - Train staff to meet the changing needs of our students, and the changing issues that affect them, such as safety and security, AIDS, campus violence, and others.
    - Recognize the barriers to attracting and maintaining high-quality professionals, and reduce the attrition rate among them.
    - Recognize that many practitioners come to our profession from other backgrounds and specialties, and adapt our professional development programs accordingly.
    - Define the core knowledge, competencies, and skills needed by all professionals regardless of preparation and specific work setting.
12. We must develop our graduate professional preparation programs in ways that reflect the changing conditions of higher education, our students, and our profession.
    - Increase the number of persons entering our graduate pro-

fessional training programs in order to meet current and projected staffing demands.
- Increase the racial, ethnic, and male representation in our professional training programs.
- Make our professional training programs fit the reality of our working professional lives.
- Improve the communication and collaboration between student affairs educators and student affairs practitioners.
- Do a better job of preparing both specialists and generalists in our field.
- Develop our professional training programs consistent with the CAS standards, focusing on administration, student development, and counseling.

Conclusion

As we stated in the beginning of this book, we are very optimistic about the future of student affairs, and we believe the next decade, leading to the next century, will perhaps be the most exciting and challenging in the history of our profession. We must, however, anticipate the new futures for student affairs and act upon them to the benefit of students. We must do so with the highest ethical standards, with the highest commitment to quality, and within a framework that acknowledges the preeminence of the academic mission of the institution.

William Allen White probably best summarizes how we feel about the future of the student affairs profession: "I am not afraid of tomorrow, for I have seen yesterday, and I love today."

Name Index

F

G

H

I

J

K

L

M

N

Subject Index

D

E

F

G

H

T

U

V

W